TROPICAL PATHS

LATIN AMERICAN STUDIES
(VOL. 2)

GARLAND REFERENCE LIBRARY
OF THE HUMANITIES
(VOL. 1555)

LATIN AMERICAN STUDIES

General Editor: David William Foster

1. The Contemporary Praxis of the Fantastic: *Borges and Cortázar*
   by Julio Rodríguez-Luis

2. Tropical Paths: *Essays on Modern Brazilian Literature*
   edited by Randal Johnson

TROPICAL PATHS
*Essays on Modern
Brazilian Literature*

edited by
Randal Johnson

GARLAND PUBLISHING, INC. • NEW YORK & LONDON
1993

Library of Congress Cataloging-in-Publication Data

Tropical paths : essays on modern Brazilian literature / edited by
Randal Johnson.
    p.   cm. — (Latin American studies ; vol. 2) (Garland
reference library of the humanities ; vol. 1555)
    "Essays . . . brought together in honor of Fred P. Ellison on the
occasion of his retirement from the University of Texas at Austin"—
Pref.
    In English, with some essays translated from Portuguese.
    Includes bibliographical references.
    ISBN: 0-8153-0780-2
    1. Brazilian fiction—20th century—History and criticism.
2. Brazilian fiction—19th century—History and criticism.
I. Johnson, Randal, 1948–   . II. Ellison, Fred P. III. Series.
IV. Series: Latin American studies (Garland Publishing, Inc.) ;
vol. 2.
PQ9603.T7 1993
869.3—dc20   91-45265
                                                   CIP

Printed on acid-free, 250-year-life paper
Manufactured in the United States of America

Dedicated to Fred P. Ellison

CONTENTS

Preface   1

Introduction, by Randal Johnson   3

Iracema: A Vanguard Archaeography, by Haroldo de Campos   11

The Lascivious Voluptuousness of Nothing: A Reading of
    Epitaph of a Small Winner, by João Alexandre Barbosa   31

Political Literature in Amazonia: Márcio Souza and
    His Predecessors, by Pedro Maligo   53

Doramundo by Geraldo Ferraz: The Problem of Talking
    about Crime, by Naomi Lindstrom   77

Masculine Vampirism or the Denunciation of Pygmalion:
    A Reading of Adalgisa Nery's *A imaginária*,
    by Affonso Romano de Sant'Anna   91

Guimarães Rosa through the Prism of Magic Realism,
    by Charles A. Perrone   101

Heteronymy in Guimarães Rosa, by Walnice Nogueira Galvão   123

In the Inter(t)sex(t) of Clarice Lispector and
    Nelson Rodrigues: From Drama to Language,
    by Ana Luiza Andrade   133

Osman Lins's *Avalovara*: A Novel of Love?, by Massaud Moisés   153

Memoirs Told to the Mirror: Autran Dourado and Darcy Ribeiro,
    by Fábio Lucas   165

Literature, Film and Politics in Brazil: Reflections on
the Generation of 1968, by Randal Johnson   183

The Prison-House of Memoirs: Silviano Santiago's
Em liberdade, by K. David Jackson   199

The Hurried Midwives of Time: Brazilian Fiction
in the 1980s, by Silviano Santiago   223

Contributors   231

PREFACE

The essays in this volume were brought together in honor of Fred P. Ellison on the occasion of his retirement from the University of Texas at Austin. Most are previously unpublished. Of the three that have appeared in Portuguese, two (Barbosa and Campos) were at least partially elaborated while their authors were E. L. Tinker Professors at Texas. João Alexandre Barbosa's essay appeared originally as "A volúpia lasciva do nada: uma leitura de *Memórias póstumas de Brás Cubas*" in *Revista USP* 1 (March-May 1989); Haroldo de Campos's was initially published as "*Iracema*: uma arqueografia de vanguarda," *Revista USP* 5 (March-May 1990); Fábio Lucas's "Memórias contadas ao espelho: Autran Dourado e Darcy Ribeiro" has appeared in his *Mineranças* (Belo Horizonte: Oficina de Livros, 1991). All are used with permission. Charles A. Perrone translated Walnice Nogueira Galvão's "Heteronymy in Guimarães Rosa." Randal Johnson translated Haroldo de Campos's "*Iracema*: A Vanguard Archaeography," João Alexandre Barbosa's "The Lascivious Voluptuousness of Nothing: A Reading of *Epitaph of a Small Winner*," Affonso Romano de Sant'Anna's "Masculine Vampirism or the Denunciation of Pygmalion," Massaud Moisés's "Osman Lins' *Avalovara*, A Love Story?," Fábio Lucas's "Memoirs Told to the Mirror: Autran Dourado and Darcy Ribeiro," and Silviano Santiago's "The Hurried Midwives of Time: Brazilian Fiction in the 1980s." In some cases--especially that of the Campos essay, with its highly creative and often neologistic poetics--the translator sought to retain a sense of the author's writing rather than transmute it into the discursive canons of English style manuals. In those essays discussing works which have been translated into English (Barbosa and Moisés) citations are from the translation. This accounts for the use of Anglicized proper names in the Barbosa piece (e.g., Braz Cubas rather than Brás Cubas, Eugenia rather than Eugênia). In all cases the translation was sent to the author for approval.

The volume's title, *Tropical Paths*, is an homage to the late Joaquim Pedro de Andrade, the Cinema Novo director whose *Macu-*

1

naíma (1969) represents such a milestone in contemporary Brazilian culture. His *Vereda tropical*, a true masterpiece, is included in the multi-episode film *Contos eróticos* (1977).

Finally, I would like to thank all the contributors for having taken the time from their busy schedules to participate in this project. More importantly, and in the name of all contributors, I would like to thank Fred P. Ellison, a true pioneer along these tropical paths, for all he has done to promote the study of Brazilian literature in this country.

INTRODUCTION

Randal Johnson
University of Florida

Interest in Brazilian literature, and particularly in Brazilian narrative, has increased significantly in the United States during the last few years. This interest is evident first of all in the growing number of novels translated into English, including writers such as Jorge Amado, Ivan Ângelo, Ignácio de Loyola Brandão, Helena Parente Cunha, Rubem Fonseca, Clarice Lispector, Marcos Rey, João Ubaldo Ribeiro, João Guimarães Rosa, Moacyr Scliar, Márcio Souza, and Lygia Fagundes Telles, among others. It is equally apparent in the marked expansion in the number of critical works published.[1]

The modern history of North American criticism of Brazilian literature is a rather short one, going back little more than fifty years and the work of Samuel Putnam, whose historical survey, *Marvelous Journey*, appeared in 1948.[2] Even more significant for the development of Bra-

---

[1] One thinks, for example, of the work of scholars such as Helen Caldwell, Bobby J. Chamberlain, Robert Di Antonio, Paul Dixon, Earl E. Fitz, David Haberly, Elizabeth Lowe, Maria Luísa Nunes, Daphne Patai, Susan Canty Quinlan, Roberto Reis, Darlene Sadlier, Raymond Sayers, Candace Slater, Irwin Stern, and Jon Vincent, not to mention many others who have published valuable articles and essays.

[2] Putnam's contribution to the study of Brazilian literature has yet to be fully appreciated. In addition to publishing one of the first histories of the subject, he also initiated the Brazilian literature section of the Library of Congress's *Handbook of Latin American Studies*. The journalistic studies he published in the 1930s and 1940s reveal an intellectual who was both intensely concerned about Brazil and its people and also deeply committed to social justice. Other early contributions to the study of

3

zilian literary studies in this country is Fred P. Ellison's *Brazil's New Novel: Four Northeastern Masters* (1954). Ellison's book introduced to the American public one of the most important generations of Brazilian writers of this century, the social novelists of the country's impoverished northeast. His book provided the first systematic studies of the writers included--Jorge Amado (the single most widely-translated Brazilian writer), Rachel de Queiroz (arguably Brazil's first important woman novelist), Graciliano Ramos (whose 1938 *Vidas secas* is a universally recognized masterpiece) and José Lins do Rego (who was perhaps Brazil's most popular writer in the 1940s)--and set a new standard in the field. The book continues to be a major point of reference for studies of contemporary Brazilian narrative.

Through his critical essays, his literary translations,[3] his development of pedagogical materials, his pioneering efforts in building an internationally recognized program of Luso-Brazilian studies at the University of Texas, and his direction of numerous theses and dissertations--including my own--Ellison's impact on the discipline has been immense. The present volume, which brings together essays by scholars from both Brazil and the United States--all of whom have some professional association with Fred Ellison--owes much to his legacy and example.

The volume is intended as a mosaic of Brazilian narrative from romanticism until the postmodern or, less abstractly, from the late 1800s until the 1980s, beginning with the pioneering work of José de Alencar and ending with the dilemmas faced by Brazilian writers today. I use the term "mosaic" quite deliberately, for contributors were invited to submit an essay on any aspect of modern Brazilian narrative, which has a long and rich tradition with a great diversity of styles, themes, and trends expressed at different moments of Brazilian history by often conflictive movements, schools, and orientations. Together, the essays exemplify

---

Brazilian literature in the United States are Isaac Goldberg's *Brazilian Literature* (1922) and David Miller Driver's *The Indian in Brazilian Literature* (1943).

[3] He translated Rachel de Queiroz's *As três Marias* (1943; *The Three Marias*, 1963), Adonias Filho's *Memórias de Lázaro* (1952; *Memories of Lazarus*, 1969), and, in conjunction with Naomi Lindstrom, Helena Parente Cunha's *Mulher no espelho* (1983; *Women Between Mirrors*, 1989), all of which were published by the University of Texas Press.

many of the central issues and concerns raised or addressed by Brazilian literature during the last century and a half: nation and nationhood, identity and alienation, modernity and tradition, memory and history, love and sexuality, crime and violence, and politics and social change. The more specifically literary concerns raised include the social nature and aesthetic configuration of discursive and symbolic practices. The essays also reveal the diversity of perspectives that currently characterizes Brazilian and "Brazilianist" criticism.

In one of his most cited articles, "Literatura e cultura de 1900 a 1945," Antônio Candido has suggested that historically Brazilian literature has developed through a dialectic of "localism" and "cosmopolitanism." On the one hand, it has shown an at times extreme concern with expressing Brazilian reality through a fictive language of cultural nationalism, on the other, it has revealed a desire to be in step with European literary fashions and trends (109).

Localism is intimately tied up with questions of national identity, which have found multiple expressions throughout Brazilian literary history. Writers of the colonial period incorporated local or regional motifs in their writing, which has often been called *nativismo*. The romantics and the modernists, in turn, sought to create a new and more authentically Brazilian literary language, the romantics as part of a project of national formation, and the modernists as a component of a program of discovery and definition of a national character in conjunction with a broader process of institutional and social modernization.

Cosmopolitanism, on the other hand, is most evident in Brazilian writers' historical infatuation with European and, to a lesser extent, American culture, as illustrated by their frequent mirroring of epochal styles, movements, and intellectual fads. In his own sardonic way, Roberto Schwarz summarizes the situation with great concision. He writes that Brazilian art and letters have always found a way to "adore, cite, ape, sack, adapt or devour" European models. The result is frequently what he calls the "cultural whiplash" with which Brazilians identify themselves (22).[4]

---

[4] Brazilian criticism has tended to follow the same pattern. In this regard, Schwarz has written the following: "Nos vinte anos em que tenho dado aula de literatura assisti ao trânsito da crítica por impressionismo, historiografia positivista, *new criticism* americano, estilística, marxismo, fenomenologia, estruturalismo, pós-estruturalismo e agora teorias da

The dichotomy, of course, is a false one. The two categories are rarely mutually exclusive. The best of Brazilian literature--Machado de Assis, Lima Barreto, Mário de Andrade, Graciliano Ramos, Guimarães Rosa, and Clarice Lispector, to mention but a few of its most prominent representatives--forges unique cultural syntheses of the two. More often than not, it is a question of emphasis rather than an exclusive option for one or the other.

If José de Alencar sought to create a literary language adequate to the expression of the new world, he did so through an implicit dialogue with and against such European writers as Chateaubriand. His effort to create an Indianist epic--part of a larger project of what Doris Sommer has called "foundational fiction"--involved a radical recasting of literary style which can only be understood against the backdrop of European canons (see the essay by Campos). If Amazonian writers have struggled to find ways of conceptualizing and transmuting into literary form what has sometimes been called the "green hell," they have often done so using categories developed by European travellers and observers (Maligo). If, in *Doramundo*, Geraldo Ferraz borrows heavily from the detective fiction genre, he does so with an original, specifically Brazilian twist (Lindstrom).

The modernists of the 1920s attained strikingly creative syntheses which are at once attuned to the contemporaneous European avant-garde *and* expressive of a concern with national identity. Mário de Andrade's *Macunaíma* (1928), subtitled *The Hero without a Character*, is perhaps the most perfect example of such syntheses. In many ways the modernists constitute this volume's "structuring absence." The essays on pre-modernist writers (Campos, Barbosa) project forward to modernism, while a number of those on later writers refer back to them.

The local/cosmopolitan dialectic subsumes other dichotomies that appear throughout this volume. One example is the opposition between a documentary tendency and an avant-garde impulse. A second dichotomy contrasts a nostalgic and memorialistic propensity (that is, literature turned toward the past) to a conception of literature as a form of political intervention (literature turned toward the future). These

---

recepção... Mas é fácil observar que só raramente a passagem de uma escola a outra corresponde, como seria de esperar, ao esgotamento de um projeto; no geral ela se deve ao prestígio americano ou europeu da doutrina seguinte" (*Que horas são?* 30).

tendencies naturally overlap. Such is the case in Silviano Santiago's *Em liberdade*, which parodically assumes a memorialistic tenor in a fictional, postmodern pastiche of Graciliano Ramos (Jackson). Darcy Ribeiro's *Migo* is another hybrid, self-reflexively alternating between *roman à clef*, memoir, and satire (Lucas). Others are Márcio Souza's *Galvez, imperador do Acre* and *Operação silêncio*, both of which revitalize Oswaldian satire and elaborate a metafictional discourse combining reflections on cultural identity and a desire for political participation (Maligo, Johnson). The documentary mode of Brazilian narrative is most evident, in this volume, in Maligo's essay on the politics of Amazonian narrative and Johnson's article on the generation of 1968. Maligo's essay joins Fábio Lucas's piece on two novelists from Minas Gerais as the only other entry focusing on a specific Brazilian region. Given its strength in the historical development of Brazilian literature, the relatively scant space devoted to regionalism--one variant of the localism mentioned above-- might be surprising, if it were not for the fact that its most prominent representatives have already been so thoroughly analyzed, beginning with the Ellison volume mentioned above. Maligo's study in fact dialogues with Ellison's later analysis of Ferreira de Castro's *A selva*.[5]

Renato Tapajós's *Em câmara lenta* (Johnson) also reveals a strong documentary tendency, especially through its implicit affiliation with what has been called the *romance-reportagem* (non-fiction novel) that gained such notoriety in the 1970s. The novel also shares many characteristics with the memoirs of political struggle that began to appear in the late 1970s and thus with a longer memorialistic tradition in Brazilian literature. Memorialism appears in a number of essays in this volume. Affonso Romano de Sant'Anna's piece on Adalgisa Nery suggests that confessional memorialism has been one of the strategies used to constitute a female narrator in contemporary Brazilian literature. In this regard, one might point to the early work of Clarice Lispector, particularly *Perto do coração selvagem* (1944), as a model. Fábio Lucas's essay on Autran Dourado and Darcy Ribeiro focuses on a certain manifesta-

---

[5] It would not be unreasonable to trace a certain intellectual genealogy from *Brazil's New Novel: Four Northeastern Masters* to my own *Cinema Novo x 5: Masters of Contemporary Brazilian Film* (University of Texas Press, 1984), to Charles A. Perrone's *Masters of Contemporary Brazilian Song: MPB 1965-1985* (University of Texas Press, 1989), and on to Pedro Maligo's work on Amazonian literature.

tion of the memorialistic *Bildungsroman* as a central characteristic of the fiction of Minas Gerais. Finally, David Jackson shows that Santiago's *Em liberdade* uses a counterfeit memorialism, in the form of an intimate diary supposedly written by Graciliano Ramos, to construct a postmodern discourse that creates a simulacrum of the real.

Santiago's novel also represents another constant in Brazilian literature throughout this century: a self-reflexive vanguardism that constantly seeks to expand and transform the possibilities of literary expression. This avant-garde impulse is evident in Alencar's search for literary solutions appropriate to the construction of an Indianist epic. Haroldo de Campos also exhibits such an impulse in his post-structuralist approach to Alencar's novel. Machado de Assis looks beyond contemporary conventions in his deconstruction of 19th-century literary and philosophical models in *Memórias póstumas de Brás Cubas* (translated into English as *Epitaph of a Small Winner*), analyzed so acutely by João Alexandre Barbosa. João Guimarães Rosa, who is the subject of studies by Charles Perrone and Walnice Nogueira Galvão, surpasses all narrative models of his time. Perrone examines the applicability of the concept of magic realism to Rosa's fiction, while Galvão draws parallels between Rosa and the Portuguese modernist poet Fernando Pessoa in their common use of artistic heteronyms. The exploration of the creative boundaries of literary expression also characterizes much of the work of Osman Lins, whose brilliant *Avalovara* is the focus of Massaud Moisés's essay.

Brazilian literature also speaks to and with other pages in Western literature through its intensely intertextual and dialogical nature. Alencar's dialogue with European linguistic canons and Machado de Assis's deconstruction of late 19th-century discursive modes exemplify this tendency. Naomi Lindstrom's essay on *Doramundo* reveals Geraldo Ferraz's "divergent example of the novel of crime" and its implicit critical dialogue with traditional genres of detective fiction, Charles Perrone discusses Guimarães Rosa in relation to Spanish American magic realism, David Jackson outlines Silviano Santiago's dialogue with Graciliano Ramos, Johnson focuses on Márcio Souza's reflections on the broader relationship between literature, film and politics, and Ana Luiza Andrade discovers a surprising inter(t)sex(t)ual exchange between Clarice Lispector, who has gained increasing international attention in recent years-- especially through the work of French writer Hélène Cixous--and the self-proclaimed reactionary of Brazilian literature, playwright Nelson Rodrigues.

Closing the volume are Silviano Santiago's considerations on the dilemmas facing Brazilian writers in the 1980s and 1990s, especially regarding their relationship to the publishing industry, the public, and criticism. Santiago implicitly asks a number of questions that are and will continue to be crucial to Brazilian literature in the years to come. What does it mean to be a writer (or a critic) in contemporary Brazil? How does the writer fit into a society flooded by the outpourings of a mass media whose rapid technological development has transformed Brazil into a society of spectacle? In such a situation, with *telenovelas* piped nightly into tens of millions of Brazilian homes, what is the social function of literature? Whom does it serve? What are the conditions of its production, circulation, and consumption? What strategies are available to writers other than accommodation with the market? What options are available for criticism, marginalized by mass media, the market, and often by its own hermeticism, other than retreat into the isolated confines of university-based discourse? The answers to these questions will go a long way toward shaping the future of Brazilian literature.

REFERENCES

Candido, Antônio. "Literatura e cultura de 1900 a 1945." *Literatura e sociedade: estudos de teoria e história literária*. 4a ed. São Paulo: Companhia Editora Nacional, 1975.

Ellison, Fred P. *Brazil's New Novel: Four Northeastern Masters*. Berkeley: U of California P, 1954.

Putnam, Samuel. *Marvelous Journey*. New York: Alfred A. Knopf, 1948.

Schwarz, Roberto. *Ao vencedor as batatas*. São Paulo: Livraria Duas Cidades, 1977.

_____. *Que horas são?* São Paulo: Companhia das Letras, 1987.

IRACEMA: A VANGUARD ARCHAEOGRAPHY

Haroldo de Campos
Pontifícia Universidade Católica, São Paulo

> Porventura não haverá no caos incriado do pensamento
> humano uma nova forma de poesia, um novo metro de
> verso? (José de Alencar, 11 June 1856)

If we undertake a reading of the Brazilian novelistic space that
is not predetermined by a Hegelian-Lukácsian eschatology of the novel
as an "agonic" form,[1] or if we adopt a Bakhtinian dialogical focus that
recognizes "the simultaneous existence in literature of phenomena taken
from widely separate periods of time, which greatly complicates the
historico-literary process" ("Forms of Time and Chronotope in the Novel"
85), then José de Alencar's *Iracema* (1865) will appear as an option not
precluded (nor negatively sanctionable) by the linear-evolutive fatalism
of that initial eschatological reading.

---

[1] That is, on the road toward disappearance: in Hegel, the transcen-
dence of art occurs in philosophy, with the death of the classical *epos* and
the displacement of the modern interest of the work of art toward reflection about the work of art itself; in Lukács--especially in the Lukács of
1935, who recasts in an optimistic key the pessimism of *Theory of the
Novel* (1914-1915)--the reconciliation of the world with meaning points
toward a new epic, that of a classless society, supposedly already near
materialization in "socialist realism," foreshadowed by the positive hero
of Gorki's *Mother*.

Constellar Reception

Alencar received the Western literary heritage, represented primarily by the "French school," in a global manner: constellate as in the contemplation of the homogeneous skies, which are in reality made of different astronomic-stellar distances.[2] Recounting his formative years, his *naïf* apprenticeship as a writer, in *Como e por que sou romancista* (1873), this "promiscuous" reader (as Araripe Jr. once called him) spontaneously relates that in his attempt to go from the texts of Fénelon and Voltaire to those of the "moderns," he read Balzac before Chateaubriand and Victor Hugo. Unable to respond to the "good form" of the Balzacian realist novel, which Lukács called "the form of mature virility," and unable to find a Brazilian form for the novel of "disillusion," in the sense of a bourgeois epopee of a world without meaning,[3] Alencar's most consequential aesthetic contribution was elsewhere on the chess board of the literary field. His most coherent space of freedom opened along the lines of least resistance toward the ideological, which permitted him to exercise his novelistic factitiousness (so fecund in works, so sparse in truly lasting achievements): the archaeographic retreat to the pre-history of the bourgeois novel, beyond the epic, to the ritual core of myth and legend, the folkloric prehistory of the novelesque, the UR-EPOS.

---

[2] Here I am using Jauss's metaphor, which reelaborates Kracauer's idea of the impossibility of a "general history" capable of unitarily and coherently integrating "eventic history" from which the "coexistence of the simultaneous and the non-simultaneous" derives on the horizon of reception.

[3] *Lucíola* and *Senhora* are his most successful attempts at confronting existential relations reified by money, finding the *pharmakós* par excellence in the objectified woman: the forced prostitute, whose revenge is the unleashing of Eros; the woman financier, who conquers the man through her own means and entangles him in an ambiguous web of despotic power and seduction.

Regressive Utopia or Philological Revolution?

It was not a question of a mere "regressive utopia," because a concrete content existed in this imaginary return to the origins, which was hampered by the period's literary praxis: the broader problem of creating a national literary language, the search for a "form of expression" which would be so important and persistent for Brazilian writers.[4] To create a new expression was to create freedom, and the negative limit of this freedom was found precisely in Portuguese vernacular purism. If at times the conservative politician and former minister of Justice of the Empire (1868-70) proclaims himself subversive, it is when he accepts Pinheiro Chagas's accusation of an "insurrection against the grammar of our common language" and responds that the "philological revolution" the Portuguese critic attributes to him is "irresistible and fatal," founded in the "popular spirit" and "shall be broad and profound, like the immensity of the seas that separate the two worlds to which we belong." His postscript to the second edition of *Iracema* (1870) and his earlier "Carta ao Dr. Jaguaribe," which serves as an afterword to the first edition, are, almost as much as Oswald de Andrade's modernist manifestos, valiant pieces of poetic combat and a call for freedom of invention. Alencar berates the "panic terror of Gallicisms," the narrow-minded avarice of those lusophile purists who "defend their sixteenth-century Portuguese, that is, their adolescence, like a garden of the Hesperides, where a profane term or phrase cannot enter." (Reread from a distance, Alencar's irony reveals a pre-Freudian matrix in the repression of the "unusual," a pubescent gesture--*de puberté difficile*--of adolescent defense against the pleasureful blemish in the text.) *Iracema*'s author proclaims the importance of writers in the transformation of the language's code, refusing to see grammar as an immutable canon, an "inalterable standard to which the writer must rigorously submit." He argues: "Compare the current rules of modern languages with those that predominated in the period of their formation and you will see the transformations they have undergone because of the action of poets and prose writers." He defends polylingual blending as a way of vitalizing Brazilian Portuguese:

---

[4] Antônio Candido discusses the question in his 1943 study on the appearance of Clarice Lispector, a polemical work, where the currency of the question is re-posed in the period of the post-modernist novel, against the frame of the regionalists of the 1930s.

We must not forget that the child of the New World receives the traditions of indigenous races and lives in contact with almost all of the civilized races that land on its soil, brought by immigration. In Portugal, the foreigner lost in the midst of a condensed population exerts little influence on the customs of the people; in Brazil, to the contrary, the foreign is a vehicle for new ideas and an element of national civilization. The agents of the transformation of our language are these representatives of so many races, from Saxons to Africans, that make an exuberant amalgam of blood, traditions, and languages on this soil.

Hybridism and the Translating Operation

Studying the origins of the novel as a "hybrid" of language, M. Bahktin writes: "European novel prose is born and shaped in the process of a free (that is, reformulating) translation of others' works" (a process which, he clarifies, may include the "transposing" of epic verses into prose). He also notes:

the germs of novelistic prose appear in the poly- and heteroglot world of the Hellenistic era, in Imperial Rome and during the disintegration and collapse of the church-directed centralization of discourse and ideology in the Middle Ages. Even in modern times, the flowering of the novel is always connected with a disintegration of stable verbal-ideological systems and with an intensification and intentionalization of speech diversity that are counterpoised to the previously reigning stable systems, an activity that goes on both within the limits of the literary dialectic itself and outside it. ("Discourse in the Novel," 378, 371-372)

Selecting fabular chronotopes with folkloric roots, *Iracema* goes back to the pre-history of the *epos*. It is articulated as a "myth of origins," structurally exposed in terms of the symbolic tale of adventures and variegated with idyllic-pastoral moments. Referring to this phase of Alencar's production, in which *Iracema*, in my opinion, is the only truly exponential text, Brito Broca has spoken of "true pastorals in which there is much of a fairytale nature." In this sense, it is a "monological" work (close to "epic monologism"), elaborated in a serio-aesthetic fashion (the "carnavalization" of this paradigm occurs in *Macunaíma*, where the fable is disguised as a farce, taking on a "parodic mode"). Still, on the plane of the signifier--a plane which, from the operational perspective of its "poetic function," should be understood in a broad sense, involving both its "form of expression" and its "form of content"--the text of the Alencarian "legend" is sliced through by polyphony, in the Bakhtinian sense of the word. The intervention of language "in a savage state," presented as a program for a critical awareness of Brazilian poetic practice, breaks with the statutes of "epic monologism." It also reveals a moment of the "romanticization of the *epos*" via language in the sense of the reeducation of the Brazilian poet through an apprenticeship of the "state of nature" via Tupinized writing. This is the moment of "experimental provocation" (Bakhtin) in *Iracema*, which reprojects it in the future, rescuing it from the secrets of "epic distanciation" where Alencar had inscribed it with an augural stroke, fascinated by the recovery of the "historical infancy" of the Brazilian (a theme capable of provoking "an eternal instigation," as Marx himself recognizes referring to those "normal children" the Greeks must have been...). In this sense, Alencar acts like a translator aspiring to radicality. He makes canonical and "verocentric" Portuguese--the language of domination of the former metropolis--"strange" by the influx of the Tupi paradigm, which he idealized as an Edenic language, with an Adamic power of naming, existing in a state of iconic, auroral primordium. The author of *Iracema*, moreover, will ultimately suggest that he sees in Adam, a "red man" of clay, the father of the "American race."[5]

---

[5] "Through what might be called a presentiment of the past, similar to the prophecy of Vieira, I think Brazil is the cradle of humanity; and that the Biblical Adam, the red man made of clay, was the trunk of this American race, which supposes the degeneration of the others when, to the contrary, it is their common ancestry." Cf. Araripe Jr., "José de Alencar," 239 n. 110. This is in an exerpt from an article by Alencar about pre-historical man, published shortly before the novelist's death. The anthropological- etymological metaphor goes back to Hebrew, where *adam* means "man," made of clay according to the Bible; *adamá* means "earth," and *adom*, correlatedly, means "red," "color of the earth." See *Theologisches Wörterbuch zum Alt Testament*, 82, and *Lexicon hebraicum et aramaicum veteris Testamenti*, 12-14.

Alencar functions as a virtual translator when he outlines his project of a "prose experiment" (also defined as an "essay" or a "demonstration," where one will find "entirely Brazilian poetry, drawn from the language of the savages"). Enunciating his program, the novelist says:

> Without doubt the Brazilian poet has to translate the ideas of the Indians into his language, even if they are uncultured and coarse; but the great difficulty is precisely this translation; civilized language must be molded as much as possible to the primitive simplicity of the barbarian language and only represent indigenous images and thoughts in terms and phrases that seem natural coming from the mouth of the savages. Knowledge of the native language is the best criterion for literary nationalism. It gives us not only the true style, but also the savage's poetic images, his modes of thought, the tendencies of his spirit, and even the smallest peculiarities of his life. The Brazilian poet should drink from this well, whence the true national poem, as I imagine it, will emerge. ("Carta ao Dr. Jaguaribe")

The translating operation ultimately becomes, irresistibly, a "barbarizing" *razzia*, which ruins the purity of the dominant, civilized language, molding it to the "etymological fantasy" (the expression is Cavalcânti Proença's) of "savage expression." Alencar distances himself from Chateaubriand who, in *Atala*, had claimed to use the *style indien* with parsimony, fearful that his tale would become something as incomprehensible for the reader as "Hebrew."[6] Instead, through a tactic of

---

[6] Some narrow-minded spirits, contemporary or later, accused *Iracema*'s author of "plagiarizing" European models. The proposition has no validity for those who understand literature as a permanent intertextual dialogue where the problem of "originality" is not reduced to a mere passive review of sources and influences. Alencar, a "creative translator," transgresses *Atala*'s paradigm in more than one sense. Linguistically, instead of civilizing indigenous language, as Chateaubriand proposes to do, he seeks to "Tupinize" Portuguese. Ideologically (in religious and ethical terms), the mestiza Atala, daughter of a Spaniard, reveals herself a Christian. In love with the Indian Chacta, she prefers to poison herself rather than break her oath of virginity and consecration to God made to her dying mother.

With *Iracema*, everything occurs in reverse. Tupã's virgin violates the tribe's interdiction and lets herself be possessed by Martim, making it possible for him to drink the sacred acacia spirits, with which the young Portuguese warrior "drugs" himself and thus deadens the restrictions of his chivalrous and Christian code of conduct. Following her natural impulses, the Tabajara virgin nestles in her lover's arms, consummating her possession in the trances of the dream. Seduced/seductress, violated/violator, the 'virgin of the sertão' is comparable, in Cavalcânti's expression, to the "vine that erotically and amorously entwines itself around the proud trunk represented by Martim." Iracema's "savage condition" freed Alencar from his conservative inhibitions and from the prejudices of his epoch, allowing him to create a female figure capable of amorous initiatives and sexual realization instead of a submissive and obstinate, nunlike maiden. Lucíola, in this sense, is Iracema's counterpart in Alencar's work. Like the Indian woman, the prostitute is also an exception, living free at the margins of social norms; but while the former is spontaneous and innocent in her rapture, the latter is divided. Dante Moreira Leite has observed that in *Lucíola* Alencar places "in the same woman, the two female images of the period: the pure virgin and the courtesan. These two women (Maria and Lúcia), although united in one, are different people: Maria is the soul, Lúcia the body."

Iracema, however, radicalizes and subverts *Atala*: Alencar goes farther than Chateaubriand. (The "Christianization" at the end of *Atala* represents, for Michel Butor, the first step of Chateaubriand's gradual effort to "denaturalize" a book--*Les Natchez*--which "in its origin was a cry of indignation against his country and his religion"). If Alencar's book-poem seems to us today to be a sugar-coated harlequin romance, we must remember that at the time it was written some saw in it (and particularly in the scene of Iracema's possession) "the most shameless materiality." The author of this censure is Franklin Távora, often considered the precursor of Brazilian "naturalism"... This moralistic reaction by the future author of *O cabeleira* coincides with that of the emperor Dom Pedro II toward *Lucíola*, who found the book's "licentiously realistic" composition to be strange. I emphasized these "transgressive" aspects of *Iracema* in relation to *Atala* in the brief text I wrote, in July 1985, on the occasion of the publication of the new French translation of Alencar's masterpiece, by Inês Oséki-Dépré. My text, "*Iracéma*: une archéologie d'avant-garde," together with Liliana Giraudon's review, "Erotisme de combative "nativism" in which the "verisimilitude" is another name for the Edenic "realism" of language understood as a "faithful portrait" of man in a "state of nature," Alencar intuitively comes close to an idea of translation as a "making strange" of the vernacular, which implies exposing the translator's language "to the violent impulse coming from the foreign language" (this is the principle of translation "as form," defended in modern times by Walter Benjamin, who bases his argument on Rudolf Pannwitz). If we consider what Mattoso Câmara Jr. says about the structure of this language, scientifically described and "de-romanticized" (20-21),[7] Alencar's "invented" Tupi results in a heteroglossic grafting of Portuguese: it proliferates in decapsulating metaphors starting from agglutinated semantemes; it unfolds in similes that iconically reproduce the presupposed concretion of the primitive world. In the historiographic "fiction" of Brazilian Indianist Romanticism, one might say that Alencar's Tupi represented, like an imaginative scriptural "counterfeiting," the "Ossianic Poem" that was lacking, by indicting, as a "strange-making" (extravagant or *extra-vagus*) "supplement," the erasure of the "origin" promoted by the repressiveness of colonial culture (we might recall, in this regard, the thesis of Joaquim Norberto, underlined by Antônio Candido as a symptom of radicality, of the presumed "existence of an authen-

---

langue," appears in *Impressions du sud*.

[7] Mattoso does not refer explicitly to Alencar, but he reproves the "naive and simplistic" technique for the understanding of the etymology of Tupi words, of which the author of *Iracema* was practically convinced. Direct and detailed restrictions concerning the novelist are found in Frederico G. Edelweiss. On page 13 of his study one reads the following: "With such precarious and fallacious resources no one is capable of discovering genuine Tupi terms, the only acceptable forms in the environment of non-acculturated tribes, in whose midst the scenes of *Iracema* unfold and which, for this very reason, errs in its very title." We learn that *Eirembé* would be the appropriate onomastic composite, instead of *Iracema* (27)... This fact is sufficient for us to evaluate the abyss of incomprehension that can open between serious research into Tupi, necessary and respectable on the scientific plane where it should occur, and the free, inventive poetics of the amateur "Tupinist" Alencar, when the scruples of the former pretend to "correct" the aesthetic project of the latter.

tically indigenous literature which, had it not been maliciously suffocated by the colonizer, could have had the formative role that was left to the Portuguese...").

From the Phonic Metaphor to the Style of Detached Clauses

By inventing his Tupi as an aesthetic device, Alencar constituted an image of his prosody, of his timbre. This has been the object of many studies, including that of Cavalcânti Proença: "It is thus clear that Alencar found in Tupi not only the vocalic resonance of this predilection, but also a plastic and sensorial language, rich in onomatopeias." Later, the same author notes: "And some of the virtues of the Tupi tongue are transmitted to that of the civilized language, primarily its prosodic sweetness, with lax and slow vowels, indifferent to the push of the consonants." And he concludes by stressing the "influence of the indigenous language on Alencar's rhythm," speaking of "Alencar's music" as if of an expression "that had already become a literary commonplace." What is less obvious, and has yet to be analyzed, is how much this idealized sonorous staff influenced what we might call *Iracema*'s "microtonal" texture. It is transformed into a program for a differentiating revitalization of Brazilian Portuguese: "All peoples of musical temperament possess a sonorous and abundant language. Brazil meets these conditions: the national influence is already being felt in the much smoother pronunciation of our dialect." From equations of similitude on the plane of the "form of content" (metaphors in generic terms or, more specifically, comparative "similes"), the immediate steps are the "phonic metaphors" or "*parafonias*" ("anagrams" in the Saussurean sense of the term) that equate and semantically magnetize phonic figures dispersed and redistributed on the "plane of expression." If many critics have observed that the key to the legend-novel is "cryptographic" (from Araripe Jr. to Wilson Martins to Silviano Santiago), one must dig deeper to perceive that Iracema is not merely the cryptogram "lips of honey," included in Alencar's glossary of Tupinisms. The name is also textually reconfigured into a subliminal cryptophony. We thus have, for example, the comparative syntagm, "Mais rápida que a ema selvagem" ["Faster than the wild rhea"], which gives us the brown virgin's name through her agile running style in the mode of a Homeric "fixed metaphor"; one hears: RApIDA EMA / IRAcEMA...

Corresponding to this phonic work, always within the Tupinizing paradigm, is the idea of "style" as "plastic art." Still concerning the influence of the Tupi language on Alencar's imagination, Cavalcânti Proença observes: "In it Alencar's imagination would find broad horizons to explore; and the visual characteristic of his spirit could only be stimulated on contact with a language which, because of its primitiveness, was concrete par excellence."

From this derives Alencar's opposition to "conjunctive style" in the polemic with Pinheiro Chagas.[8] To the copulative style, which he considers "abusive" ("the use of the copulative to join distinct ideas and complete sentences is an abuse"), *Iracema*'s author prefers the style of "detached clauses," proposing the substitution of that conjunctive style ("so aligned with conjunctions") by a "more simple and concise phrase": the "separation of clauses denotes the succession and contrast" of "various impressions," instead of tending toward the "accumulation of colors" and toward "crude pastiche." The example that Alencar exhibits in the "Post-scriptum" to the second edition of *Iracema*, from the occurrence of this "style of detached clauses" in the classics themselves (the description of the island of Ceylon by Lucena), is a paradigm of the *ready-made* of "Brazil-wood poetry," as Oswald de Andrade would systematize it in his "montage style" cutouts during the heroic years of Modernism. Here I partially rewrite it with typical Oswaldian "pauses":

As pedreiras criam os mais finos rubis,
safiras, olhos-de-gato e outra muita sorte de pedrarias.
O mar, além de muito pescado, é, como já dissemos,
um dos três tesouros das pérolas e aljofras do Oriente.

It is the defense of asyndetic writing, the beginning of the revolt of parataxis against hypotaxis, on the level of aesthetic information, that begins to be outlined with Alencar the "Tupinist." This defense is supported by an argument extracted from the translating process. In the same "Post-scriptum," Alencar, acting as an intertextual (intralingual) transla-

---

[8] "In the opinion of the honorable man of letters [Pinheiro Chagas], the nerves of style are the particles, especially the conjunctions, which weave the sentences of classical authors and serve as links to the long series of phrases which pile up in a single sentence. For my taste, however, instead of fortifying the style and giving it vigor, this accumulation of phrases linked together by conjunctions weakens the sentence, rendering thought diffuse and languid."

tor, demonstrates how to transpose the "old" style into the modern. He presents an excerpt of Fr. Luís de Sousa's classical prose "disguised as modern"; then, he dresses an excerpt from *O Guarani* in "the old style" (in classical form). In this operation of rewriting, quite precisely understood as a "cross-dressing," in the first demonstration he compacts the text in fewer sentences (from eight to six) in order to make it more "concise" and "terse"; in the second, he exemplifies the "style of detached clauses" (an embryo of syncopated modernist prose?). All of this converges toward a program of a "barbarizing" making-strange: "the civilized language must mold itself as much as possible to the primitive simplicity of the barbarous language." As Soares Amora has noted, this is fundamentally a program of "translation":

> Alencar did not hesitate in taking full advantage of indigenous words, playing with their sonorous values and their metaphoric and symbolic content, and in seeking, in Portuguese phraseological structure, with all its resources of euphony, expressivity and impressivity, a 'translation,' the most faithful possible to the spirit of the Tupi language (from the literary point of view). No matter that the solutions found by Alencar may be more valid in the light of literary aesthetics than of linguistics--what matters is that his discoveries were perfect and responded integrally to the spirit, the character, and the poetic intentions of the work.

The idea of "fidelity," which is regulatory in the citation, can now be rethought in Benjaminian terms as "fidelity to the reendowment of a form": the semiotic form of Tupi aesthetically idealized as an Adamic language, leading Alencar to the hybridizing transgression of canonical Portuguese. The most radical stage of this heteroglossic project will be completed by Guimarães Rosa in "Meu tio, o Iauaretê," a true conclusion of *Iracema*'s "philological revolution." There the Indian virgin who ran agilely through the woods of Ipu and then nurses her son with the milk of breasts bleeding from the offspring of the tayra, is reincarnated in a real "tigress," the female jaguar Maria-Maria, coveted by the manly zeal of the jaguar/jaguar hunter Tonho Tigreiro, who roars and bellows in Tupi. A lexographical eye can discover the name "Jaguareté" in one of Alencar's notes, defined as "the greater devourer;" a lover of phonic consonances can find an echo of "Moacir," the "son of suffering," in the final appeal, "Remuaci" (friend, half-brother), of the agonizing jaguar-Indian. In a certain possible interpretation, this is the hybrid text generated and "donated" by Alencar in his attempt, emphasized by Araripe Jr., to decipher the enigma of the origin ("...decipher it, give it form, and, vaguely, reduce it to the concrete...").

The Refusal of the Epigonal Form of the Epic

In André Jolles' conception, *Mythos* and *Logos* coexist "oxymoronically." The desire to know through "elucidation," oriented toward the object and its relations, which aspires to universally valid judgements, unfolds in another "mental disposition" from which the "myth" results. It is a form capable of creating the universe, things, and their relations through an interrogation and a response, based not on its truth content, but rather on the "veridical prophecy" (Jolles stresses that in German *fragen*, "to ask," comes from the root *freh*, also involving the meanings of *forschen*, "to desire," "to search for," and *fordern*, "to demand"). To this human questioning, which is translated into a desire and a demand, the universe responds as a "form," the myth, whose messenger is the "symbol."

Alencar's gesture of return to the UR-EPOS (the resumption of the impossible *epos* in the bourgeois era, by a Brazilian novelist who was incapable, in turn, of coherently writing the "prose of the world" molded in a "strong" form and in Balzacian realism's paradigm of "truth") occurred through this paramythological mode of "veridical deciphering," by resorting to fabular structure shaped by the mediation of folklore and the oral tradition. Discussing *Iracema*'s historical argument--which he calls a "legend" and not a "historical novel" when he systematizes his complete work--Alencar points toward the oral tradition as an "important source of history, and at times the most pure and truthful one." Cavalcânti Proença notes: "The roots of Alencar's work are in folklore; thus the structure of the popular stories is strongly projected in their fabulation. As in the stories of Trancoso, some of his characters receive vague denominations--*a very poor lad, a king, the Indian, the witch*" (thus the error of those who seek a psychological exploration in *Iracema*: this would be like asking for psychological depth from Homeric Hellene or from the heroine of a fairy tale...).

With the example of *Atala* in sight, and coexisting--in the dialogical literary space of the coexistence of the nonsimultaneous--with the work of Balzac, who died in 1850, Alencar made his "regressive" option

in the available field of literary possibilities and provoked both an antici-
patory and a productive moment. His movement was regressive/pro-
gressive if we consider what comes afterwards (the "prose of comparative
conjunction" or of "simile" of Raúl Pompéia and Clarice Lispector, on the
one hand; Macunaímic "carnivalization," in a parodic-anthropophagic
mode, on the other; the "Tupinizing" radicalization, within the "seri-
ous-aesthetic" orientation of Rosa's "Iauaretê," at a third moment).

The epic poem in the manner of Camões, exhausted by successive epigonal dilutions, from the short-winded *Prosopopéia* to the *Cara-
muru* and to *A confederação dos tamoios* (to limit the discussion to the
Brazilian context), had been exhausted as an effective intertextual standard, without Brazilian poets themselves realizing it. Discussing the recently published *A confederação dos tamoios* (Gonçalves de Magalhães,
1856) at the request of Dom Pedro II, Magalhães's Maecenas, Alexandre
Herculano notes the formal deterioration of the epic poem:

> None of the great contemporary poets, Goethe, Byron,
> Manzoni, Hugo, Lamartine, Garret, has attempted, to my
> knowledge, the epic. It is because their highly refined poetic
> instincts reveal to them that such an endeavor would be more
> than arduous, it would be impossible. The human epopee,
> which was no longer appropriate in the last century (Voltaire's
> genius gave sad testimony to this), is even less so in this one.
> The past still possessed the anger of philosophism; the present
> century looks at everything that is heroic and sovereign with the
> cold disdain of indifference and skepticism.

Intuitively, Alencar moves toward the rejection of the epigonal,
neoclassical form of the *epos* in poetry, taken by the same impulse of
refusal of "Portuguese of the Court," in which Magalhães had written his
poem ("a beautiful subject which, enhanced by the grandeur of an unhap-
py race and by the scenes of our land's splendid nature, would have
provided the theme for a divine epic if it had been written by Dante").
In his polemic against the Camões-like composition of the courtly bard
he affirms: "If one day I were a poet and I wanted to sing the song of my
land and its wonders, if I wanted to compose a national poem, I would
ask God to make me forget for a moment my ideas of a civilized man."
This "forgetting," although still nourished by the dream of writing "a
poem," resulted in *Iracema*. Thus, to capture "savage thought" (this
expression, which today recalls Lévi-Strauss, is in the "Carta ao Dr. Ja-

guaribe"), the writer decides on an "experiment in prose." Alencar seems to be bringing together, in the same programmatic purpose, the two prime motives (or the two extremities) of his polemic. On the one hand, the need to "barbarize" (read "Tupinize") Portuguese to submit it to indigenous "modes of thought," and thus, thanks to a translating process oriented toward the plane of the signifier, arrive at the linguistic sources from which the "true national poem" would derive. On the other, that sentiment, which is not completely formulated in terms of a program, but rather strongly perceived in terms of the rejection of a worn-out form, which makes him first attack *A confederação dos tamoios*, and later, in the "afterword" to *Iracema*, exempt Gonçalves Dias while at the same time criticizing his use of "classical language" in his attempt at writing a "Brazilian epic" (*Os timbiras*, 1857):

> Gonçalves Dias is the national poet par excellence; no one can compare to him in the opulence of imagination, in the fine labor of his verse, in his knowledge of Brazilian nature and primitive customs. In his American poems he took advantage of many of the most beautiful indigenous traditions; and in his unfinished poem *Os timbiras*, he proposes to describe the Brazilian epic. Nevertheless, the savages of his poem speak a classical language (...); they express ideas appropriate to civilized man, and which they would not likely have in their state of nature.

The inadequacy of Dias's language, resolved by Alencar on the expressional plane through a mechanism of radical translation, making-strange (no matter if it is philologically "false" and idealized in terms of his conception of Tupi), gave way to a different, complementary formal solution to resolve a typological impasse: accede to the poem by way of prose. The failure to reassume the *epos* in versified form (and inevitably modelled on Camões, even if in blank verse) dictated such a distinctive choice, whether in regard to the unfinished *Os timbiras* by Gonçalves Dias, the "national poet par excellence," or in regard to the awkward flight of Magalhães's *A confederação dos tamoios*, protected by renitent imperial favor. Alencar's scriptural praxis confirmed the failure of his personal project for an epic, attempted in 1863:

> When writing some letters about *A confederação dos tamoios* I committed the imprudence of saying: 'the indigenous traditions provide the material for a great poem that perhaps

some day someone will present without clamor or ostentation, as a modest fruit of their vigils.' That was sufficient for some to suppose that the writer was referring to himself and that he already had the poem in hand; several people asked me about it. This raised my literary mettle; without calculating the minimal efforts necessary for such a large task, which overwhelmed the two illustrious poets, I outlined the plan of the book and began with such vigor that I took it to the fourth canto in one breath. This breath was sustained for nearly five months, but it then died down...

This did not occur without profound vacillations. The idea of going from verse to prose involves, for Alencar as for the Chateaubriand of *Atala*, who inspires him to a certain extent, a trace of "depreciation," of "degradation."[9] Alencar, in turn, on renouncing the epic initiated and in full expansion ("a book where there are still and there will remain incubated around two thousand heroic verses"), does so by way of an "alibi," an astute theoretical reflection which invokes the possible misunderstanding of the poem being elaborated as a decisive argument for abandoning the undertaking: verse would increase the project's difficulty, making the task of molding "savage thought" to Portuguese more complex. The "prose experiment" would function as a first step, a "test" for the work begun in verse ("On the other hand one would know the effect the verse would have by the effect of the prose"). The consolation of poetry lost (and invious) to viable prose is consummated in this declaration of intentions: "If the reading public likes this literary form, which seems to me to have some attractions, then I will make an effort to finish the poem I began, although the verse has lost much of its primitive charm." If not, the "un-

---

[9] In the preface to the first edition of *Atala*, after defining his book--"C'est une sorte de poème"--Chateaubriand is quick to clarify it through a note: "At a time when everything in terms of literature is perverted, I feel obligated to warn that, if I use the word 'Poem' here it is because I do not know how to make myself understood any other way. I am not one of these barbarians who confuse prose and verse. The poet, no matter what they say, is always a man par excellence; entire volumes of descriptive prose are not worth fifty beautiful verses of Homer, Virgil, or Racine."

redeemed" poet adds, the unfinished verses would be relegated to the "drawer of old papers" as "autobiographical relics"; that is, if the public's incomprehension made the author renounce this "genre of literature" as well. Although he did not soon find popular success (see the testimony of Machado de Assis, in 1866, referring to *Iracema* as a "work of the future"), the "prose experiment," Alencar's vicarious poem ("essay" or "demonstration") both supplemented and effaced, in the writer's spirit, the vocational inaptitude for versified epic. This leaves him with a painful balance of "two thousand heroic verses," which seem to him, in the intervals of lucid self-criticism, to be inferior, because of their vulgarity and monotony, to "so much awkward prose" he had "committed to paper"; at a moment of less rigor, the clever alibi recrudesces, tinged with proud constraint, and he then formulates it as a fear of wasting time uselessly "writing verses for half-breeds," a variant of that same justification according to which he should abandon the project of "writing a poem that would be prolonged," thus avoiding "the risk of not being understood." In this second self-explanation, the "savage" project is punished by the civilized "bad conscience." The poem's epic breath (the Camonian mold is implicit) does not correspond to the "savage mind." The "verses for half-breeds" would risk not finding a sufficiently perceptive audience to discern the "scruple of fine gold" (...) "unearthed from the deep layers where an extinct race sleeps"; an audience capable of preferring, "to the images in fashion," the "wild flowers of Brazilian poetry," "the image or thought" so tirelessly "polished" by the author; an audience able, finally, to recognize the aesthetic validity of the translating, hybridizing operation of civilized language in the molds of the barbarous language, dared by the poet-prose-writer in the moment of radicality that governs this very project.[10]

---

[10] In his 1882 book about Alencar, Araripe Jr. captured well the "strange sensation" that *Iracema* aroused, giving it an "inimitable tone": "It is not an aboriginal song; but also a European would be incapable of writing it. It is an entirely creole product." And he emphasizes the "fact of its untranslatability"--a characteristic generally attributed to poetry--as the "most evident proof" of the "original character" of this prose, resulting, in turn, as we have seen, from an operation of translation, in the broad sense of the term.

The Greatest Indianist Poet

Whatever the *post-festum* breaks by which the novelist Alencar is divided as a thinking subject, in relation to the experience of *Iracema* the truth is that through the dislocation of the epic project, from epigonal verse to "inimitable" prose, he resolves vocational chance into a morphological necessity (and the regressive movement into a progressive one): from an inhibition toward or an incompetence with verse is born the proposal of a new "literary form," erected on the exhaustion of an obsolete model ("Because of its dignity and nobility, verse does not allow a certain flexibility of expression that fits quite well, however, with the most elevated prose. The elasticity of the sentence would thus permit one to use indigenous images with greater clarity, so that they are not unperceived."). *Iracema*, the poem-substitute, the "song without meter" in the unrefined melody of "savage thought" ("Who cannot illustrate his native land, sing its legends, without meter, in the unrefined melody of its ancient sons"), corrodes and erodes the "nobility" of the epic in verses as such, which will only leave autobiographical limbo for the posthumous museography of specialized pages. *Os filhos de Tupā* (1863), in decasyllabic verses, planned for XII Cantos, is the lackluster rough-draft of this frustrated appetite for the "dignified" epic, in traditional molds. The diamond-like culmination of this psychic impulse (the metaphor here is not Mallarmean, but rather Alencarian: "Nature suffers the influence of powerful tropical irradiation, which produces diamonds and genius."), now rectified in its course or inflection, is manifested in *Iracema* (1865). Thanks to a sort of crystallographic mutation, which results in the turning of the frustrated poem into surprising prose ("a transformation of coal into a diamond"). From the minacious chrysalis where two thousand decasyllables toil in a potential state of epic proliferation, there emerges a little book of thirty-three synthetic chapters, a prose of "unagglutinated metaphors" and "detached clauses," in the rhythm of an imaginary Tupi. Here Alencar, the prose writer by destiny, overcomes the poets by election, beginning with Gonçalves Dias himself.

Paraphrasing Walter Benjamin's comment about German Romanticism ("Die Idee der Poesie ist die Prosa"), I could say that the idea of poetry of Brazilian Indianist Romanticism was prose. In a school in which poetry provided the tone, prose provided the form (the "method," explains Benjamin). Jakobson observed, speaking of Pushkin and Liérmontov, of Maiakovski and Pasternak, in their respective moments of Russian literature, that in periods of prosaic epigonism, of the repetition of classical models, the innovative breeze, the precursor of unsuspected directions, normally comes from the exceptional prose of poets. Perhaps in the Brazilian case we are faced with a symmetrically opposite hypothesis. The greatest Indianist poet (the only fully readable one today, if we do not consider the inside-out Indianism of Sousândrade) was a prose writer: José de Alencar. This is not a novelty. Augusto Meyer (in a pioneering essay in which he rebels against the impoverishing reading of Alencar in accordance with the strict model of realism) had already observed: "*Iracema* would be enough to enshrine him as the greatest creator of Romantic prose, and the greatest Indianist poet, in the Portuguese language."

REFERENCES

Alencar, José de. *Iracéma, légende du Ceará*. Tr. Inês Oséki-Dépré. Aix-en-Provence: Alinéa/UNESCO, 1985.

Araripe Jr. "José de Alencar." *Obra crítica 1*. Rio de Janeiro: Ministério de Educação e Cultura/Casa de Ruy Barbosa, 1958.

Bakhtin, Mikhail. "Discourse in the Novel" and "Forms of Time and Chronotope in the Novel." In *The Dialogical Imagination*. Ed. Michael Holquist. Tr. Caryl Emerson and Michael Holquist. Austin: U of Texas P, 1981.

Câmara Jr., J. Mattoso. "Da natureza das línguas indígenas." *Revista de Letras* [Faculdade de Filosofia Letras e Ciências Humanas de Assis] 3 (1962): 17-29.

Campos, Haroldo de. "*Iracéma*: une archéologie d'avant-garde," *Impressions du sud* [Aix-en-Provence] 11 (January 1986): 53

Edelweiss, Frederico G. *José de Alencar / O tupinista segundo as notas do romance Iracema*. Salvador: Centro de Estudos Baianos, Universidade Federal da Bahia, publication no. 87, 1979.

Lexicon hebraicum et aramaicum veteris Testamenti. Org. F. Zorell S.J. Rome: Pontificium Institutum Biblicum, 1968.

Theologisches Wörterbuch zum Alt Testament. Vol. 1. Org. G. J. Botterweck and H. Ringgren. Stuttgart: Verlag W. Kohlhammer, 1973.

THE LASCIVIOUS VOLUPTUOUSNESS OF NOTHING: A READING OF *EPITAPH OF A SMALL WINNER*

João Alexandre Barbosa
Universidade de São Paulo

I

In a letter dated 11 December 1852, little more than a year after having initiated *Madame Bovary*, Flaubert wrote to Louise Colet:

> Je commence par te dévorer de baisers, dans la joie qui me transporte. Ta lettre de ce matin m'a enlevé de dessus le coeur un terrible poids. Il était temps. Hier, je n'ai pu travailler de toute la journée... A chaque mouvement que je faisais (ceci est textuel), la cervelle me sautait dans le crâne et j'ai été obligé de me coucher à 11 heures. J'avais la fièvre et un accablement général. Voici trois semaines que je souffrais horriblement d'appréhensions: je ne *dépensais* pas à toi d'une minute, mais d'une façon peu agréable. Oh oui, cette idée me torturait; j'en ai eu des chandelles devant les yeux deux ou trois fois, jeudi entre'autres. Il faudrait tout un livre pour développer d'une manière compréhensible mon sentiment à cet égard. L'idée de donner le jour à quelqu'un *me fait horreur*. Je me maudirais se j'étais père. Un fils de moi! Oh non, non, non! Que toute ma chair perisse et que je ne transmette à personne l'embêtement et les ignomies de l'existence![1] (*Oeuvres complètes* 62-63)

---

[1] The letter was unpublished until the 1927 edition. In English translation: "I begin by devouring you with kisses, I am so happy. Your letter of this morning lifted a terrible weight from my heart. It was high time. Yesterday I could not work all day. Every time I moved (literally), my brain throbbed in my skull, and I had to go to bed at 11 o'clock. I was

31

No reader of Machado de Assis would fail to see in the last two lines of Flaubert's letter an echo of the final negatives which end the *Epitaph* of Braz Cubas.

Although the terms are different (Flaubert particularizes annoyances and ignominies, Machado generalizes by speaking of human misery), as are the respective verbal modes (in Flaubert the future subjunctive; in Machado the preterite perfect), the two texts are similar, even in their formulation of that which is or will be denied: the idea of the genetic transmission of a negative worldview, expressed as "stupidity," "ignominy," or "legacy of our misery."

Of course a more basic distinction exists between the two: whereas Flaubert expresses a personal fear--the suspicion that Louise Colet planned to modify their relationship through maternity--the fictional Braz Cubas attempts to settle accounts with his very existence. The "deceased author" says:

> Adding up and balancing all these items, a person will conclude that my accounts showed neither a surplus nor a deficit and consequently that I died quits with life. And he will conclude falsely; for, upon arriving on this other side of the mystery, I found that I had a small surplus, which provides the final negative of this chapter of negatives: I had no progeny, I transmitted to no one the legacy of our misery. (223)[2]

Braz thus sees the negative as a positive balance: more than just a confirmation of a biological order, this statement functions as one of the *Epi-*

---

feverish and completely despondent. For these past three weeks I have suffered from horrible apprehensions: I never stopped thinking of you, but in a way that was scarcely pleasant. Yes, the thought tortured me; once or twice I actually saw stars before my eyes--on Thursday, among other days. The idea of bringing someone into this world fills me with *horror*. I would curse myself if I were to become a father. A son! Oh, no, no, no! May my flesh perish utterly! May I never transmit to anyone the boredom and the ignominies of existence!" (*The Letters of Gustave Flaubert* 174).

[2] Translator's note: All citations in translation are from the English edition, listed in Works Cited.

taph's structuring principles. Read backwards, that is, between death and death, the book leaves little intact, save the enormous exception of the book itself. As for Mallarmé, destruction was Machado de Assis's Beatrix.

In this sense, the novel that remains standing among the ruins it itself created ends up by being the true and final negative: the affirmation of a fictional discourse made possible only through the negation of an artistic manner of doing and saying (like the Romantics and the first realist/naturalist works) that sought the justification for its discourse in other discourses (historical, political, philosophical, etc.).

The *Epitaph*, published between March and December 1880 in the *Revista brasileira*, represented the affirmation of a way of seeing literature which not merely negated its own previous nature, but also made this nature the nourishment of the worm that gnawed the "cold flesh" of the "deceased author." By doing so, it permitted the appearance of the "author who writes after death." It therefore has nothing to do with two phases of a single writer. It is, rather, the way in which, to use the terms of the epitaph, the present work, "gnawed" by the previous one, creates the space where it is possible to make the change: to install negativity in the interstices of the work itself.

But what does this creation mean, and where, in the work, are its identifying traces? First, these traces are not exhausted in the thematic planes of the work, but rather should be sought in the discourses that create them. The negativity is not merely in the "peevish pessimism" noted both by Braz Cubas himself in the warning "To the Reader" and by Machado de Assis in the "Prologue to the Fourth Edition," but also in the dismantling of those discourses that represent such "peevish pessimism" and which constitute their thematic planes.

This is evident in the compositional perspective in which the author acts as editor, associating his discourse with the tradition of Sterne, Xavier de Maistre or Garrett. The initial eight chapters rectify what is said there by insisting that the *Epitaph* is a work from beyond the grave. In "To the Reader," Braz Cubas himself notes the unusual nature of the compositional process, shunning his experience and excusing himself for the necessity of a short prologue, affirming: "Hence I shall not relate the extraordinary method that I used in the composition of these memoirs, written here in the world beyond" (17).

Starting with the selection of point-of-view, therefore, the work includes, as a compositional principle, a critique of the Romantic hypertrophy of the self by constructing an "author who writes after death" rather than "deceased author" as in Chateaubriand. Perhaps for this very reason, Augusto Meyer could see ultra-romantic features in the *Epitaph*, culminating in the seventh chapter, "The Delirium" (161).

The narrative discourse adopted in the *Epitaph* involves discordant stylistic traits that provoke the simultaneous appearance and dissolution of signifieds and through which irony and humor organize the space of negativity. Thus even in the initial chapter, the graveside elegy, using analogies with Nature ("a fine drizzle, steady and sad") for the commonplaces spouted by the orator ("This sombre air, these drops from heaven, those dark clouds covering the blue like a crepe of mourning, all manifest the harsh and cruel grief that gnaws at her deepest entrails") undergoes a radical reading by the narrator who destroys it by suddenly shifting to a lower level: "I shall never regret the legacy of twenty government bonds that I left him" (19-20).

This procedure pervades the work from beginning to end. Still in this first chapter is another passage as efficient as the previous one, albeit more subtle--the sentence in which the narrator, so to speak, chooses the noises of his last moments above ground: "At present, I wish to die calmly, methodically, hearing the sobs of the ladies, the soft words of the men, the rain drumming on the taro leaves, and the piercing noise of a razor being sharpened by a knife-grinder outside in front of the door of a leather craftsman" (20). The last phrase, in contrast to the muffled and soft sound of the previous ones ("sobs," "soft words," "the rain drumming"), as well as the choice of objects designated ("razor," "knife-grinder," "door of a leather craftsman"), creates a fundamental discordance that obligates the reader to read in the previous clauses a set of conventional epithets extracted from the traditional way of organizing the sounds of death.

At the other extreme, chapters II and IV, "The Plaster" and "The Fixed Idea," broaden the procedure in two senses: they reveal the necessary articulation between the critique of discourses and that of the ideas they represent, and they point toward the disorientation of the positions and opinions created by the story. Together, both senses provide the tone and the substratum of the *Epitaph*. Thus, it is the "fixed idea" of the invention of the plaster which, on the one hand, provokes reflections on the uncertainties of historical discourse and, on the other, it is the more developed and configured critique of the very fertility of theories that absorbs the narrator and which will later serve as the foundation of Quincas Borba's Humanitism. Little is actually said about the plaster;

its purpose is more important: "an anti-melancholy plaster, designed to relieve the despondency of mankind" (21).

Starting from the affirmation of a generalized pathological state--the melancholy from which one should relieve humanity--the narrator skips to a reflection on history: the plaster as an *idée fixe*, as diffuse as the sickness to which it is destined, composes the terms of the metaphor with which he searches for a definition of history. Between the adjectives that qualify Nature ("immensely whimsical") and history ("eternally irresponsible"), the movement is of identification if one pays attention to the fact that, in the following paragraphs, history is treated as "voluble" since the narrator finds nothing that can serve as a comparison to the fixed idea: "I cannot think of anything so fixed in this world: perhaps the moon, perhaps the Egyptian pyramids, perhaps the late Germanic Diet" (24).

This absence of stability and fixity prepares the suture between the *Epitaph*'s novelistic core (which, in fact, begins only with chapter X) and the proliferation of theories which attempt to substitute the realization of the *idée fixe*. An example is the "theory of human editions," in chapter VI, where Virgília appears for the first time and which is only explained in chapter XXVII, where the main character and, therefore, the *Epitaph*'s primary novelistic vein, reappear. This theory points, like all those that pass through the *Epitaph*, toward the relative, the indecisive, the unstable, the compensatory, the transitory, the uncertain, where a trench is opened between the desired but always frustrated fixity of history and the human discourse that makes it into something that is "voluble," "eternally irresponsible." The narrator says:

> ...It is this very capacity that makes us masters of the earth, this capacity to restore the past and thus to prove the instability of our impressions and the vanity of our affections. Let Pascal say that man is a thinking reed. He is wrong; man is a thinking erratum. Each period in life is a new edition that corrects the preceding one and that in turn will be corrected by the next, until publication of the definitive edition, which the publisher donates to the worms. (77)

But the threads dispersed in this first part of the *Epitaph* are reconnected in the emblematic description, in chapter VII, "The Delirium," of the difficulties that the narrator will face and the strategies he will use to overcome them.

Since it is a delirium, and since the narrator himself calls attention to his ill condition ("reflections of a sick brain" or "a sick man's thoughts" [31]), it is possible to find, in a Freudian condensation in dreams, the subtext of a reading in a double articulation: Nature and history, identified as "voluble" by his conscience, are translated through a discourse that joins romantic and realistic traits, finally resolved through the corrosion of humor. The chapter is prepared by chapters II and IV, in which the relationship between history and Nature is suggested, as well as by the immediately preceding chapters--V and VI--in which the image of Virgilia concretizes the relationship, melding Nature and history in a dizzying personal movement.

The return to the past in chapter VI (which inspires the "theory of human editions") is the platform from which Braz Cubas's delirium takes off: that which will be unresolved in his relationship with Virgilia--the stages their love will pass through before and during her marriage and after the death of her husband, going from indifference to indifference, passing through passion--is now perceived through the allegory.

By inverting the lines of Corneille's play used as the chapter's title, the "author from the dead" accentuates the contradictions that can lead to the full realization of love. In *Le Cid*, the words of the chapter title ("Chimène, qui l'eût dit? Rodrigue, qui l'eût cru?") follow the torment of Chimène, dilacerated between filial fidelity and her love for Don Rodrigue, and the two questions are posed after Don Rodrigue's expression, "Que de maux et de peurs coûteront nos pères," and after other expressions interpreting his dilaceration: while Don Rodrigue speaks of a "miracle d'amour," Chimène speaks of "comble de misères" (Acte III, Scène IV, 798).

By giving precedence to Don Rodrigue's speech, inverting the terms of Corneillian movement between believing and saying, the narrator presents that which in fact provokes the delirium: the transformation of Buffon into a sparrow hawk, which, besides including a reference to the author of the *Histoire naturelle*, also recalls the famous statement about style. It occurs starting from Virgilia's comment, thus described by the author: "As we touched casually on an illicit love affair that was half secret and half overt, I heard her speak with scorn and with a little indignation about the woman in question, who happened to be a friend of hers" (30).

Interpreting the satisfaction of Virgilia's son on hearing "these stout and worthy opinions" is when Buffon's line appears in the subtext, defining not only Virgilia's style, but also qualifying the extent to which her posture is rapine, anticipating, in a certain sense, the "universal law" expressed by Nature in the following chapter: "The tiger kills the lamb because the tiger's philosophy is that, above all, it must live, and if the lamb is tender so much the better" (34). The circle is complete: the inverted readings of Corneille and Buffon point toward the indifferent reversibility between Nature and history, articulated through that which is "whimsical" and "voluble" in one and the other.

In chapter VII itself, the reader soon confronts the arbitrary nature of oneiric images: the relationship between "a Chinese barber" and a mandarin, Saint Thomas's *Summa theologica* and a hippopotamus that serves as the narrator's guide. But arbitrary only on the surface, as in all oneiric images: how can one not see in the narrator's transformations a critical allusion to the period's evolutionist science, with even a reference to the sensations of life in death, as we find in the note on the awareness of immobility in the episode dealing with the *Summa theologica*, in which there exists the same mesmerism so carefully cultivated, for example, by an Edgar Allan Poe?

The very destination of the voyage on which the narrator is taken by the hippopotamus points toward such an allusion: "to the beginning of the ages." In fact, without perceiving the purpose of the journey, "abandoning [himself] to fate," the narrator indicates his indifference, affirming: "I am not ashamed to confess that I felt a certain itch of curiosity to know just where the beginning of the ages was, whether it was as mysterious as the origin of the Nile, and above all whether it was more important or less important than the end of the ages" (31).

Everything appears through images of desolation: between the whiteness of the snow and the silence (through which the shadow of Pascal passes), Braz Cubas sees man's reduction in an inverted process of evolution (which had already been revealed in the dialogue with the hippopotamus about the passage from Eden to Abraham's tent): "one might have said that the life in things had become stupefied in the presence of man" (32).

Precisely after the critical reading of evolutionism the central figure of the delirium appears: Nature, or Pandora. The passage occurs without great interruption, except that imposed by silence: "Did it fall from the air? Did it rise from the earth? I do not know. I know only that an immense shape, the figure of a woman, then appeared before me, with its eyes, shining like the sun, fixed upon me" (32).

It is possible, as Otto Maria Carpeaux suggests, that this part of
the chapter is filtered through Machado de Assis's reading of Leopardi's
Operette morali, especially the "Dialogue of Nature and an Icelander,"
just as one may recognize the presence of Schopenhauer or Pascal (48-
52). But more to the point and more internal is to recognize in this
chapter the transformation and the amplification of a metaphor found in
a poem Machado had published two months earlier, in the same *Revista
brasileira*, titled "Uma criatura" and later included in his *Ocidentais*. It
is the metaphor of Nature as a conciliator of opposites, nourishing itself
with death to make life possible and thus permitting a reading of divergent and contradictory signifieds.

In the poem's last five tercets (it is composed of eight tercets
and a final conclusive distich in alexandrine verse), one may grasp the
essential elements of the metaphor, whose fragments are spread through
the chapter of the *Epitaph*:

> Friamente contempla o desespero e o gozo,
> Gosta do colibri, como gosta do verme,
> E cinge ao coração o belo e o monstruoso.
>
> Para ela o chacal é, como a rola, inerme,
> E caminha na terra imperturbável, como
> Pelo vasto areal um vasto paquiderme.
>
> Na árvore que rebenta o seu primeiro gomo
> Vem a folha, que lento e lento se desdobra,
> Depois a flor, depois o suspirado pomo.
>
> Pois essa criatura está em toda a obra:
> Resta o seio da flor e corrompe-lhe o fruto;
> E é nesse destruir que as forças dobra.
>
> Ama de igual amor o poluto e o impoluto:
> Começa e recomeça uma perpétua lida,
> E sorrindo obedece ao divino estatuto.
> -- Tu dirás que é a Morte; eu direi que é a Vida.
>   (*Poesias completas* 447-448).

I am concerned less with showing a parallelism between the
poem and the *Epitaph* than with pointing out the fact that the conception

of Nature as "immensely whimsical" is affirmed differently in each case, although the terms used are essentially the same. Thus, Nature's indifference and impassiveness, which fill the first three tercets transcribed, echo in the description of her face in the *Epitaph*: "Then for the first time I could see her enormous face close up. Nothing more pacific in the world; no violent contortion; no suggestion of hate or ferocity. Its sole, all-pervasive expression was that of eternal isolation, of changeless will, of the impassivity of complete egoism" (33).

In the same way, the destructive sense in the last line of the fourth tercet is translated in the part of Nature's speech which justifies death:

> Time finds interest not in the minute that is already passing, but only in the minute that is about to come. The new-born minute is strong, merry, thinks that it carries eternity in its bosom; it brings only death, and perishes like its predecessors. Egoism, you say? Yes, egoism; I have no other law. Egoism, self-preservation. The tiger kills the lamb because the tiger's philosophy is that, above all, it must live, and if the lamb is tender so much the better; this is the universal law. (34)

What is the difference between the two texts? In the poem the metaphor is used to transmit a meaning--the contradictory and ultimately conciliatory character of Nature, life and death at the same time--through a subject of the enunciation that assumes the knowledge of the contradiction. In the *Epitaph* two discourses are articulated, that of Braz Cubas, whose paradigm is an interpretation of Nature with a romantic substratum, and that of the Nature, who affirms the destructive and "whimsical" tenor that owes so much to a naturalist and evolutionist interpretation of history. Thus also the difference in the two texts' literary nature. In the poem a conciliatory lesson undoes the intensity of a few (rare) images, pushing the text toward the common grave of philosophizing good sense. In the novel the force of the contradiction (now not merely of signifieds but of discourses that mutually criticize one another) creates a space through which the reader experiments the vertiginous or "delirious" tension of the ruptures with the narrator's discourse.

From the angle of the delirium and madness it is possible to see the story as an uninterrupted passing by of "afflictions and joys" in which neither science nor imagination can act as instruments of the creation of intensity. Here is the notable passage: "The history of man and of the earth had thus an intensity that neither science nor the imagination could give it, for science is too slow and imagination too vague, whereas what I saw was the living condensation of history" (34).

Thus, between the slowness of science and the vagueness of the imagination is the condensation that only deliria, madness or dreams can provide. What Braz Cubas sees in the first place, "the several forms of a single malady, which would attack now the viscera, now the psyche," ends up by creating a "nebulous and elusive figure made of patches--a patch of the intangible, another of the improbable, another of the invisible--all loosely sewn together with the needle of imagination" (34-35). Being "the chimera of happiness," there is nothing left but the emptiness of the historical centuries that fill the chapter's final paragraphs, where one retakes the useless voyage "to the beginning of the ages" guided by the hippopotamus. But this last vision is preceded by Braz Cubas's laugh after the first vision, a laugh of despair, "immoderate and idiotic" (35), and the speech with which he addresses Nature or Pandora is, at the same time, one of challenge and acceptance:

> 'You are right,' I said, 'the thing is amusing and worth seeing; a bit monotonous, perhaps, but worth seeing. When Job cursed the day he had been born, it was for want of seeing the show from up here. All right, Pandora, open your belly and devour me; the thing is amusing, but devour me.' (35)

Digested by Nature, but a "whimsical" nature that includes the volubility of history, and not merely the postive Nature as spectacle of the romantic paradigm, the narrator can deliver himself to the "voluptuousness of nothing" through deliria, madness, or dreams, woven by the "needle of imagination." The same needle that now adds another thread to the delirium, the madness and the dream: the very text that is constructed starting from the voluptuous lasciviousness of nothing.

II

From the point of view of narrativity, starting with chapter X the *Epitaph* takes on a diachronic organization, going from Braz Cubas's birth to the final balance of his existence in chapter CLX. However, so numerous are the interruptions, the turns of the text upon itself, the dislocations and substitutions between narrator and reader--in short an intense intertextuality--that the resulting impression is one of discontinuity. The plot unfoldings are so proliferous that the question of a central thread that impels the reader of fiction, that "reading for the plot", to use Peter Brooks' expression, is disconcerting. One might say that the narrator summarizes and magnetizes everything if it were not for the fact that he is also the subject of an incessant mobility, denying the reader the tranquility of a fixed and calm perspective.

Combined with these general characteristics, which might make us think erroneously of an absence of compositional method, is a rigorous narrative plan establishing precise relationships between chapters, demanding an incessant rereading to understand the author's method precisely in the sense the narrator describes it: "although the system is indispensable, one should use it in a spirit of looseness and informality, in one's shirt-sleeves and suspenders, like a person who does not care what the lady who lives across the street, or even the policeman on the block, may think of him" (38).

An example of this compositional rigor, in which textual space transforms contexts of meaning through the use of repeated signifiers, occurs in chapter XI. There, dealing with his master-slave relations with Prudencio, "a little colored house-slave," the narrator describes the way he used the boy as his "horse":

> [...] he would place his hands on the floor and would take a rope (as a rein) between his teeth; and I would climb onto his back with a little stick in my hand, would beat him, and would turn him this way and that, and he would obey--sometimes groaning, but he would obey without a word or, at the most, with a 'Gee, Nhonhô!' to which I would reply, 'Shut your mouth, beast!' (40)

In chapter LXVIII, "The Master," the same master-slave relation reappears, in the figure and voice of the former slave Prudencio who, now free, punishes one of his own slaves. The repetition is not casual: the expression of master-slave relationship serves as the vehicle of articulation between the narrator's experience as a child and the reflections of the adult about the compensations man uses to overcome past suffering:

> Now, however, that he was free and could move his arms and legs when and as he pleased, now that he could work, relax, sleep, as he willed, unrestrained, now he rose and became top

man: he bought a slave and paid to him, in full and with interest, the amount he had received from me. (129)

If the reader correctly understood the expression of master-slave relations, his or her perception, after fifty-seven chapters, forces a re-reading so the transmitted signifieds can be fully absorbed. In this way, a strong solidarity exists between chapters XI and LXVIII, such that the expression of such relations, which involve both, translates on the level of the signifier that which, on the level of the signified, is expressed by the chapter titles: "the child is the father of the man" comes to refer as much to the narrator as to "the whip," a synecdoche for "a little colored house-slave." Internally, the reiteration of the signifier accentuates the repetitiveness of human acts, the nucleus of the narrator's pessimistic irony.

The narration lets one perceive perfectly delimited nuclei, shuffled, of course, by the text's sinuosity. Starting with chapter X, which initiates the second part of the *Epitaph*, the following moments are distinguishable: the adventure with Marcella, the European experience, the return to Brazil, the adventure with Eugenia, the encounter with Virgilia, the separation from Virgilia, the appearance of Quincas Borba, that of Nhan-loló, the period of isolation and reflection, and the onset of madness.

Each moment, however, is interrupted by chapters that deepen the meanings of experience, creating spaces that will be filled or recovered in the following moments. The work with literary language itself, which makes the analysis possible, constructs the discontinuity in such a way that it is only possible to extract signifieds in the very articulations between the diverse moments, primarily because the discontinuity does not occur only on the temporal plane, but also involves the recapturing and critique of the language used in one chapter and, later, in an expanded fashion, in another.

Take, for example, chapters XIV and XV. In the former, "The First Kiss," the beginning of the narrator's relations with Marcella is constructed with images borrowed from Romanticism, explicitly defined as such by the narrator, and immediately contrasted with Realism, which mimeticizes the movement of their relations. The passage to the following chapter represents an intensification in the sense of a "capitalist" degradation of the love affair between the naive young man and the experienced woman. In chapter XIV the narrator writes:

At all events, I was a handsome lad, handsome and bold, and I galloped into life in my boots and spurs, a whip in my hand and blood in my veins, riding a nervous, strong, high-spirited courser like the horse in the old ballads, which Romanticism found in the medieval castle and left in the streets of our own century. The Romanticists rode the poor beast until he was so nearly dead that he finally lay down in the gutter, where the realists found him, his flesh eaten away by sores and worms, and, out of pity, carried him away to their books. (50)

At the beginning of chapter XV, "Marcella," the imagetic transformation, in the form of an intertextual allusion, anticipates the change in the relationship: "It took me thirty days to go from the Rocio Grande to Marcella's heart, riding not the war-horse of blind desire, but the wily, stubborn ass of patience" (51). Between the war-horse and the ass, the space is created to begin chapter XVII with the phrase that represents the apex of degradation of the love with which the relations between Braz Cubas and Marcella had begun: "...Marcella loved me for fifteen months and eleven contos, nothing less" (55).

One must note, finally, the reiteration of the opposition between the languages of Romanticism and Realism in the following chapter (XVIII), recalling of a scene from *A Thousand and One Nights*, which favors the narrator's romantic and dreamy side, starting from what he perceived to be Marcella's "mocking" gaze in the face of promises and vows of love. They are, in truth, more than oppositions. They are vertiginous dislocations that account for the uneasiness and hallucinations resulting from the reencounter with Marcella and that run through chapters XXXVIII, XXXIX, XL and XLI, in which the woman, disfigured by pockmarks but always possessing a pratical and "capitalist" sense, is confused, in chapter XLI, with the sweet Virgilia of the early years. Everything points toward the transitory nature and the weakening of passions. One thus sees how temporal continuity finds its counterpoint in intratextuality, configured as successive retakings and critiques of the very narrative elaborated by the "deceased writer," as he insists on accentuating in the famous chapter CXXXVIII, "To a Critic."

This type of procedure accounts for one of the novel's fundamental aspects: the unstable play between reason and madness that gives the book both its style ("this book and my style are like a pair of drunks: they stagger to the right and to the left, they start and they stop, they mutter, they roar, they guffaw, they threaten the sky, they slip and fall"

131-2) and the vertiginous nature of the proliferous "theories" and "*idées fixes*" in Braz Cubas's relationship with reality. Quincas Borba's Humanitism summarizes that relationship, which finds its final and mortal unfolding in the "*idée fixe*" of the plaster.

Only by situating the writing between reason and madness, woven by the "needle of the imagination" and, therefore, permitting a tense and non-exclusive co-existence, could Machado de Assis find a possible way of approaching, through literature, a precisely located reality (Brazil between the beginning and middle of the 19th-century) that would not allow itself to be read merely according to rational schemes or their negation.

Between one and the other, literary language creates the space of fictionality that maintains intensity in the reading of the different values inhabiting it. Thus, a partial reading of the "philosophy," or the "psychology," or the "sociology"--all in quotation marks--of the *Epitaph* is not viable: what one calls the book's humor or irony is nothing less than the transformation into verbal material of that which the narrator's epoch could offer as kinds of "philosophy," "psychology," or "sociology," still in quotation marks. In this sense, they are as much creations as personages, plots, and situations; they are the results of the poetic work with language and not passive references to rhetorical treatments.

For all of these reasons, and as if to rectify the previous affirmation, once the fictional nature of the text is recognized, it is possible to remove the quotation marks and say that the philosophy, psychology or sociology of the *Epitaph* are closer to being these kinds of knowledge depending on the degree of rigor with which Machado de Assis distends the very possibilities of poetic signification, making the instability between reason and madness a way apprehending, through the delirium of signifiers, how much delirium exists in the signifieds. In each of the nuclear moments mentioned above, the presence of such a procedure lends the reflections a coherence that overcomes their digressive tenor, à la Sterne, preserving at the same time the zig-zagging nature of writing in the *Epitaph*.

The segment dealing with the trip to Europe, after the frustrations of his relationship with Marcella, is composed of a single chapter (XIX), "On Board," in which all of Braz Cubas's reflections, seeming to insist on the way he managed to free himself from the anguish of separation, centers on his analysis of the distance between the experience and its poetic realization. To this end he uses the suffering of the ship's captain in the face of the illness and death of his wife and the way in which from a severe sailor there emerges a man who is sensitized by everything related to life at sea and who takes on, moreover, the role of a poet capable of composing a "Horacian ode," sonnets, and, finally, a "dirge."

Seeming to fulfill himself through poetic accomplishment, the captain's suffered experience is, so to speak, degraded by his sentimental usage of poetry, on which Braz Cubas's narration confers an ironic and destructive tenor. This is the case, for example, of the paragraphs in which he narrates and comments on the captain's expressions after his wife's death and burial at sea:

> He wiped away an importunate tear with his sleeve; I sought consolation for him in poetry. I spoke to him about the poems that he had read to me, and I offered to have them printed. The captain's eyes showed a little animation. 'Perhaps I'll accept,' he said, 'but I don't know... they are poor verses.' I swore that they were not. I asked him to put them all together and to give them to me before the disembarkation.
>
> 'Poor Leocadia!' he murmured without reply. 'A corpse... the sea... the sky... the ship...'
>
> The next day, he read to me a freshly composed dirge in which the circumstances of his wife's death and burial were commemorated. He read it in a voice quavering with emotion, and the hand that held the paper was trembling. When he had finished, he asked me whether the verses were worthy of the treasure that he had lost.
>
> 'They are,' I said.
>
> 'They may lack poetic inspiration,' he remarked, after a moment's hesitation, 'but no one can deny them sentiment-- although possibly the sentiment itself prejudices the merits...' (64)

Observe the complexity of the play between sentiment and poetry in the captain's melancholic expression, beginning with the evocation of his wife's name and ending with the enumeration of images ("a corpse... the sea... the sky... the ship...") through which he anticipates the composition of the dirge he will bring to Braz Cubas the next day.

In the same way, in the chapters where Braz narrates his European experiences, either at the Universidade de Coimbra, "engaging in practical romanticism and theoretical liberalism" (65), or on his obligatory post-university touristic pilgrimages, *living* romantic poetry "for I could not write it, in the hospitable bosom of Italy" (68), there passes a sense of useless availability that, seemingly a reflexive enrichment, in truth slowly intensifies that hypochondriac "flower of melancholy" that gnaws from the inside Braz Cubas's way of relating to reality.

This becomes denser in chapter XXV, "In Tijuca," which, starting from a phrase by Shakespeare, progressively completes that which had initially appeared in "The Delirium":

> I pressed my silent grief to my breast and experienced a curious feeling, something that might be called the voluptuousness of misery. *Voluptuousness of misery.* Memorize this phrase, reader; store it away, take it out and study it from time to time, and, if you do not succeed in understanding it, you may conclude that you have missed one of the most subtle emotions of which man is capable. (72)

Between the yearning for fame and hypochondria, both responsible for the *idée fixe* of the plaster, the "voluptuousness of misery," like the nothingness expressed by Nature or Pandora, explains the dispersive activity of Braz Cubas, who metamorphoses into a capitalist, a journalist, a federal deputy, and the writer of his *Epitaph*.

This is not limited to thematic planes, but rather finds its correlative in the *Epitaph*'s very composition. In chapter XXVI, Braz's hesitation in relation to the possibilities of marriage and a political career, leaving him with the "voluptuousness of misery," finds resonance in the suggestion of Virgilia's name in the initial verses of the *Aeneid*, a creative process in which the unkempt movements of writing correspond to the narrator's uncertainties and receptivity while they accentuate the vertiginous fortuity of human actions.

The digressions that occur thereafter, starting with chapter XXIX, which encapsulates other digressions, constitutes a novelistic segment concerning the irresponsible and brutal way the narrator establishes a relationship with Eugenia, whose designation, "The Flower of the Thicket," repeats the essence of an episode in chapter XII, which recounts the narrator's revenge by denouncing the kiss exchanged between Villaça and Dona Eusebia, Eugenia's mother, who had "entered a little thicket" (47).

One thus sees how the narration establishes the relationship of distant chapters through the exploration of verbal possibilities--in this case, the expression "flower of the thicket" refers to the result of the clandestine relations between Villaça and Dona Eusebia, ironically translating into the crippled Eugenia--and not merely through thematic confluences. Or, more precisely, the dependency between one and the other is of such an order that the reader understands the totality of the later chapter's meaning only by rereading the earlier one and vice-versa.

The allegory in chapter XXXI, which ends with the narrator observing that if the butterfly were not black, but rather blue or orange, "I might have pierced it with a pin and kept it to delight my eyes," and, subsequently, that "I think that it would have been better for the butterfly if it had been born blue" (82), is only perceived entirely if related to Eugenia's physical defect. This makes the chapter avoid the reader's characterization as "some sort of joke or just an unsavory incident" (83), as the narrator notes in the following chapter.

In sum, through all of these chapters there occurs a meditation on determinism, whether referring to the color of the butterfly or to Eugenia's physical defect, "born lame," which finds its full textual realization in the final sentences of chapter XXXV, where the imperative anaphoric construction articulates reason and delirium: "I kept telling myself that it was right to obey my father, that it was desirable to embrace a political career... that the constitution... that my bride-to-be... that my horse..." (87).

The segment that goes from chapter XXXVII, whose title--"At Last!"--represents an intratextual commentary on the various appearances and disappearances of the *Epitaph*'s central female personage, until chapter CXIV, whose title, "End of a Dialogue," recalls the famous dialogue without words of chapter LV, "The Venerable Dialogue of Adam and Eve," constitutes, from a novelistic perspective, the central part of the *Epitaph*. In fact, it is here that there occurs the initial meeting with Virgilia, her loss to Lobo Neves, the death of his father (with the definitive characterization of Braz Cubas as a capitalist), the reencounter and deepened relationship with Virgilia, the encounter with Quincas Borba, the frustrated trip of Lobo Neves and Virgilia to accept a provincial presidency, the reappearance of Quincas Borba in the guise of a philosopher (and a capitalist, thanks, as Braz Cubas supposes, to an inheritance), Virgilia's frustrated pregnancy, the appearance of Nhan-loló and, finally, the ending of Braz's relations with Virgilia.

Permeated by reflexive catalyses in the already mentioned proliferation of "theories" or "philosophies," invariably initiated with instances of caustic humor--those which stand out are the recurring "theory of human editions," the "solidarity of human misery," the tip of the nose, the "equivalence of windows," the theory of legs, of the whip, the bibliomaniac, that of botany, of moral geology, that of the relationship between Nature and feminine dress--what dominates is the sense of frustration that corrodes all the novelistic segments and which will drag the narrator, in the following section, to the counterpoint of Quincas Borba's Humanitism.

Here a fundamental aspect in the novel's composition begins to become clear: as the occurrences slowly lead the narrator toward frustration and futility (see how, after trying everything, his most brillant phase is said to be that in which he serves as a brother of the Third Order!), the *Epitaph* tends to accentuate the value of textuality itself as a space in which one can enjoy at least a moment of true creation and, therefore, freedom.

In this sense, the book expounds an essential dialectic: the more deeply Machado de Assis explores the uselessness of searching for coherence among the delirous signifieds of the Brazil of his and the narrator's time, the more he affirms the voluptuousness of writing itself, which points toward a fleeting moment of resolution between the flowers of melancholy and the nomination, of which the plaster as an "idée fixe" was incapable. It would thus not be an exaggeration to see in the *Epitaph*, as a textual space, a synonym of the effective creation of Braz Cubas's true plaster, as a sort of revenge, through literature, against the state of things that disorients the narrator. As he notes in chapter CIX: "This pulling and pushing between different mental attitudes put me off balance. I wanted to wrap Quincas Borba, Lobo Neves, and Virgilia's note in one over-all philosophy and send them as a gift to Aristotle" (177).

This disequilibrium always finds a means of compensation in the novel's composition, and does not merely wrap everything in the "same philosophy": the construction of a literary fabric by the "needle of the imagination," exposing itself as a rigorous literary creation, articulates the signifieds of reason and madness that disorient the narrator. It is not a question of the expression of a "philosophy" (in quotation marks) that the narrator's pessimistic irony or humor opposes to signifieds that knock it off balance. If that were the case, the only option would be a philosophical reading, through which, as so often happens, what would remain would be the residuals of a second-hand philosophy, destitute of any greater interest for literature. The examples given above point in this direction, that is, in the direction of a strong interdependence between literary creation and the values (social, psychological, philosophical or historical) that it transmits.

A reading of chapter LXXXVII, "Geology," will help complete this basic notion. Reflecting on the death of the miser Viegas and the hopes that Lobo Neves and his wife Virgilia nurtured toward a possible inheritance, Braz Cubas indicates the complexity of Lobo Neves' character, in which, according to him, "there was (...) a certain basic dignity, a stratum of rock that resisted the impact of daily commerce" (151). From the beginning of the chapter, however, an intratextual commentary serves as a means of passage to what will be said thereafter. Considering the superficial layers of Lobo Neves' character, the narrator repeats an image he had already used in chapter XXIII, where life is compared to a torrent, now with the addition of the adjective "perpetual." This provides the opportunity for the narrator's commentary: "And God alone knows the power of an adjective, especially in new, tropical countries" (151). This instability, recognized in the use of the adjective in tropical lands, will be the chapter's object of analysis, referred to the relativity of personal probity. This analysis proceeds as follows:

> I shall say only that the most honest man I ever met was one Jacob Medeiros or Jacob Valladares--I do not exactly remember his name. Perhaps it was Jacob Rodrigues; anyway, Jacob. He was honesty personified. He could have become rich by a small violation of one of his minor scruples, but would not; he let no less than four hundred contos slide through his fingers. His honesty was so exemplary that it became petty and irritating. One day, when he and I were alone in his house enjoying an agreeable conversation, a servant announced that Dr. B., a tiresome fellow, had come to call on him. Jacob ordered the servant to say that he was not at home.
>
> 'It won't work,' shouted a voice from the hallway, 'I'm inside already.'
>
> And indeed, Dr. B. soon appeared at the door of the room. Jacob went to greet him, saying he had thought it was a different person and not Dr. B., adding that he was greatly pleased with the visit--which gave us an hour and a half of mortal boredom, and so short a period only because Jacob consulted his watch, causing Dr. B. to ask him whether he was going out.
>
> 'With my wife,' said Jacob.

Dr. B. retired, and we breathed again. After a few breaths, I called Jacob's attention to the fact that he had just told four lies in the space of less than two hours: the first, by saying he was not at home; the second, by pretending to be happy with the importunate fellow's visit; the third, by saying that he was going out; the fourth, by adding that his wife was going, too. Jacob reflected a moment and then confessed the justice of my observation, but he excused himself on the ground that absolute truth is incompatible with an advanced state of society and that peace and order can only be achieved at the cost of reciprocal deceit... Ah, now I remember: his name was Jacob Tavares. (151-152)

Starting with observations of a psychological nature about Lobo Neves, the chapter ends as a meditation that is not only philosophical, but also historical and social, about the necessity of those little lies, or "reciprocal deceit," as the narrator prefers, that restore society's equilibrium. More important, however, is the efficacy with which the author manages to reveal, in his uncertainty about the very name of the "most honest man" he ever knew, the sense of insecurity and instability that confers on the chapter poetic, creative resistance, through which it is possible to read the philosophical, social and historical values of the narrator more intensely.

Only by configuring that superficial layer of Jacob's character, as he had insinuated to Lobo Neves, is the name recalled: "Ah, now I remember: his name was Jacob Tavares." That is, both the proliferation of possible adjectives and the uncertainty regarding the name itself, textually translate social and historical instability, giving the philosophical reflection a literary consistency that *is* of interest to literature.

This procedure, the nucleus of the essential dialectic referred to above--a bearing toward literariness itself to the extent that a sense of ruin begins taking over the novelistic segments of the *Epitaph*--becomes accentuated starting from the denouement of the narrator's relations with Virgília. Beginning with chapter CXV, despite the frustrated possibility of a marriage with Nhan-loló and the attempts at journalism and politics, the *Epitaph*'s movement is marked by liquidation: the deaths of Lobo Neves, Dona Plácida, and Marcella, Eugenia's decadence, the death of Quincas Borba, and so on. Although some "theories" still recur, such as the "philosophy of old leaves," "Helvetius' theory," the "theory of benefits," or the "philosophy of epitaphs," all expressions of decadence or nostalgia, this final part of the book is dominated by Humanitism, which finds expression in the failures or the ridiculousness of its practical applications, such as Braz Cubas's project to "diminish the size of the shakos worn by the National Guard," or the casual demonstrations of its applicability, such as the scene of the fighting dogs or the "pride of servitude," which is the title of chapter CLVI.

In fact, Quincas Borba's Humanitism is a grotesque amplification of the narrator's disorientation, jolted between the *idées fixes* that attempt, through an "immensely whimsical" nature, to explain history, which is "eternally irresponsible." It is thus not unusual that Quincas Borba doubts the narrator's sanity: the transformation of Humanitism into a method for "a social, religious, and political revolution that would make the Archbishop of Canterbury a tax collector in Petropolis (217), as one of Braz Cubas's deliria suggests, is a restating of the *Epitaph*'s initial chapters about the limits between reason and madness.

Braz Cubas seems to know that this is a discussion without end: in the important chapter CXXVII, "Formality," between the spirit and the letter, his option is for the letter: "The reason is that, contrary to an old absurd saying, it is not the letter that kills; the letter gives life; it is the spirit that causes doubt, interpretation, controversy, and therefore struggle and death" (196).

The terrain is thus prepared for the appearance of the book's great, final paradox: nothing as a balance, as a book, which is as Machadian as it is Flaubertian (it suffices to recall *Bouvard et Pécuchet*) or Mallarmean. A book where nothing is serious because that which is serious is nothingness. In this sense, writing his posthumous memoirs,

the romantic Braz Cubas, through the modern hand of Machado de Assis, opened the doors of the future to the *Sentimental Memoirs* of the modernist Oswald de Andrade. Our tradition was beginning in earnest.

REFERENCES

Brooks, Peter. *Reading for the Plot: Design and Intention in the Narrative*. Oxford: Clarendon Press, 1984.

Carpeaux, Otto Maria. "Uma fonte da filosofia de Machado de Assis." *Vinte e cinco anos de literatura*. Rio de Janeiro: Civilização Brasileira, 1968.

Corneille, Pierre. *Le Cid. Thèâtre*. Texte préfacé et annoté par Pierre Lièvre. Paris: Gallimard, 1950.

Flaubert, Gustave. *Oeuvres complètes. Correspondence*. Nouvelle édition augmentée. Troisième série (1852-1854). Paris: Louis Conard, Librairie-Editeur, 1927.

_____. *The Letters of Gustave Flaubert, 1830-1857*. Selected, edited, and translated by Francis Steegmuller. Cambridge: The Belknap Press of Harvard University, 1979.

Machado de Assis, Joaquim Maria. *Memórias póstumas de Brás Cubas*. Rio de Janeiro: MEC/INL, 1960. English edition: *Epitaph of a Small Winner*. Tr. William L. Grossman. New York: Noonday Paperbacks, 1952, 1956, 1959.

_____. *Poesias completas*. Rio de Janeiro: Civilização Brasileira/INL, 1976.

Meyer, Augusto. *A chave e a máscara*. Rio de Janeiro: Edições O Cruzeiro, 1964.

POLITICAL LITERATURE IN AMAZONIA: MÁRCIO SOUZA AND HIS PREDECESSORS

Pedro Maligo
Michigan State University

To judge from the growing number of materials currently made available about Amazonia in the printed media, on television, and in academic settings, it is fair to assume that the debate over said part of South America has taken decidedly international contours. Based on recent findings that seem to point to the macro-scale interdependence of living systems and their supporting environments throughout the planet, and in spite of the oversimplification generally detected in the approach to the subject (of which equating Amazonia with a single forest located in Brazil is but an example), worldwide attention is being paid to information involving Amazonia, from the murders of individuals such as Brazilian union leader Chico Mendes to the major economic and social issues that help to shape life--and death--in that region.

Before becoming current news and the object of scrutiny of articles, documentaries, and round-tables, however, Amazonia had been for over three centuries a powerful catalyst for imaginations and topic of a continuing intellectual debate. Indeed, as early as the sixteenth century, the arrival of European explorers--who doubled as Amazonia's first civilized chroniclers--represented only the start of countless efforts to describe, interpret, and fictionalize the region which have transcended geographical and cultural boundaries. In the scope of Brazilian literature, those attempts can be detected in the works which I will isolate in this study, namely, that segment of fictional prose whose markedly political contents offer an understanding as to how Amazonia has been used historically to reflect primary concern with the discussion and transmission of ideologies.

It is no less true, however, that Brazilian fictional literature dealing with Amazonia has not yet been studied adequately.[1] A brief historical overview of Amazonia-related prose with ideological implications would take us back to the mid-1800s, when a series of books were published that recounted the experiences of several researchers in and around the region. Together with mythical accounts of Amazonia found in earlier explorers such as Carvajal and Acuña, the scientific texts contributed to the making of a corpus of knowledge that would permeate to early fictional literature as obligatory references in the creation of an image of Amazonia. Owing to a style that revealed a desire to emulate the metaphorical extraction of artistic literature (Henighan 23-24), the majority of the scientific texts were structured around two distinct modes: an objective mode of observation of phenomena, and a subjective mode of account of impressions. The latter houses ideological discourses that ultimately point to the authors' political and economic desires vis-à-vis their object of description. Thus, while in the Agassiz study a prediction of the future of Amazonia states that a day would come when the world would claim the region into the ranks of industrialized nations (341), in Wallace one finds that a long poem describing an acculturated Indian village was written "in a state of excited indignation against civilised life in general" (176). Indeed, although favoring a discourse that praised material progress as a reflex of the rapid accumulation of scientific knowledge in the second half of last century, some scientists were able to offer sobering thoughts about the need to guide change to Amazonia from the standpoint of respect for local cultures and environments. An example is Santa-Anna Nery's *Land of the Amazons*, first published in 1899, where a point is made emphatically that "scientists should precede

---

[1] Studies focusing on Amazonia-related Brazilian literature are limited to Péricles Moraes' *Os intérpretes da Amazônia*, originally published as an essay in his *Legendas e águas fortes* (1935), and Peregrino Jr.'s chapter in *A literatura no Brasil* (1935), edited by Afrânio Coutinho. The latter's usefulness lies in its attempt to devise an operative division of periods. Of truer critical spirit, but limited in their regional scope, one finds Mário Ypiranga Monteiro's *Fatos da literatura amazonense* (1976) and *Fases da literatura amazonense* (1977), and Márcio Souza's well-known *A expressão amazonense* (1977). Silvano Peloso's recent *Amazzonia: mito e letterature del mondo perduto* (1988) is an encompassing historical anthology that includes some analytical commentaries.

colonists in those virgin lands, in order to determine the resources of the country and to watch over their preservation" (60), therefore expressing a view that gains popularity today in the wake of conservationist movements. The texts of these authors are representative of the scientific literature up to the turn of the century; they show that one of the main concerns was with the discussion of Amazonia, rather than its factual documentation.

If we follow the chronological evolution of literary prose about Amazonia, it becomes apparent that, in spite of the stylistic and substantive transformations brought about by different artistic movements, the scientific text represented a major source of both information and inspiration for Brazilian writers. As one would expect, however, the impact of the scientific text is less diluted in works that fall within literary Naturalism. In fact, starting with Inglês de Sousa in the 1870s, the works of Euclides da Cunha, Alberto Rangel, Gastão Cruls, and Raimundo Morais, ranging collectively from 1904 to the late 1930s, were highly dependent on a dialogue with the scientific text. In it, those writers found the bulk of their arguments as they participated in the debate--mainly about economic and social issues--that surrounded the period known as the first Rubber Boom.[2]

Literature of that period is structured along the three main lines of (a) factual documentary intention, (b) social commentary, and (c) ideological projection. Factual documentary intention occurs at the level of immediate signification of the text, itself conveniently organized around a string of *casos* or *cenas*.[3] Social commentary is linked to the historical discourse but depends, to a certain extent, on the metaphorical depiction of Amazonia, thus being closer to the connotative level; this is apparent as the region is portrayed as a place of exile. Finally, ideological projection belongs entirely to the level of connotation, as Amazonia, initially presented as space apart through the use of the mythical text, is then created or conquered linguistically. As Ellison notes in his study of the process of composition employed by Ferreira de Castro in *A selva*,

---

[2] For historical and analytical accounts of this important period in the economic life of Amazonia, see Benchimol and Weinstein.

[3] Meaning *episodes* or *scenes*, these terms usually refer to a common organizational feature of realist literature.

linguistic analysis makes it possible to identify the parallel existence of such levels:

> Together with language appropriate to the historical re-creation and subjective description of such culture areas as the Amazon, there are numerous instances of mythological and Biblical imagery that help to create an atmosphere akin to magic realism. (105)

One can readily see that all three lines depend, in varying degrees, on the notion of Amazonia as space apart.

Such a notion did remain as a valuable instrument of modernistas Mário de Andrade and Raul Bopp, whose *Macunaíma* (1928) and *Cobra Norato* (1931), respectively, presented Amazonia as a cultural repository which yielded several of the allegorical and linguistic elements that the writers employed in their attempts to portray what they perceived as a primitive, truer Brazilian character.

Along with the economic desire of the turn of the century and the aesthetic desire of the modernists of 1922, a third line of literary expression of the intellectual debate over Amazonia is to be found in the documentary intention of Amazonia-born writers. The latter transcends fixed periods and, even if considered by individual author, lacks the specificity as an expression of desire that can be detected in *infernistas* and *modernistas*. Over the years, literature produced by Amazonian writers appears to have been guided by a more abstract impulse, to reflect and join in the mainstream of Brazilian literature. The prose of authors such as Inglês de Sousa, Raimundo Morais, and Dalcídio Jurandir represented their attempt to write within the boundaries of the literary canon of their day. By conforming to their schools, they aimed at using form as the means to bring universality to a personal interpretation of Amazonia. This attempt is more apparent in Sousa and Jurandir, while Morais' flawed literary technique makes his texts stand out mainly as vehicles of an ideological posture that finds its justification in a dialogue with the traditional *infernista* literature, on which it is quite dependent.

The three lines ultimately express political attitudes, whether as reinforcement or as criticism of the *status quo*, literary or otherwise. As such, literature of the Rubber Boom reflected nationalistic aspirations for the economic and populational integration of Amazonia; modernist literature incorporated an aesthetic view of Amazonia into a proposed new interpretation of Brazilian culture starting with the arts; and the literature of native writers demonstrated a measure of critical awareness exemplified by Inglês de Sousa's naturalistic documentary of small-town politics, Raimundo Morais' stance toward the debate over the image of Amazonia, and Dalcídio Jurandir's examination of one of Brazil's regional societies in line with fiction from the 1930s to the 1950s.

These attitudes are political insofar as they contain an individual's response to a given social issue or program. In the remainder of this article, however, I wish to identify political attitudes in those works that deal mainly with the relationships between individuals and government. *Political* is not used in its broader sense as one would find in the writers mentioned above; rather, it is a term that I apply to texts that present critical views of structures of power, public administration, forms of government, and so on. This would comprise the fourth relevant aspect in the historical representation of Amazonia, namely, the region as symbolic territory for criticism directed at the Brazilian sociopolitical structure and government.

A few comments on the most important features of the critical debate in these texts will give the reader an idea of the preferred themes and approaches over time. While Amazonia was perceived historically as an ideal territory for the projection of economic, social, and aesthetic programs, it is also possible to trace its use as a ground of political debate to Euclides da Cunha's criticism of the central government's measures concerning land occupation and social welfare, as one can see from his journalistic articles.[4] It is in the 1930s, however, that one comes across works that employ Amazonia as the realistic setting for

---

[4] Of those written before his trip to Amazonia, "Entre o Madeira e o Javari" (1904) is the most noteworthy since it establishes the linguistic nuclei of Euclides' later articles. Between 1906 and 1909, after returning from Amazonia, Euclides wrote a series of articles in which, with visionary concern, he denounced the exploitation of the rubber-tappers and called for corrective social measures, such as in "Impressões gerais":

> Dela ressalta impressionadoramente a urgência de medidas que salvem a sociedade obscura e abandonada: uma lei do trabalho que nobilite o esforço do homem; um justiça austera que lhe cerceie os desmandos; e uma forma qualquer do *homestead* que o consorcie definitivamente à terra. (1976: 112).

literature of overwhelmingly critical tone, intended to present and defend political views that derive from partisan preferences. The model for such texts appears to have been *A selva* (1930), a novel by the Portuguese writer Ferreira de Castro in which the plot, of semi-autobiographical extraction, is that of a political exile in Amazonia who ends up as a miserable rubber-tapper and later bookkeeper in a *seringal* up the Madeira River.

A selva is generally considered the paradigmatic contemporary novel that uses an Amazonian setting (e.g. Moraes, Peregrino Jr., Souza), an appraisal that, in my view, typifies a far-reaching situation of cultural colonialism of which the mechanisms of the editorial market in Brazil can be seen as a reflex.

Prior to the appearance of *A selva* in 1930, the bulk of Green Hell literature had already been published, as illustrated not only by Alberto Rangel's landmark short stories of *Inferno verde* (1908), but also by Rodolfo Teófilo's *O paroara* (1899) and Carlos Vasconcelo's *Deserdados* (1921). Both *O paroara* and *Deserdados* are novels that contain the basic plot of outsiders who are annihilated by life in a *seringal*, and both are structured around a string of *casos* that are standard in Amazonia-related literature of that period: the rainy season and consequent flooding of the rivers, an explanation of the legends of the *boto* and of the *Cobra Grande*, a description of a steamer sailing by a settlement on the banks of the river, a fishing trip, the work and character of the *regatão* are all examples of passages included in the texts with documentary and aesthetic purposes.[5]

Similarities between *A selva* and its predecessors are linguistic (e.g. the parasitical *apuiseiro* as metaphor for the exploitation of labor,

---

[5] *Boto* (*Inia geofrensis*) is the dolphin found in the main rivers of Amazonia. Popular belief links it to a male figure who seduces unwed women, thus explaining their pregnancy. *Cobra Grande*, or *Boiúna*, a snake capable of appearing under different bodies and disguises, is considered to be the most important and complex mythical figure in Amazonian culture, usually associated with danger and destruction. The best source of references about the two figures is Câmara Cascudo's *Dicionário do folclore brasileiro*. The *regatão*, or river merchant, is always depicted as a greedy, dishonest male Arab or Turkish immigrant whose boat is a true emporium that caters to the scattered population along the rivers. See José Alípio Goulart's *O regatão*.

in chapter 15 of *Deserdados* and chapter 8 of *A selva*), documentary (e.g. sodomy, in chapter 7 of *Deserdados* and chapter 11 of *A selva*), and ideological (e.g. *caboclos* as incompetent and *cearenses* as creatively energetic). Based on its literary language, however, critics consider that *A selva* epitomizes literature about Amazonia. According to Márcio Souza,

> A vivência, para Ferreira de Castro, foi a fórmula visível que condensou seu romance. Em *Inferno verde*, de Alberto Rangel, não há um suporte vivencial e a selva está manifesta pelas palavras carregadas. Vivência e linguagem, escritor e personagem, em *A selva*, estão unidos neste desvelamento da ostentação. É um romance estudado que nada oculta, e desarma a própria natureza, como Euclides da Cunha tinha desarmado tudo pelas palavras escolhidas. (1977: 125)[6]

Sharing a similar opinion, Peregrino Jr. also based his judgement of *A selva* partly on biographical facts: "Depoimento veraz sobre a terra e a gente que ele conheceu de perto. . . . Poucas obras tão exatas na fixação do homem e da terra da Amazônia. Raros escritores brasileiros conseguiram dar-nos da Amazônia um quadro tão denso, colorido e dramático" (1955: 162). It is worth noting that critics utilize biographical criteria to validate views which coincide with the Green Hell stream, while biography is not enough to legitimize (on the contrary, it is a reason to suspect) an Amazonian writer's view of the region as Green Paradise. For instance, Eneida de Morais, a poet from Pará who sided with Raimundo Morais in the defense of the Green Paradise position, is dismissed in two sentences by Peregrino Jr.: "De Eneida de Morais tivemos em 1930 um livro lírico sôbre a Amazônia--*Terra Verde*. É mais do que tudo um canto alegre e ardente, uma louvação literária da Amazônia" (162). Both Souza--whose study does not concern writers from the state of Pará--and Moraes ignore Raimundo Morais and Eneida. Thus a problem remains in the validation of criteria: just as biography is used inconsistently, it appears that value judgements based on contrast of styles of different periods are equally inaccurate, albeit seem-

---

[6] A similar opinion can be found in Moraes (27-28), who nevertheless acknowledges Vasconcelos's precedence.

ingly acceptable to critics who prefer the relatively modern text of *A selva* over those which informed it.

I am inclined to think, however, that this preference is the product of a colonized mentality or, at least, of problems of commercial distribution (although the latter would not be necessarily devoid of relationship with the former). I believe that an indication of this can be found in Souza's remark to the effect that with Ferreira de Castro "a literatura marcou o seu primeiro encontro público com os leitores do mundo" (1977: 124). Although the statement appears to show that primacy given to the European novel derives from the assignment of literary value to texts of disparate periods, it can be explained realistically by the fact that the regionally-published Teófilo and Vasconcelos did not have the marketing opportunity for such a public encounter. Indeed, the issue of quality is secondary in critical texts about *A selva* because, as Ellison points out, the book is read mostly for its documentary value: "It is curious, however, that the great majority of critics have emphasized *A selva*'s worth and importance as social novel dealing with the economic exploitation of the *seringueiros* or rubber gatherers of the Amazon" (101). If not from commercial distribution, it appears that the critics' choice of a paradigmatic text originates from arbitrary, personal preference based on the belief that biography (and, by extension, perceived documentary accuracy) is sufficient indication of merit, with the aforementioned exception of Amazonian writers, in which case the criterion seems to lose its appeal. Given this impressionistic scenario, it is not surprising that the critics who have examined literature on Amazonia were not interested in linguistic analysis as the starting point for detecting the creation of images whose continued, stereotypical presence in later works would serve as a *bona fide* literary yardstick. To locate such a study in the scope of Brazilian criticism, one would have to turn to Wilson Martins, whose encyclopedic *História da inteligência brasileira*, albeit far from detailed literary analysis, suggests a reading of Vasconcelos and Ferreira de Castro oriented toward the function of language and its lasting impact. About *Deserdados*, he writes:

> Muitas cenas e episódios são claramente introduzidos para 'completar' a lista das peculiaridades amazônicas; deve-se observar, entretanto, que *Deserdados* apareceu oito anos antes de *A*

selva e que são muito mais vigorosas as suas descrições de contatos e conflitos humanos. (6: 249)[7]

Indeed, when contrasted with the literature that followed, *A selva* has to be considered the least politicized of all, since its critical intention is more or less limited to the traditional approach of documentation. It is only at the end of the story that a political act surfaces, although generated by the frustration of a single individual rather than representing the culmination of collective strategy: the *barracão* is set on fire by a rebellious employee, "whose vengeance upon Juca Tristão for his punishment of recaptured runaway workers reflects the only clearly articulated social awareness in the novel" (Ellison 107).[8] Whether modeled after *A selva* or previous texts, the basic characteristic of the critical literature of the 1930s is an omniscient narrative voice that is instrumental in the development of a thesis novel of neo-realist type, whose focal point is the presentation of political ideology. Different from that of the *infernistas*, who saw documentation of reality as a critical goal in itself, this approach goes beyond documentation in order to propose and defend solutions that require political participation and decision-making. Abguar Bastos' fiction provides an example of such literature. Envisaged as a cycle to which the writer gave the overall title of *Os dramas da Amazônia*, his three novels aimed at reshaping historical and literary perception of the region. The title of the first novel, *A Amazônia que ninguém sabe* (1929), serves as an indication of that objective, whose political view was presented in the form of rhetoric against outsiders in Amazonia and, by metaphorical extension, Brazil. Renamed *Terra de Icamiaba* in its second edition (1934), it was part of a reaction to Mário de Andrade's *Macunaíma*, whose mythical approach to nationalism was

----

[7] In a review contemporary to the appearance of *Deserdados*, Alceu Amoroso Lima wrote that Vasconcelos's attempt to examine the epic of the exiles after Euclides da Cunha, Alberto Rangel, and Rodolfo Teófilo had resulted in "páginas ardentes, vigorosas, estonteantes, onde sangre uma realidade de inacreditável violência," to conclude that "[o] livro do Sr. Carlos Vasconcelos não é 'um' romance, mas 'o romance' do cearense na Amazônia" (343-44).

[8] A *barracão*, the main building in a *seringal*, houses offices, storage, and the company store used by the employees.

considered by Bastos to be a politically irresponsible, escapist attitude in the face of what he saw as the need to represent Brazilian culture from the standpoint of reality and not symbolism. In order to challenge the modernists' position, Bastos even launched a manifesto: "[O] Flaminaçu, em que caldeava 'o latino ao índio' num 'movimento' que parece não ter ultrapassado a sua própria pessoa," writes Martins (6: 427). Joaquim Inojosa appraises Bastos's manifesto differently, in the context of the influences of the modernist movement on the intellectual life of Northern Brazil: "Não deixou, entretanto, o *Flami-n'Açu* de constituir um documento de forte significação dentro da temática renovadora da época..." (275). He agrees, however, with Martins's commentary that the general lines of the manifesto were to push nationalism in the arts still further: "*Flami-n'Açu* constituía um apelo de ordem nacionalista, de um nacionalismo bem amazônico, com todos os ímpetos do escritor criado naqueles assombrosos verdes tropicais" (274). Of interest to us is that Bastos's attempt reveals that the representation of Amazonia as symbolic territory is part of an intellectual debate. In fact, the very circularity of language in this literature illustrates how most authors employ the notion of competence to try to validate their own texts, whether in artistic terms or as reinforcers, or innovators, of ideological discourse. In Bastos, this strategy continues not only in the manifesto but also in his two other novels, such as the reference in *Certos caminhos do mundo* (1935) to Euclides da Cunha as incompetent, "um sujeito que andava pedindo notas" about Amazonia (9), or in the comical appropriation of Mário de Andrade's visit to the region in *Safra* (1937).[9]

---

[9] Criticism of Euclides da Cunha stems mainly from the fact that during his travels on the Purus he had met Plácido de Castro, who had been the leader of the armed movement that had resulted in the independence of Acre from Bolivia and its 1902 annexation as Brazilian territory, and who briefed Euclides on *seringais* and their operation. When Euclides' "Entre os seringais" was published in 1906, Castro accused the author of plagiarism. As usually happens when the subject is Euclides, the versions of the story vary according to the personal bias of the critic or biographer. A short, pro-Euclides account is found in Velloso Leão (65-66). Mário de Andrade appears as a character who, in the first edition of *Safra* (1937), presents himself as "Mário d'Almeida, paulista" (178), although from then on he is called Mário d'Almada, a name maintained in the book's second edition (1958). Abguar Bastos

Metalanguage goes only as far as satirical humor, however, because Bastos' Amazonia is but a collage of traditional images that oscillates between detailed Naturalism and telegraphic Modernism. The space apart of the naturalists still exists in Bastos, although understood mainly as a bountiful territory. In such a space, danger to human beings does not come from nature itself, but from the exploitation imposed by an outside economic order. Such a view leads to a basic ideological contradiction, apparent in *Certos caminhos do mundo*, but rendered even more visible as one reads that novel and *Safra*. The contradiction occurs because at the same time that he writes against the migration of outsiders to Amazonia, Bastos suggests that Brazilian territorial and economic expansion into Bolivian Acre is an irreversible event explained by the willingness of the land to surrender to the outsider. In the context of his nationalistic discourse, Bastos claims the defense of the territory from intruders without realizing that the logic with which he justifies the takeover of Acre is based on the same expansionist attitude that he sets out to criticize. On the other hand, if political logic fails his stance, the logic of the imagery which underlies such a posture reinforces my conclusion to the effect that language is the main instrument for an author's construction of Amazonia. Thus, in *Certos caminhos do mundo*, which carries the subtitle of *Romance do Acre* and whose main theme is the conquest of that territory, an image of Acre while it still belonged to Bolivia is made up entirely with referents taken from the naturalist tradition in its representation of a space apart: it is "o outro lado," and man wonders about the "mistério tenebroso da região" (43-45). Still in line with the naturalists' code, the land is also personified as a female that prefers the foreigner over the Amazonian character: "Estava provado. A terra não tinha amor ao seu dono. Com as suas florestas des-

---

wrote a whole chapter of *Safra*, "A rainha do café," to make fun of Andrade, his *Macunaíma*, and the modernists. Several references, including the title of the chapter, were taken directly from *O turista aprendiz*, Andrade's Amazonian travel diary, while fictional dialogue is interspersed to reinforce the comical. In one such dialogue, d'Almada asks a native:

-- Conhece Macopapaco?
-- Nunca ouvi falar.
-- Vai ser o herói do meu próximo romance.
Um caboclo, ao lado, gemeu:
-- Ai! que preguiça! (137)

grenhadas e as suas sombras lascivas, preferia entregar-se ao estrangeiro," writes Bastos, who continues the use of erotic vocabulary in the
definition of Amazonia as "plagas adúlteras" that are oblivious to the
caresses of its owner (47). Since the owner in the quotation is the Bolivian, the deterministic logic of the image transforms the Brazilian *cearense*
into à justified agent of nationalist expansion.

In *Safra*, whose main theme revolves around the extractive
economy of Brazil nuts, xenophobic discourse is developed to include
outsiders who are in a position to harm Amazonia due to their greater
economic and political power. Therefore, in Bastos's Amazonian cycle,
hostility toward the outsider that was generalized in *A Amazônia que
ninguém sabe* (Martins, 5: 466-67) results somewhat subdued in the
praise of the *nordestino* in *Certos caminhos do mundo*, but is rekindled
in *Safra* as the author's political thought appears to have developed in
the direction of considering class struggle more relevant than a group's
ethnic or geographical origin. Accordingly, Bastos makes extensive use
of dialogic structure in the latter novel, with the aim of expressing political criticism:

> Dizem que o atraso dos outros Estados é porque todo o din-
> heiro do Brasil vai pra São Paulo. E enquanto São Paulo vive
> na fartura os outros vivem na desgraça. O Govêrno até hoje
> não pagou aos amazonenses a indenização do Acre. Ficou-se
> com êle e babau. Dizem que São Paulo come, e Bahia, Rio
> Grande e Minas ajudam na comilança. Li essa história num
> jornal oposicionista. É verdade, Dr. Teotônio? (142)

Thus a didactic function prevails in order to denounce the economic
exploitation of the poor by the rich, and of Amazonia by Brazil.

Equally didactic, Lauro Palhano and Francisco Galvão were too
involved with politics, however, to be concerned with issues of literary
creation such as metalanguage. Palhano's *O Gororoba*, considered by
Martins as "o protótipo perfeito de toda uma série de 'romances proletá-
rios'" (6: 515), has the traditional plot of a *nordestino* who heads for
Amazonia in search of a better life after the drought of 1877, although
he settles in the city of Belém instead of ending in a *seringal*. While the
book can be read as testimony of the political thought of a socialist
author in the 1930s, the changes to the text between the first edition in
1931 and the second in 1943 are what provide the most revealing document of all, for the latter has been altered to eliminate the closing dia-

logue that discusses political action and, more importantly, to add the author's preliminary note: "A Amazônia de Gororoba foi um vasto garimpo. Hoje, sob os auspícios do Estado Novo, transforma-se em fábrica, esplendente forja de trabalho profícuo e útil."[10]

Just as *O Gororoba* finds its thematic and structural model in *O paroara* and *Deserdados*, Galvão's *Terra de ninguém* (1934) is an almost exact reproduction of *A selva*, from the middle-class main character who decides to try his luck in a *seringal* to his attraction to the owner's daughter, a communist who has returned from Rio de Janeiro sporting "cabelos soltos à Jean [sic] Crawford" and "um decóte moderno, aberto sobre os seios ponteagudos" (76). The only noticeable difference from *A selva* is the emphatically partisan discourse "com muitas palavras marxistas e pouca profundidade ideológica" (Souza, 1977: 193). This makes the end of the story, in which rebellious *seringueiros* kill their boss and set fire to the *barracão*, assume the symbolic political meaning whose lack Ellison detected in Ferreira de Castro's novel. Therefore Amazonia, the imagined territory of economic and aesthetic programs, is still depicted as a space apart, this time by authors who use it as a microcosm in their universalizing ideological discussion. That the themes could have been taken from other contexts of economic exploitation (as indeed they were by other politically engaged authors writing about different Brazilian regions, e.g. Jorge Amado's early texts) reinforces the fact that, in this literature, regional features exist mainly to provide an exotic documentary background, as if they were a device to keep the reader's attention.

It is not until 1976, when Márcio Souza publishes his first novel and gains national exposure with it, that political issues are examined as they relate primarily to an Amazonian context, although language may allow for their reading as metaphors of a broader Brazilian scene.[11]

---

[10] Although overlooking the change to the final chapter, Martins cites the addition of the preliminary note (6: 516). Palhano's observation does not take into consideration that Amazonia's relative economic resurgence at the time was due mostly to an external factor represented by increased demand for rubber during the Second World War.

[11] Three novels, pertinent to my study, concentrate on Amazonian themes: *Galvez, Imperador do Acre* (1977), *Mad Maria* (1980), and *A resistível ascensão do Boto Tucuxi* (1982). Souza's literary production is large, however, and while other novels incorporate Amazonian issues

While previous literature employed archetypal situations, such as life in a *seringal*, in order to convey a message that would apply to Amazonia only insofar as transformation of the political and economic system would ultimately affect Amazonian reality, Souza's fiction treats historical events from the standpoint of their specific significance to the region's political universe. In other words, while older literature reproduced the naturalists' and modernists' attitude of looking to the outside of Amazonia, Souza returns to the approach of his Amazonian predecessors by proposing an examination of the region's internal problems.

My reading of Souza's fiction uses as a framework his critical views in *A expressão amazonense* (1977). In it, Souza analyzes literary history in the state of Amazonas from an economic perspective to conclude that, similar to the economy, such literature has been shaped historically by an extractive mode. When applied to literature, he uses the figure of extraction to signify the imposition of outside cultural values combined with the natives' perception that, in order to participate in cultural production, they must cater to imported, established tastes. Although he tries to identify this *extrativismo* in the language of individual texts of all periods, Souza often is guided by extra-literary considerations, of which his assessment of Ferreira de Castro, quoted earlier in this article, is an example. In any case, he pioneered (and stressed) the notion that both *amazonense* literature and literature set in Amazonas have had little to do with local cultural realities. About the Rubber Boom, for instance, he states:

> A sociedade do látex obteve o consumo do entulho europeu e também um incrível amontoado de palavras que aparecia diariamente nos jornais como poesia, construções retóricas de palavras que pretendem simbolizar um indefinido sofrimento, mas que na verdade eram a demonstração de uma aberração: a cultura como forma de exploração. (1977: 123)

Extrativismo represents, therefore, the major organizing idea in Souza's fiction. The word itself is used denotatively in reference to a

---

(e.g., *A ordem do dia* [1983]), his drama is eminently Amazonian (e.g., his plays "A paixão de Ajuricaba" [1974] and "As folias do látex" [1976]). For an account of Souza's theatrical production, see his *O palco verde* (1984).

mode of economic production, and connotatively to represent acculturation and political domination. More importantly, he literally extracts the
thematic and formal elements that make up his text from history and
literature. By doing so, Souza intends to reinterpret events from the
standpoint of a native who has chosen to denounce the harmful effects
to regional culture and economy that resulted from historical dependence
on the outside.

Started as a modernist strategy to enable a critical commentary
of a given contemporary situation (e.g, the chapter "Carta pras Icamia-
bas" in *Macunaíma*), the technique of appropriating older texts and styles
is employed by Souza in a slightly different manner, because he is also
interested in the examination of historical causes *per se* and in the interpretation of events in their own time. While the modernists created
scenarios onto which they collated an historical text or reference, Souza
recreates historical events and applies modern commentary as the displacement factor, thus suggesting a critical reading of tradition. Criticism
of the present in the *modernistas* becomes criticism of past and present
in Souza. This attitude is an integral part of the latter's "extractive"
writing, whose metalinguistic nature is apparent in his cannibalization of
the modernists' technique.

In order to give literary form to this process, Souza adopts in
Galvez and *Boto Tucuxi* the basic structure of the *feuilleton*, in which
short fragments or chapters encapsulate a more or less complete episode
in the adventurous life of a hero--or, in the case of Souza's appropriation, anti-hero.[12] At the same time, language represents the corrosive
vehicle of the narrator's critical consciousness. For instance, the first
sentences of *Galvez* explain that "[e]sta é uma história de aventuras onde
o herói, no fim, morre na cama de velhice. E quanto ao estilo o leitor
há de dizer que finalmente o Amazonas chegou em 1922" (15).[13] Such

---

[12] A shorter version of *A resistível ascensão do Boto Tucuxi* was
actually printed as a Sunday *feuilleton* in the newspaper *Folha de São
Paulo* from May 1981 to March 1982, thus preceding its publication as
a book.

[13] Both *Galvez* and *Boto Tucuxi* owe to a picaresque tradition, although with minor formal variations; for instance, only *Galvez* is autobiographical and neither Galvez nor Boto Tucuxi, the main characters in the
novels, are servants or tyrannical masters. In *Boto Tucuxi*, Souza ac-

an opening statement is of utmost importance, since it shows the writer's concern to bring Amazonas into a larger Brazilian and literary context (represented by the modernist movement of 1922), therefore constituting the opposite of the traditional attitude of superimposing outside models on Amazonia. As the writer uses the mainstream to his technical advantage, his syntax has Amazonas as the performer of the action--*chegar*--instead of its object. Language is the device with which the narrator critically oversees the past (at the purely denotative level of actions) while interpreting its effects on the present (at the connotative level of political commentary). As a result, Souza's text is very consistent with the "extractive" notion that language is everything; just as he saw the traditional depiction of Amazonia as an accumulation of outside linguistic models, he now proposes a fictional representation based on the appropriation of those models. The preoccupation with language as mediating ground continues into the remainder of the first fragment of *Galvez*, which clarifies the movement that starts with a metalinguistic past and extends metaphorically into the present:

> Em 1922 do gregoriano calendário o Amazonas ainda sublimava o latifoliado parnasianismo que deu dores de cabeça a uma palmeira de Euclides da Cunha. Agora estamos fartos de aventuras exóticas e mesmo de adjetivos clássicos e é possível dizer que este foi o último aventureiro exótico da planície. Um aventureiro que.... confirmou de cabeça o que a lenda requentou. Depois dele: o turismo multinacional. (15)

Since a palm tree suffering from headache is also a hyperbolic figure of the kind that one would find in Mário de Andrade's travel impressions, the initial fragment of *Galvez* clearly introduces to the reader the language around which the image framework of the text will be constructed: naturalist rhetoric recycled through modernist prose. Perhaps the best example of such a combination is a fragment of *Galvez* in which that character reflects about literature after he is cast away on a beach of the Amazon:

------

knowledges the influence of that style: "Estamos de volta ao picaresco, literatura de crise. Não é por nada que o Lazarillo de Tormes nunca tirou diploma de economia em Chicago" (13).

> Estou prisioneiro de uma paisagem. A praia era a terra de
> ninguém, e comecei a pensar no desafio que aquela paisagem
> devia representar para a literatura. Ora vejam como eu era
> civilizado! Eu estava abandonado na selva e pensava em proble-
> mas literários. Problemas que, por sinal, ainda não consegui
> superar. Sei apenas que a preocupação com a natureza elimina
> a personagem humana. E a paisagem amazônica é tão compli-
> cada em seus detalhes que logo somos induzidos a vitimá-la com
> alguns adjetivos sonoros, abatendo o real em sua grandeza. (84)

To denounce the victimization of landscape by language is an objective
only to the extent that it defines metalanguage as the paradigm for
textual composition. In fact, the few descriptions of natural settings are
but a reminder of the narrator's awareness of traditional literature: "Meu
olhar era uma figura de retórica," explains Galvez as he sits down to look
at the scenery (85).

On the other hand, the passage above clearly states the narrator's concern with the human character, whose actions will refer as
metonymy to a social universe. Character portrayal in Souza comes in
sharp contrast to that of his sources, however, especially when ap-
proached from the understanding that myth is a unifying element where-
by the *seringueiro* as an Oedipal figure or as a Hercules, and the native
as *Macunaíma* or *Cobra Norato* defined the character in absolute terms.
But since Souza does not portray any character as intrinsically mythical,
language aims at explaining how he or she ends up being perceived as
such, within an historical Amazonian context. Thus he does not write
about what a mythical entity did, but how a mythical entity was constructed. This means that, in fact, the author dismantles myth in order
to expose how it came to be.

Souza always attributes mythical status through a mediating
stance, normally represented by the perception that a group has of a
character. In *Galvez*, the main character is a Spaniard who, after a series
of adventures in Belém and Manaus, finds himself heading a revolution
that in 1899 proclaims the independence of Acre with the ultimate goal
of bringing it to Brazil. Crowned Emperor of the new territory, he
recounts the reaction of his astonished subjects: "Alguns acreditavam que
eu era Dom Pedro I que retornava ao trono do Brasil" (177). In *Boto
Tucuxi*, the narrative voice alerts the readers from the beginning that
"[e]ste folhetim procurará reproduzir no melhor e mais depurado estilo
extrativista, as peripícias de um herói mítico chamado pelo povo de Boto

Tucuxi" (14). *Mad Maria,* whose story revolves around the construction of the Madeira-Mamoré railroad in the first decade of this century, further illustrates the process. Here, the narrative offers a glimpse of a character's perception of the jungle:

> Tudo o que lhe vinha na (sic) cabeça, sempre, era esta sensação de estar deslocado no tempo.... Collier sentia-se na pré-história do mundo.... A bruma e o vapor transformam tudo numa ilustração de paisagem pré-histórica, isto todos os dias.... Estamos no rio Abunã, numa manhã qualquer, em 1911, no verão.
> No período cambriano devia ser assim. (16)

This last passage demonstrates a development of the organizing principle found in the opening fragment of *Galvez,* namely, to bring Amazonia to temporal existence by explicit reference to dates. That the character sees the scenery mythically as a land that time forgot is the author's strategy to stress the idea that such perception is but literary device. Resulting from the clash between reference to an historical present and to a mythical past, the call to reality is reinforced by resumption of the action; the continuation of the passage informs that "Collier estava enfrentando os piores momentos de um trabalho tecnicamente simples" (16-17). The passage is extremely revealing since it enables us to see the difference in ideological points of view between *infernistas* and Souza. The character's labors, which would have been construed by the former as ritual sacrifice required by progress, are dismissed by Souza from the standpoint of historical displacement as a greedy foreign enterprise that cost the lives of thousands of people, an interpretation that becomes more apparent as the plot advances.

While in the literature of the Rubber Boom the land proved to be receptive to outside forces as a sort of *tabula rasa* where natives were practically nonexistent, Souza's Amazonia is a territory where the mythical embodiment of a source of power, generally represented by an external agent, is made possible by the ignorance of the region's political elite. In Souza, ignorance represents an Amazonian sign, one that is politically equivalent to the naturalists' clean slate. Such is the case in *Galvez,* for instance, where the Spaniard remarks that "[e]ra inútil tentar compreender o mundo do extrativismo pelas regras estabelecidas. Nem Aristóteles, nem Maquiavel; toda a minha ciência de clima temperado estava inutilizada pelos trinta graus do Amazonas" (135). Thus, Souza develops the notion of ignorance and presents it as a quality of the native society.

His caustic depiction of Amazonian economy and politics consists of the interplay of the natives' erroneous perception that they exploit the outsiders and the reality of their exploitation by outsiders who take advantage of the native society's inability to get organized around an ethical system founded on other than "extractive" beliefs. In *Boto Tucuxi*, for instance, several passages point to what is, in Souza's view, this basic feature of Amazonian behavior; they range from metalinguistic references, such as in the explanation that the compiler of the text seemed to employ a technique of automatic writing, "sem ter consciência do que fazia, o que era bem amazonense" (20), to direct commentary about the hypocrisy that underlies ignorance as "um dos mecanismos de defesa da elite extrativista, nunca saber realmente o que está acontecendo" (194). Both levels are combined to reinforce the idea that Amazonian society is not prepared to deal with the values it adopts from the outside. Therefore, the suggestion is that such society itself creates the world apart in which it dwells and that allows for its exploitation by the producers of the culture it attempts to mimic. Regarding the style of the narrative in *Boto Tucuxi*, for instance, one reads:

> Trata-se não exatamente de um 'roman à clef,' ou mesmo de uma narrativa no estilo dos 'bildungsroman,' nem mesmo é um humilde 'erziehungsroman,' ou até mesmo um 'roman fleuve,' pois o professor Azancoth psicografou um folhetim na exata estatura de Manaus. (20)

Such inability (or hypocritical unwillingness) to understand global realities explains the possibility of corruption, defined as the product of adaptation to a context that lacks logical and ethical standards. Corruption is not only the intelligent exploitation of ignorance ("[E]m terra de crise permanente o dinheiro ainda era o melhor argumento ideológico," *Boto Tucuxi* 101), but also the difference that transforms normal behavior into mythical behavior. The issue for Souza is, then, how a host of corrupt characters or enterprises could have been seriously perceived as mythical in the scope of their realities, that is, as they were viewed from the perspective of their own time. Indeed, Galvez, whose only mundane excesses at the start of the story were sexual escapades, soon realizes that there is a fortune to be made as mock emperor; in *Mad Maria*, one of the story lines focuses on an individual's moral decadence in the jungle while another follows the corruption of national political leaders in Rio de Janeiro; and *Boto Tucuxi* is about the rise to power of the most corrupt politician of Manaus. For the most part, his conclusion is naturalistic: a corrupt environment should generate corrupt behavior, in a cycle that pervades the history of Amazonia up to the 1970s, when "Manaus deixou de ser modorrenta, pacata e francófona: é uma cópia brasileira da despudorada Saigon" (*Boto Tucuxi* 197).[14]

Souza's literature represents, therefore, an historical answer to the Rubber Boom. It is a delayed response that takes advantage of knowing the consequences of a bankrupt system, and one that appropriates themes and styles from different periods in an attempt to suggest that artistic expression derives directly from an economic mode of production. It also evidences the Amazonian writer's belief that deflation of an external discourse about the region must be achieved through metalanguage. Souza's political attitude addresses the fact that interpretation of Amazonia was never oriented towards its own contexts, a tradition which the author suggests be broken, since the outsiders are those who reap the dividends of the natives' ignorance. Or, as Galvez puts it, in a fragment appropriately called "Tradição:"

> Na ilha de Marapatá os aventureiros costumavam deixar a própria consciência antes de se entregarem à caça. Fui o único aventureiro a entrar em Manaus com a consciência bem ativa. Nunca me arrependi. (*Galvez* 106)

As one examines the bulk of this literature, the overriding conclusion comes to be that Amazonia is seen often as the vehicle of a group's desires: for those looking in from the outside, it represents a territory where a new order--economic or aesthetic--may be established; from the opposing stance, it is the provider of themes whose artistic transformation may help to put the author, his agenda, or even the region, on the map. Amidst this layering of definitive opinions, the representation of Amazonia is constantly oriented toward an ideological debate, which now assumes increasingly international proportions.

---

[14] Still in *Boto Tucuxi*, the author had forewarned the readers: "E como toda história encerra um fundo de moral, vamos logo afirmando: esta é uma história amazonense onde por isto mesmo nenhuma moral pode encerrar. Ninguém dá aquilo que não tem" (14).

REFERENCES

Agassiz, Luiz and Elizabeth Cary Agassiz. *A Journey in Brazil*. New York: Praeger, 1969.

Andrade, Mário de. *Macunaíma (o herói sem nenhum caráter)*. 16a ed. São Paulo: Martins, 1978.

_____. *O turista aprendiz*. São Paulo: Duas Cidades; São Paulo: Secretaria da Cultura, Ciência e Tecnologia, 1976.

Bastos, Abguar. *Certos caminhos do mundo (Romance do Acre)*. Rio de Janeiro: Hensen, n.d.

_____. *Safra*. 2a. ed. *Os dramas da Amazônia 3*. Rio de Janeiro: Conquista, 1958.

_____. *Terra de Icamiaba*. 2a. ed. Rio de Janeiro: Andersen, 1934.

Benchimol, Samuel. *Amazônia: um pouco-antes e além-depois*. Manaus: Umberto Calderaro, 1977.

_____. *O cearense na Amazônia: Inquérito antropogeográfico sobre um tipo de imigrante*. Rio de Janeiro: SPVEA, 1965.

Bopp, Raul. *Cobra Norato*. Ed. Alfonso Pintó. Barcelona: Dau Al Set, 1954.

Cascudo, Luís da Câmara. *Dicionário do folclore brasileiro*. Rio de Janeiro: Instituto Nacional do Livro, 1954.

Castro, Ferreira de. *A selva (romance)*. 2a. ed. Rio de Janeiro: Moura Fontes & Flores, n.d.

Cunha, Euclides da. *Um Paraíso perdido: reunião dos ensaios amazônicos*. Petrópolis: Vozes; Petrópolis: MEC, 1976.

Ellison, Fred P. "The Myth of the Destruction and Re-creation of the World in Ferreira de Castro's *A selva*." *Luso-Brazilian Review* 15:suppl. (Summer 1978).

Galvão, Francisco. *Terra de ninguém (romance social do Amazonas)*. Rio de Janeiro: Andersen, n.d. [1934].

Goulart, José Alípio. *O regatão (mascate fluvial da Amazônia)*. Rio de Janeiro: Conquista, 1968.

Henighan, Tom. *Natural Space in Literature: Imagination and Environ ment in Nineteenth and Twentieth-Century Fiction and Poetry*. Ottawa: Golden Dog Press, 1982.

Inojosa, Joaquim. *Os Andrades e outros aspectos do Modernismo*. Rio de Janeiro: Civilização Brasileira; Brasília: INL, 1975.

Leão, Veloso. *Euclides da Cunha na Amazônia (ensaio)*. [Rio de Janeiro]: São José, 1966.

Martins, Wilson. *História da inteligência brasileira*. 7 vols. São Paulo: Cultrix; São Paulo: Universidade de São Paulo, 1977-78.

Monteiro, Mário Ypiranga. *Fases da literatura amazonense*. Manaus: Imprensa Oficial, 1977.

_____. *Fatos da literatura amazonense*. Manaus: Universidade do Amazonas, 1976.

Moraes, Péricles. *Os intérpretes da Amazônia*. Coleção Araújo Lima. Rio de Janeiro: S.P.V.E.A., 1959.

Nery, [Barão de] Santa-Anna. *The Land of the Amazons*. Trans. George Humphrey. New York: Dutton; London: Sands, 1901.

Palhano, Lauro. *O Gororoba (Cenas da vida proletária)*. 2a ed. Rio de Janeiro: Irmãos Pongetti, [1943].

Peloso, Silvano, ed. *Amazzonia: Mito e letteratura del mondo perduto*. Roma: Albatros-Riuniti, 1988.

Peregrino Jr., [João]. "Grupo Nortista." *A literatura no Brasil.* Ed. Afrânio Coutinho. Vol. 2. Rio de Janeiro: Sul Americano, 1955.

Rangel, Alberto. *Inferno verde (Scenas e Scenários do Amazonas).* 4a ed. Tours: Arrault, 1927.

Souza, Márcio. *A expressão amazonense: do colonialismo ao neoco lonialismo.* São Paulo: Alfa-Omega, 1977.

_____. *Galvez, imperador do Acre.* São Paulo: Círculo do Livro, n.d.

_____. *Mad Maria.* São Paulo: Círculo do Livro, 1980.

_____. *A ordem do dia (Folhetim voador não-identificado).* Rio de Janeiro: Marco Zero, 1983.

_____. *O palco verde.* Rio de Janeiro: Marco Zero, 1984.

_____. *A resistível ascensão do Boto Tucuxi (Folhetim).* Rio de Janeiro: Marco Zero, n.d. [1982].

Teófilo, Rodolfo. *O paroara (scenas da vida cearense e amazonica).* Ceará: Moderna a Vapor, 1899.

Vasconcelos, Carlos de. *Deserdados (Romance da Amazônia).* 2a ed. Rio de Janeiro: Leite Ribeiro, 1922.

Wallace, Alfred Russel. *A narrative of travels on the Amazon and Rio Negro.* New York: Greenwood Press, 1969.

Weinstein, Barbara. "Persistence of Caboclo Culture in the Amazon: The Impact of the Rubber Trade, 1850-1920." *The Amazon Caboclo: Historical and Contemporary Perspectives.* Studies in Third World Societies 32. Ed. Eugene Philip Parker. Williamsburg: College of William and Mary [Department of Anthropology], June 1985.

DORAMUNDO BY GERALDO FERRAZ: THE PROBLEM OF TALKING ABOUT CRIME

Naomi Lindstrom
University of Texas

Doramundo, the 1956 novel by Geraldo Ferraz, exercises its unusual appeal in large measure because it functions both as an exploration of social problems, particularly the social causation of violent crime and the modern vestiges of the honor code, and as a lyrical, critical meditation on the difficulty of formulating an adequate expression of these concerns. The novel is one in which numerous voices are heard to speak. In many cases, the topic of the utterances is crime and its underlying causes. (Perhaps an equal amount of commentary is dedicated to problems of sexuality and its expression or repression, another major nucleus of meaning in *Doramundo*, interdependent with the focal theme of criminal violence. In accordance with the specialized emphasis of this study, the discussion topic of crime will be, for the most part, somewhat arbitrarily separated out from that of sexuality.)

So prominent is the element of talk that, while the plot would most likely be described as hinging on a series of murders, the killings themselves occupy a less important place in the text than do the comments they elicit from the novel's characters. The fundamental situation is quickly made evident in the first pages. Cordilheira, less a town than a site where a powerful foreign company sends its workers on location, has recently seen a string of murders. All the victims are single men, and it is common knowledge that their murderers are married men avenging conjugal infidelities. *Doramundo*'s plot traces several efforts to investigate, control, or remedy the problem; though these attempts prove fruitless, the novel has a satisfying resolution: a loving couple transcends the cycle of violence.

This reading of *Doramundo* sees the novel as equally a commentary on crime in its social context and on related issues of communication, including both non-artistic assertions made about murder and murderers and the more implicit and oblique statements generated by works of art. The problem *Doramundo* takes up (among others) is: how do people achieve, or fail to attain, an adequate expression of critical and human understanding when they verbalize their beliefs and observations about violent crime and the factors behind it? The novel contains a number of assertions about specific crimes or the general phenomena they reflect, uttered by a variety of characters. These formulations range from the bluntly pithy to the expansively meditative. Through this sample, certain patterns emerge, giving clues to the ways in which social problems are transformed into the raw material for verbal exchanges and the degree of success such discussion achieves.

Beyond characters' statements, viewed globally, *Doramundo* constitutes an experiment in artistic ways of discussing lawless violence. By following some of the practices customary to the hard-boiled detective novel and departing from others, it draws attention to the traditional strengths of the subgenre and suggests modifications to enhance its ability to speak of crime with critical awareness and with a minimum freight of hidden, unacknowledged ideological interferences. As Fredric Jameson observes, every text that presents an interpretation should contain implicit within it a justification of why it deserves to have been brought into existence: "every individual interpretation must include an interpretation of its own existence, must show its own credentials and justify itself: every commentary must be at the same time a metacommentary as well" (10). Here Jameson's immediate reference is to secondary texts interpreting literary works. Yet the same principle legitimately applies to works of creative writing, considered in their function as suppliers of, among other things, criticism and interpretation of a diversity of social and cultural texts. By presenting itself as a public, published text, *Doramundo* makes the tacit suggestion that its way of talking about crime constitutes a step toward an adequate and competent discourse on this topic. At the very least, it offers itself as less repugnantly saturated with ideology than the many samples of commentary the novel displays as reprehensible examples.

The novel includes representative comments on the crimes besetting Cordilheira, articulated by local and visiting observers. These appear not only in dialogue as such--continuous exchanges between individual characters--but also as stray, isolated remarks. The latter may be attributed to a single source or may be offered as a representative composite of the utterances of an entire group of commentators. For example, discussion of the town's troubles among those passing through by train is synthesized into such unattributed observations as "Vingança dos casados, falta de mulher, é isso" (87).

Among the many points established by the diverse examples of overheard speech, one is the accuracy, and at times eloquence, with which observers possessing no special training or expertise often succeed in formulating their diagnosis of the town's ills. Common knowledge, and its manifestation in speech, receive respectful treatment in this populist novel, with a corresponding disparagement of expertise and talk devised to sound expert. On some occasions, the expressive skill of ordinary speakers consists principally of frankness and of a pared-down statement of only the essential, as in the just-cited "Vingança dos casados, falta de mulher." In other instances, their ability goes beyond plain speaking, as the local characters generate memorably apt analogies. A seamstress being questioned by investigators suddenly departs from assertions of fact to provide a metaphorical characterization of the anomie in which the settlement's much-displaced residents exist: "Em Cordilheira sinto-me como nunca em campo inimigo, ao mesmo tempo em viagem--tantos trens, trens que vão para o interior, que vão para o mar, de longas viagens. Quando chegará a hora de partir, estrangeiro?" (105). A group of local men, searching in their informal conversation for a way of characterizing Cordilheira's situation, hit upon one of the most apt metaphors for the town under its current conditions, comparing life in the murder-plagued settlement to wartime existence (145-46; note that the seamstress's above-cited words hint at the same correspondence). The extraordinary measures officials have taken in an effort to establish control, the suppression of potentially demoralizing information (the speakers believe the company to be covering up some of the murders), as well as the conflicting interests of groups resulting in multiple killings, make the analogy fit the case. This metaphor, sketchily formulated by its originators, is taken up again and given a greater lyrical elaboration in the final passages of the novel. In these closing meditations, a voice more self-conscious in its mode of expression, but still local, confirms the acuity of the equivalence: "Este chão negro e pedregoso, manchado de sangue de uma odiosa guerra..." (203).

What is implied is not only an homage to the eloquence of simple people (whose verbal dexterity is, of course, augmented through the artistic heightening of *Doramundo*). Untrained observers can do well in explaining social problems and their personal impact because these matters are not difficult to perceive if one is really concerned to do so and not deterred from the task by the drive to serve other interests. As

Bob Dylan (in the frequently-excerpted phrase occurring in the lyrics to his "Subterranean Homesick Blues") formalized a principle central to *Doramundo*: "You don't need a weatherman to know which way the wind blows."

The above-summarized tenet holds especially true in the company settlement of Cordilheira, where the most casual observer might readily identify the social forces that make the town a likely spot for disaffected, enraged, violent behavior. The firm goes to little or no trouble to disguise its power over its workers' lives and indifference to their well-being. The headquarters of the enterprise, known baldly as A Central, shifts employees abruptly from one desolate site of operations to another. Cordilheira is a toxic environment shrouded in coal dust and clogged with a thick grime that continually coats the investigators and obscures the evidence.

While characters' brief, accurate comments are among the most memorable in the novel, not every issue involved in Cordilheira's crime wave lends itself to such laconic summation. Particularly refractory to swift explanation is the tangle of problems concerning society's constraints on the expression of sexuality and the relations between infractions of such rules and violence. These age-old questions are made newly vivid by the wave of murders by jealous husbands and by the introduction of an officially-sponsored brothel in a miscalculated attempt to quiet the town.

The local people's brief reflections on this enigma are, in most cases, eloquent, but they deal with only one small aspect of the matter and testify to the extreme difficulty of obtaining a conceptual or verbal purchase on its complexity and multiplicity. For example, the spinster seamstress, who dedicates obsessive but often quite thoughtful attention to the town's numerous adultresses, provides the investigators with the insight that these women have no interest in preventing their husbands from murdering their lovers. Heroines in narratives of crimes of passion, "Pois ficaram muito importantes" (104). For a wider picture of the expressive problem treated in *Doramundo*, it is necessary to examine the novel's more fully elaborated examples of speech about crime.

*   *   *

Doramundo's many more extended utterances on this topic could be classified in a number of different ways. The text directs attention to such features as speakers' social class, the degree of affective distance they exhibit toward those involved in the killings, and the special interests represented in talk. While taking these factors into account, the present study focuses above all on the overarching issue of how talk about crime appears as inadequate to the problem or, alternatively, as pointing toward a competent and constructive way of seeing and referring to the phenomenon. First examined will be samples of talk that *Doramundo* clearly presents as deserving the reader's disdain and typifying a wrongheaded approach. In the next section, the emphasis will be on *Doramundo*'s examples of commentary that offers the beginnings of both critical awareness and understanding of the human dimension of social phenomena.

A number of voices are heard to make incompetent, callous, or self-serving comments about Cordilheira and its difficulties. To return for a moment to the briefer and sketchier remarks, the simplest case of inadequate discussion is that of the anonymous middle-class traveler who, passing through the town and appalled by the sight, tries to soothe a personal and shared sense of disquiet with the formulation: "Mas sabe, vivem numa tranqüilidade, quem me dera a tranqüilidade e a paz das consciências deles" (22). This comment, repeatedly recapitulated and derided by a more knowing voice, represents simple ignorance of the problem and the self-servingly evasive style typical of an aloof middle class.

Only somewhat above the convenient ignorance of the bourgeois traveler is the apathy and self-centered careerism of one of the more verbalizing characters, a figure representing the criminal-investigations hierarchy. This detective has been charged with solving Cordilheira's by now multiple homicide cases--an assignment that he hopes will give a boost to a career in danger of stagnation. Addressed as *doutor* and carrying an aura of respected expertise, this mechanized product of the police bureaucracy makes no effort to establish a relation of genuine interest and concern with the human drama unfolding all around him. An only slightly mediating narrator voices the sentiments this officer might have expressed if not closely constrained by his role: "Odiava o crime pelo trabalho que dava. Gente sangrada, sujeitos querendo ter razão de eliminar" (56-57). The narrator reveals the detective's stonily uncaring habit of referring to the subjects of his professional inquiries as "lombrosianos" (56). While carrying out the procedures stipulated for an investigation, the official is overheard muttering to himself remarks that indicate a profound contempt for all who are party to the violent events: "Para mim tudo isso é cara de lombrosiano" (63; direct quote).

These and other comments manifest a cold, disaffected unwillingness to engage one's critical faculties with the problem at hand and to muster an element--obviously needed, according to *Doramundo*--of human concern and involvement. The novel also highlights more sophisticated, complex examples of misguided ways of thinking and speaking about Cordilheira's crime problem. Particularly important as a negative example is the effort to schematize and control Cordilheira's difficulties by making them the raw material for a discourse that is markedly and elaborately clinical in character. This pseudo-scientific mode of expression is the one *Doramundo* most overtly presents as the butt of mockery and the one most plainly discredited by the events of the novel's plot. The source of the clinical discourse about crime is Álvaro Flores, a self-appointed proponent of social hygiene. Presenting this individual, the narrator uncharacteristically takes the liberty of adding touches that indicate an attitude of disdain. Flores is referred to as "O subalterno" (117) and "o funcionário Flores" (119). In Flores's first real introduction in the novel (his favorite phrase and concept, the "abcesso de fixação," has already appeared in the text without much explanatory context), the narrator derives sly humor from the potentially humiliating interview situation in which the character finds himself. He has come to promote his pseudo-medical ideas to a local official of the firm that operates Cordilheira; the latter is eager to make a show of his superior status by means of a "secretária enorme com papéis ordenados," a large sign reading "SUPERINTENDENTE," and a calculated distance. Flores's smile, which displays to excess his "dentadura tratadíssima em gengiva cor-de-rosa," unnerves his superior and becomes a ludicrous non-verbal sign for the discourse he is about to set forth, in which the concept of preventive medicine is the governing notion and *abcess* is the predominant metaphor.

The interview follows a progression in which Flores overcomes his initial disadvantage and forces his superior to accept his clinical line of talk, as well as the plan of action it serves to expound, support, and legitimate. As soon as the superintendent realizes that Flores is speaking of the crimes in Cordilheira, he attempts to dismiss him on the grounds that crime is no proper topic to bring up with a businessman; Flores should instead direct his remarks to the police. Flores counters with the first of his medical-sounding allusions: "Não é com a polícia, é um preventivo" (118). This authoritative phrase instantly captures the superintendent's ear; rather than eject Flores, he now promises to reward him if his plan proves workable. Flores, in his exposition, relies heavily on lexical choices that will shore up his right to be heard as a provider of expert counsel: "estudei na base do que a polícia deixou de fazer," he says, leading him to "uma lógica muito clara" (118). After revealing his central idea--the need for a brothel--Flores has managed to win a seat in the superintendent's office, but continues to drive home his status as an expert on society's health with sizable appropriations from clinical speech: "Tinha a medicina uma forma de concentrar-se uma infecção, a que chamavam abcesso de fixação. Em Cordilheira, essa infecção generalizada é que invade a honra dos lares com o adultério..." (121).

Flores's medicalization of Cordilheira's crimes and his much-prized clinical metaphor for the brothel are perhaps the most thoroughly lampooned elements in a novel laced with satire. To begin with, Flores delivers his speech in the ridiculous ambience of an office ostentatiously equipped to impress and intimidate, and the entire scene is charged with the petty status-seeking that occurs in any hierarchical organization. Flores prevails over his superior with his seemingly scientific logic, but the plan he persuades the company to adopt turns out to be miserably ill-conceived. The scheme fails to take into account the disorder of passionate human reactions and the considerable influence still exercised in Cordilheira by a Catholic outlook. These factors, inimical to Flores's hygienic style of analysis and speech, cause the plan to misfire and throw the town into a spectacular crisis.

Flores's mode of expounding his scheme provides a satirical, but not grotesquely exaggerated, examination of a type of strategy that has often been studied from different perspectives. A general treatment occurs in Stephen Potter's famous mock guidebook to the ascension of social hierarchies, *Oneupmanship* (1952). This treatise ironically urges the reader to borrow allusions, regardless of their relevance, from high-prestige areas of knowledge. The practice of adorning speech with status-bearing loaned items is recommended for its efficacy in building up the speaker's authority and diminishing that of competing discussants (Potter). It is appropriate to cite this popular and at one time best-selling work, given *Doramundo*'s fundamental premise that the significant features of society are perceptible and comprehensible to the non-specialist observer willing to see with critical eyes.

However apropos Potter's mordant pseudo-manual may be, a more thorough and detailed correspondence could be mapped out between the satire *Doramundo* directs at clinical expression and Foucault's historical critique of experts who win the authority to define phenomena by subjecting them to a specialized frame of reference. While similar ideas appear in several of Foucault's works, the most germane here is surely the 1963 *Naissance de la clinique*. This history of clinicians' steadily increasing ability and authority to shape perceptions and formulate them in words stands out, not only for Foucault's assertions, but for the many well-chosen samples of clinical speech. While Foucault is not particularly sanguine about the curative achievements of medicine, his citations document clinicians' progressively strengthened ability to describe their observations in convincingly sharp, verisimilar detail and thus maintain perceptual and linguistic dominion over the many phenomena they come to claim as part of their expanding terrain of expertise. Although Flores is a clinician at a metaphorical remove--his specialty is hygiene for the aggregate social body--he exhibits the same vigorous drive manifested by the physicians Foucault cites. In each case, the experts' ambition and accomplishment lie in claiming and exercising their control over the set of matters they have staked out as their territory.

* * *

The most determined and frank effort, of the many inscribed in *Doramundo*, to grasp the tangle of crime-related issues by setting them out in words occupies a number of pages (91-114). The passage in question is the tormented account of "seu" Moura (Rolando), half notes on his investigation and half autobiography. His reflections are not successful in resolving anything but the question of what he is doing in Cordilheira: attempting a personal exorcism through criminal investigation. Yet, in correlating his previous knowledge of women marked as sinful with Cordilheira's spectacle of faithless wives and avengers, he skillfully identifies the simultaneously social and sexual problems behind the crimes. These passages have the capacity to engage sympathy in large part because the speaker does not falsify his involvement in the issues under discussion and is scrupulously careful to state, rather than hide, the agenda that motivates him. He makes a point of revealing where he and the discourse he is producing are "coming from" and identifying the debts his perspective owes to past personal and cultural experiences.

Though both local observers and outside investigators can produce memorable, reflective comments on Cordilheira and its problems,
the most powerful statements any character utters are not in the category
of commentary at all. These are the purposeful and pragmatic utterances Dora (Teodora) makes in her efforts to break out of the seemingly
intractable pattern of narcissistic adultery and male-honor revenge. Like
other wives of Cordilheira, Dora is involved with one of the town's single
men and knows her husband is eager to kill him. Unlike the others, who
keep both passion and crime plunged in silence, Dora cries out to her
fellow townspeople to gain their support in freeing herself and her lover
Mundo (Raimundo) from their expected fates. She first calls for help in
the most literal sense, mustering a squad of local men to halt the mur-
der-in-progress of Mundo by her husband. With the wounded Mundo
rescued, Dora then calls on the sympathetic assembly of helpers and
onlookers to bear witness to her testimony. She accuses her husband of
the assault, freely and spontaneously making the type of declaration no
previous townswoman would make even under the press of interrogation.
The silence-breaking accusation includes another element that startles
listeners out of their long-held assumptions: Dora's affirmation of her
love for Mundo, and a statement of her intention to flee Cordilheira with
him.

Dora's words, electrifying to the listeners, are brief and principally intended to bring about immediate effects: to win the assistance
and sympathy of those at hand. But to take on the powerful meanings
they evidently have by the time the story is told, her utterances and the
actions that accompany them must be interpreted and utilized as the raw
material of myth. The transformation of Dora and Mundo's plans into
a legendary flight to redemption requires the accretion over time of
interpretive retellings, imaginative heightening, and added commentary.
The labor of comprehension and mythification is the collective work of
the residents of Cordilheira, whose latent sense of community is stirred
into life by Dora's appeals. This notion of forming a collectivity is then
manifested verbally by the creation and transmission of a common myth:
the local legend of Dora and Mundo.

* * *

In discussing *Doramundo* as a divergent example of the novel of
crime and investigations, and one that comments upon such texts' ability
to speak of crime, it is important not to underestimate the divergence

that crime fiction's conventions normally allow to occur. Reading individual works, whether classical narratives of detection or those of the hard-boiled variety, can suggest that convention is rigid and rupture is easily achieved. But the subgenre's history is full of rulebreaking. The Sherlock Holmes stories offer such deviant turns as Holmes discarding and disparaging his own narratives as meaningless and Holmes and Watson competing for control of the material (as noted by Wilson). The modern whodunit was scarcely formalized before Agatha Christie's 1934 *Murder on the Orient Express* (British title *Murder on the Calais Coach*) brought in the profoundly variant element of collective guilt for crime. Since then, it has been relatively common to alter the formula by identifying the guilty party early in the plot, leaving the investigators to search for other information, such as incriminating evidence. With hard-boiled fiction, a new set of conventions brings new deviations, such as crimes whose solution is of no value or is ignored by authorities, and investigations that yield no results.

Far from subverting or rupturing the subgenre, these variants enable it to survive. As Geoffrey Hartman has observed, the ideal goal of a classical tale of detection is to offer the reader almost nothing but the pure mechanics of construction (Hartman 83); new patterns are required to distinguish fresh entries. In hard-boiled crime fiction, as well, monotony and the fossilization of conventions pose more of a threat to the form's survival than does any unexpected twist. The text that introduces new features is more likely to be bringing productive emendations to a model accepted as generally valuable than to be tearing down its fundamental structures. Even a novel like *Doramundo*, a highly original literary treatment of crime, can best be considered a commentary upon the accumulated repertory of narratives of crime and detection and an effort to increase such fiction's ability to speak honestly, in the sense of laying bare its own cultural and ideological biases.

Without labeling *Doramundo* as a Brazilian hard-boiled crime novel, which would serve no purpose, it is fair to say that it stands in a quickly recognizable relation to this largely U.S. subgenre and constitutes a special type of commentary upon it. *Doramundo* is in many respects an homage to hard-boiled fiction. Yet it is a critical tribute that questions certain conventional practices of this subgenre as potentially ideologizing or, at the least, betraying a reluctance to level with the reader about the origins and distinctive slant of the text. Throughout *Doramundo*, there appear frequent reminders that its implicit program is attuned to that of the socially conscious hard-boiled narrative; particularly salient

are notes reminiscent of the work of Dashiell Hammett, the most criti-
cally-minded practitioner of the subgenre. These echoes range from the
investigators' knowing, sarcastic recapitulation of the townspeople's
disingenuous testimony (46) to the reiteration of the term *safra* to allude
to the bodies regularly harvested from the railroad tracks. Not only is
the title of Hammett's 1929 *Red Harvest* evoked, but so is, more broadly,
the U.S author's typical practice of combining rawly realistic description
with powerful and exceptional metaphors designed to bring out the social
meanings of the events of the plot--significances that could easily be lost
amid the rapidly-paced action and the descriptions of ambiences redolent
of decay and erosion.

Strong as these tributes become, *Doramundo* subjects all such
elements to thorough transformation. First, it is made plain that the
novel comes out of the specific context of Brazilian, isolated, small-town
poverty. The urban U.S. hard-boiled novel alludes to the appurtenances
of a well-supplied society--one in which the widespread ownership of
automobiles and the general availability of consumer items profoundly
affect life. In *Doramundo*, attention is repeatedly drawn to the lack of
goods, technology, and provisions for the public's convenience. The
murder weapon in Cordilheira is invariably a rusty, begrimed length of
iron taken from the rubble that covers large portions of the town--a vivid
contrast with the handguns whose free circulation is integral to many
U.S. hardboileds. There are frequent reminders that any form of police
activity is anomalous in Cordilheira and that the authorities are conduct-
ing the investigation with the barest resources; even such standard matters as fingerprint identification prove impossible. These features are not
directly a corrective to existing U.S. hard-boiled fiction, which by general
consensus is unusually effective in giving a picture of the social background behind the events of the plot. However, they are a reminder that
fiction on crime needs continual adaptation to maintain its attunement
to the society that originates it. This principle, which might on the face
of it seem self-evident, is routinely ignored in texts that reproduce the
conventions developed during the heyday of the hard-boiled novel but
make little or no effort to show that their own provenance is a very
different society. Indeed, the society of origin may be willfully disguised,
as in Latin American crime novels full of English proper names. (The
issue briefly sketched out here is a central topic of Simpson's book; see
References.)

Doramundo more importantly extends the hard-boiled crime
novel by relaxing the strict rule of artlessness that has long been in force.

The best of the hard-boiled narratives are, of course, continually generating a mythical and metaphorical portrait of society along with a realistic one. Consider, in this regard, the physical objects that become charged with meanings, as the Maltese Falcon and glass key that give two Hammett novels their titles. The similarities between the search undertaken by the hard-boiled detective and the quests of mythical knights at times stand out distinctly. Indeed, Raymond Chandler makes such an identification all but overt in his much-cited essay of 1934, "The Simple Art of Murder": "Down these mean streets a man must go who is not himself mean, who is neither tarnished nor afraid. He is the hero; he is everything" (Chandler 533).

However great the crime narrative's reliance on myth and trope, though, the standard protocol has been to downplay and disguise anything that is art. Authors typically kick over the traces, as it were, of the influence of previous literary treatments of crime, and the hard-boiled crime novel often seems to present itself as a text without significant textual antecedents or roots in the accumulated cultural repertory. Readers ought not to be aware--and here literary critics ought perhaps to be disqualified as readers--of nonmimetic forces at work; attention is to be directed away from these elements and toward realistic representations of society.

Doramundo is an homage to this type of novel, but a critical homage and a correction to a certain degree. While the more standard hard-boiled novel conceals its mythical and lyrical strengths, *Doramundo* plainly sets forward these elements. In so doing, it implies an exhortation to hard-boiled fiction to be less hidden-handed concerning its status as art. The message at times becomes nearly overt, as in *Doramundo*'s elaborate recapitulation of the metaphor that gives *Red Harvest* its eloquent title. In *Doramundo*'s treatment, the figure Hammett expressed in one phrase becomes the starting point for lyrical passages that take *safra* from its most obvious reference, the human wreckage left behind by violence, to involve the seasons of the agricultural year and the hope of springtime renewal. The figure of the *safra* is a recurring one, along with its associations of gathering in the dead and the long and frustrating wait for spring.

The implicit criticism of the hard-boiled crime novel is consistent with a critique that *Doramundo* directs toward all talk about crime, ranging from casual remarks to fully-elaborated meditations and the artistic speech that makes up a novel. *Doramundo* drives home the point that none of this talk has as its origin a pure or neutral space; all of it is contaminated by some type of ideology, however inchoate, and all of it is sedimented with the residue of a past repertory of experiences and influences. *Doramundo* is scrupulous to reveal its own perspectives. It is overtly populist and bitingly critical of hierarchical social structures and the cult of expertise. In offering a view of crime, the novel is often found referring the reader to society for the root causes, as witness the denunciatory descriptions of the company's abuse and neglect of its workers. At the same time that *Doramundo* includes a strong vein of verisimilar representation and critical appraisal of the social causation of crime, it is no deterministic study. A strong humanistic vein runs through it as well, and again at an overt and manifest level. The resolution of the cycle of crime does not come through any movement of social reform, but through a love that rises above social conditions. Both the populist, denunciatory, and the transcendently humanistic, lyrical-mythic underpinnings of the novel are kept in plain sight of the reader. In this sense, *Doramundo* offers itself as a better way of talking about crime in that it strives to recognize the inevitable presence within its own discourse of ideological and cultural biases, sources, and indebtedness.

REFERENCES

Chandler, Raymond. "The Simple Art of Murder." *The Simple Art of Murder*. 1934. Boston: Houghton Mifflin/Cambridge: Riverside Press, 1950. 519-33.

Ferraz, Geraldo. *Doramundo*. 1956. São Paulo: Melhoramentos, 1975.

Foucault, Michel. *Naissance de la clinique*. Paris: Presses Universitaires de France, 1963.

Hartman, Geoffrey H. "The Sacred Jungle 2: Walter Benjamin." *Criticism in the Wilderness: The Study of Literature Today*. New Haven: Yale UP, 1980.

Jameson, Fredric. "Metacommentary." *PMLA* 86 (1971): 9-17.

Potter, Stephen. *Oneupmanship. Being Some Account of the Activities and Teaching of the Lifemanship Correspondence College of One-upness and Gameslifemastery*. London: R. Hart-Davis, 1952.

Simpson, Amelia S. *Detective Fiction from Latin America*. Rutherford, N.J.: Fairleigh Dickinson UP, 1989.

Wilson, Edmund. "Mr. Holmes, They Were the Footprints of a Gigantic Hound!" 1945. *A Literary Chronicle: 1920-1950*. Garden City, N.Y.: 1956. 346-53.

MASCULINE VAMPIRISM OR THE DENUNCIATION OF PYGMALION: A READING OF ADALGISA NERY'S *A IMAGINÁRIA*

Affonso Romano de Sant'Anna
Pontifícia Universidade Católica, Rio de Janeiro

Histories of Brazilian literature strangely make no mention of Adalgisa Nery (1905-1980), either as a poet or a fiction writer, despite the fact that she published seven books of poetry, one volume of short stories, and two novels. Her first novel, *A imaginária* (1959), is a fundamental text for studying the constitution of the female narrator in modern Brazilian fiction.[1]

Now that numerous researchers are reevaluating women's cultural production in Brazil, a rereading of Adalgisa Nery can no longer be postponed. Besides her literary work, she had an active presence in the literary and political fields. She was married to Ismael Nery, one of the mythological figures of modernist poetry and painting, and she thus had the opportunity to associate with a group of intellectuals that gathered in her house, including Murilo Mendes, Leonel França, and Jorge de Lima. After her husband's death in 1934, she married, in 1940, Lourival Fontes, who directed the Departamento de Imprensa e Propaganda (DIP) during Getúlio Vargas's Estado Novo. In her many trips abroad she got to know Rivera and Orozco (who painted portraits of her), Siqueiros, and Chagall, among others. She represented Brazil diplomatically in numerous ceremonies abroad and in the 1950s she became a

---

[1] Adalgisa Nery's published works include: **Poetry**: *Poemas* (1937), *A mulher ausente* (1940), *Ar do deserto* (1943), *Cantos da angústia* (1948), *As fronteiras da quarta dimensão* (1952), *Mundos oscilantes* (1962), and *Erosão* (1972); **Prose**: *Og* (1943; short stories), *A imaginária* (1959), and *Neblina* (1972). I cite from the 3rd edition of *A imaginária* (Rio de Janeiro: José Olympio, 1970).

political commentator. She was twice elected state deputy in Rio de Janeiro by the Brazilian Socialist Party.

Besides its fundamental role in the constitution of a female narrator in Brazilian literature, other elements must also be mentioned. *A imaginária* is a densely psychological novel that occupies a place between biography and fiction. The introductory chapters (the first six deal with her childhood, when she was considered an "imaginative" and "imprudent" girl. But her life is commonplace, with a passage through a boarding school, the death of her mother, a difficult relationship with her stepmother. Her adolescent readings reveal her future: "Eu era uma menina que se interessava pelas leituras das histórias do *Arco da velha*, pelas *Travessuras de Sofia*. Adorava ouvir lendas fantásticas. As sobrinhas de minha madrasta tinha a mesma idade que eu, mas as suas leituras eram diferentes" (79).

Many points of contact unite Adalgisa and the character Berenice. In the novel, Berenice marries at the age of 15, Adalgisa at 17. The original family situation is also similar: both had a difficult relationship with their stepmother. In addition, the description of Berenice's conjugal life reproduces Analgisa's co-existence with Ismael Nery. She was fascinated by her husband's intelligence, despite the fact that he oppressed and humiliated her in the years before his death of tuberculosis. The novel ends with the death of Berenice's husband, "my husband," as he is called throughout, as if he were a simple entity, just as other characters appear as entities--"my husband's mother," "my husband's sister," "my family"--without necessarily having names, but rather mere dramatic functions.

Much has been written about the fact that women often adopt the diary as a form of confession and produce a more confessional form of writing than do men. It has also often been said that the novel, starting in the 19th-century, has served as an escape valve in a male-dominated society where women possessed only the space of their imagination. Perhaps there is a relationship between this and the title of Adalgisa Nery's novel, the "female imaginary." And here one could apply psychoanalytic concepts to see in the "imaginary" a woman who attempts to create herself as a subject through the construction of her own symbolic language.

My intention here is to indicate possible paths for future study rather than undertake an exhaustive textual analysis. The first, explicitly indicated in the novel through an illustrative reference to the film *The Vampire of Dusseldorf*, has to do with vampirism.

In one part of the story, narrating the climate of madness in which they lived--the couple cohabited with a sister and the husband's insane mother, whose outrageous behavior recalls expressionist theater-- the narrator says:

> À noite, pedi ao meu marido que saíssemos, a fim de cortar a linha da loucura que eu já sentia tão perto de mim. Lembro-me de que fomos a um cinema assistir a um filme--*O Vampiro de Dusseldorf*. Sentada, eu tinha dois movimentos com os olhos: um, para a tela, outro, para a nesga da porta de saída onde eu via os trilhos do bonde. A angústia crescia a ponto de sentir-me oscilar. Num dado momento quando no filme o vampiro asso-biava, como sinal máximo de luta contra ele mesmo, como o limite da sua consciência para a inconsciência, num debate espantoso de alma, emaranhado no mais doloroso conflito eu olhei para os trilhos da rua, fiz um movimento de quem deseja levantar-se para sair, atirar-me contra o primeiro instrumento de morte que me desse repouso. (117)

Although the writer does not develop the metaphor, the novel deals with the power of masculine vampirism on the woman's soul, the vampirism men have used through the centuries, as if every woman were a kind of sap that men should naturally and rightly consume.

In this sense, *A imaginária* is a novel of formation. Of formation or deformation?, one might ask. A story that illustrates how society and men imprint the marks of domination and repression on women. At the same time, it is a narrative of how women undertake their painful jour-ney of liberation from this massacre. This passage from the text should make this clearer:

> Meu marido pouco saía de casa. Recebia os amigos todas as noites. Vivíamos rodeados de escritores, pintores, músicos e personalidades interessantes. Tínhamos diariamente dez, quinze pessoas variadas e inteligentes em nosso convívio. Eu ocupava-me da casa, dos filhos, pequeninos, e passava entre eles com simpatia e cordialidade. Muitas vezes deixavam-me ficar ouvindo as conversas, as deduções e observando o maior ou menor grau de compreensão de sensibilidade daqueles ho-mens jovens que debatiam vários assuntos sempre com franque-za e convicção. Jamais opinei. Era quase muda. Um padre

jesuíta, sábio com uma personalidade e cultura fascinantes, realizava semanalmente uma conferência só para homens. Meu marido comparecia acompanhado de um grupo de amigos. Terminada a conferência às onze horas da noite, vinham todos para a nossa casa e ficavam até madrugada alta, discutindo o tema explanado pelo conferencista. Recordo-me que eu ficava sentado num divã escutando os comentários sem que a minha presença perturbasse aquele comício. Sempre me encontrei atraída pela inteligência. Essas reuniões significavam para mim um prazer indescritível. Meu marido rebatia as conclusões dos amigos com uma lógica e acuidade acima de toda expectativa. Vê-lo dominando os argumentos dos outros, quase todos com uma cultura cem vezes maior do que a sua, constituía para mim uma vaidade e uma vitória. Eu vibrava em silêncio, com a certeza absoluta de que a sua palavra esclarecedora anularia outras inteligências. Nunca me decepcionei ou me desencantei com meu marido quando ele revelava inteligência e sensibilidade artística. Centrava o problema com tal clareza que os outros não encontravam argumento para as suas opiniões. Foi-se então construíndo ao seu redor uma espécie de respeito à sua palavra e alguns o consideravam mestre. Em consequência dessa homenagem à sua inteligência, o meu marido foi ficando dominado por um narcisismo inconcebível. Passou a viver num plano em que todas as coisas se deviam movimentar e realizar em torno de sua pessoa. Eu notava mais esse desconcerto. Ele sentia-se acima de todas as conjunturas da vida. Opinava drasticamente. Lembro-me de um fato importante para mim naquela época. Um dia um amigo nosso, poeta extraordinário, vendo-me e sabendo que eu não tinha convivência de amigas, conhecendo a minha vida entre alucinados, sem distrações normais, perguntou ao meu marido se ele não receava que eu, uma mulher tão jovem, vivendo unicamente entre homens, viesse a ter preferência por um dos seus amigos. Recebeu a resposta: 'A minha mulher é como a minha mão. No dia em que ela gangrenar, eu a decepo e continuo a viver com o resto do corpo.'

Sim, eu não passava de um detalhe que não fazia grande falta ao todo. Mal sabia ele que o meu mundo era grandioso, o meu mundo estava na sua vida e na sua alma separado por um silêncio que ele mesmo provocara. Muitas vezes comentou para os amigos, na minha frente, que eu 'era ótima companheira, mãe cuidadosa, boa dona de casa', mais que era 'destituída do mínimo de poesia, de romantismo e de vibração'. (121)

The vampirism mentioned above could be related to another metaphor explored mythically and psychologically in literature: the relationship between Pygmalion and his creation. The reference is to the myth in which Pygmalion, the king of Cyprus, fell in love with and married a statue which he himself had sculpted, as well as to the archetypal utilization of the myth as elaborated by George Bernard Shaw in the play *Pygmalion*, where the man is the craftsman and sculptor of his chosen woman's soul. Read within the framework of contemporary feminist concerns, the myth of Pygmalion becomes a syndrome of male domination in which he attempts to make woman into an object in his own image and likeness.

This ancient masculine behavior is exemplified in the story of Berenice/Adalgisa and is obvious today because of the contemporary critical eye's more acute detection of social prejudices. In this sense the husband/Pygmalion becomes such a domineering person that even the fact that the woman begins to sing without his authorization seems like a threat:

Um dia amanheci criança e, sem explicações para um alegria, comecei a cantar baixinho. A meu lado, o meu marido inspecionou-me por instantes e, depois, com ar de desprezo, falou:
-- Como você está ficando banal e comum! Eu pensei que poderia fazer de você uma mulher fora do vulgar e encontro-a superficial! Você tem todas as qualidades de uma boa dona de casa e boa mãe, mas não tem um traço de espírito. Tem uma notável propensão para a vida destituída de profundidade. A razão está em que lhe falta uma coisa muito importante--poesia. A sua insensibilidade não deixa ver as grandezas da vida. É necessário acabar com o horror que você tem de aceitar a loucura de minha mãe, acabar com essa repulsa às coisas fortes e violentas da existência, essa tendência em diminuir os choques com o argumento de que são passageiros. Isso demonstra a sua qualidade comum de pessoa. Sensibilidade não é coisa que eu possa ensinar ou dar. Inegavelmente, você tem qualidades e virtudes, mas a minha mulher precisa ser violenta

> por uma seqüência de choques, a ponto de tornar-se um ser
> quase criado à minha semelhança. (160)

To this observation the narrator adds her denunciatory reasoning concerning the operation-massacre unleashed by Pygmalion:

> O narcisismo tinha chegado ao máximo. Quanta ignorância na
> boca de um homem notavelmente inteligente, quanto desconhe-
> cimento da mulher que há doze anos vivia ao seu lado, trans-
> parente, sem escaninhos e sem esconderijos. Era de pasmar!
> Dizer que eu era destituída de romantismo, de poesia e de
> sensibilidade, era a maior monstruosidade que eu poderia ouvir.
> (160)

In effect, responding to the accusations that she lacked poetic sensibility, after Ismael Nery's death Adalgisa would write seven books of poetry. Her suffocation had ended, and the writer became the author of herself and her destiny.

The husband's words about his wife's uselessness except in domestic activities, the narrator reveals, were often said in front of his friends. They were obviously a formula for expressing social condemnation and seeking male society's approval for delimiting female space. The process of the contention and destruction of the married woman's ego in this story passes through several stages, illustrated through a triangular relationship--husband/wife/lover--in the novel's final scenes.

The tubercular and hospitalized, yet truly haughty, husband takes a lover whom he sees when he has the chance to leave the hospital and visit his family. The affair, however, has elements of affective perversity. One day the husband reveals the affair to his wife: "Eu tenho um caso com uma mulher. Nos encontramos, nos correspondemos e diariamente nos falamos por telefone" (151).

However, what could be a healthy conversation about something that happens in the life of couples becomes, for the husband, an exercise in sadism, thinking he is being sincere, but perhaps as a way of punishing his wife and himself:

> ...revelou então como e quando eram os encontros.
> Disse-me o nome da criatura, o nome do marido, onde morava
> e os filhos que tinha. Descreveu o seu físico, o seu caráter, as
> suas virtudes, a sua inteligência, a sua meiguice e os passeios

prolongados, quando descia do sanatório pelas manhãs e só aparecia em casa pelas madrugadas. Terminou dizendo:
    -- 'Ele parece uma menina. Tem os cabelos caídos pelos ombros e espera-me sempre com uma fita cor-de-rosa guarnecendo a sua cabeleira. Tem olhos de gata, oblíquos e esverdeados. É de uma ternura e uma meiguice impossíveis de serem descritas. É muito infeliz com o marido e não merece porque é uma mulher interessante e boníssima. Falam muito mal da sua conduta, dizem que é mulher largamente experimentada em casos amorosos mas, quando eu pergunto, ela se mantém uma irredutível negativa e não há porque não acreditá-la.'
    Neste momento eu tive uma infinita piedade do meu marido. (151)

The husband's sincere revelation of his extra-marital affair, that might be laudable if it occurred in such apparently simple terms, if he had not already reacted violently, in a passage cited above, to the hypothesis that his wife might also be interested in another man. But he had said that he would consider his wife a gangrened limb to be extirpated.
    Nevertheless, the young wife is humiliated despite her feeling that her love for her husband was dying. She might have even accepted the humiliation as a means of accelerating its destruction from within. She thus agrees to carry a message from her sick husband to his lover. In a scene of extraordinary female psychology, the two women are face to face, studying each other and talking in a dignified duel, with careful words and observations that demonstrate their superiority of spirit in relation to their male counterparts. Berenice gets out of a cab where her husband would await her with news of the other woman, goes to her rival's house, sees her "olhos esverdeados, com desenho oblíquo, cabelos soltos e uma fita enfeitando a sua cabeça" as her husband had described her. There follows an ironic analysis of the lover's furniture, "os bibelôs de mau gosto, um vaso com rosas irritantemente artificiais. Pareciam repolhos coloridos." A conversation ensues with "o intuito de ser cruel em cada palavra, em cada vírgula." The lover shows her the gold chain she had received from Berenice's husband. The wife, in turn, agrees to provide the financial help her husband had promised, gently humiliating her with generosity. Everything proceeds with elegance, without letting the lover's husband, who was already suspicious, know what was occurring. After Berenice's return to the taxi where her husband waited, she

was again perfect in her description of details, praising her rival's hair, but expressing reservations about the house's cleanliness.

The refined cruelty continues, for her husband "queria saber se ela se havia interessado pela sua saúde, se não havia estranhado a falta das suas chamadas telefônicas. Eu disse que sim, apesar de nada disso ter acontecido. Não propriamente para lhe dar prazer, mas para que mais tarde ele sofresse ao constatar a verdade das intenções daquela mulher." In effect, having become certain that his lover would be with him on his death bed, after his conversation with his wife she never again called or visited.

The novel still moves forward with other facts. After her husband dies, her mad mother-in-law tries to steal her children, but in the end she manages to free herself from her husband's family: "Uma tarde, meu pai levou-me para a sua casa. Durante treze anos estivera afastada da sua convivência..."

The end marks a denunciatory trajectory: the return to masculine space, to dependence on the father. Berenice is 28 years old and has lived through a dramatic cycle of transformations. She has completed a cycle of existential purification and learning. The fact that the narrative's critical awareness describes the experiences through which the character passed reveals that she was able to differentiate, advance, and transform herself along the way.

In this sense, the text is a journey, a metaphorical journey of female sensitivity searching for identity in the confrontation with the vampiresque ego or the false constructions of Pygmalions who imprison the female mind in the masculine imaginary. To reconstruct the imaginary through writing is one of the forms of recovering identity in both fiction and reality.

REFERENCES

Nery, Adalgisa. *A imaginária*. 3rd ed. Rio de Janeiro: José Olympio, 1970.

GUIMARÃES ROSA THROUGH THE PRISM OF MAGIC REALISM

Charles A. Perrone
University of Florida

Since the appearance of *Sagarana* (1946) critics of Brazilian literature have searched for terms to classify and conceptualize the prose fiction of João Guimarães Rosa and the enormous innovations he brought to narrative practice. Such terms as transrealism, poetic realism, transcendental regionalism, and instrumentalism have been used to assess Rosa's works and his place in national fiction. The author's unique status was underscored by Gunter Lorenz, who made Rosa a category unto himself by calling contemporary Brazilian letters "the literature of a sole personality."[1] The taxonomic challenges that Rosa's work represents confirm the complexity of his imaginative world. His standing in the Brazilian canon is a given. But how to understand this central writer in the broader contexts of modern Latin American fiction and world literature? What is Rosa's relation to his counterparts in Spanish America, the novelists of the so-called "boom"? What do their works share that might illuminate the processes of twentieth-century narrative of the Americas?

Such questions may lead us without much delay to one of the most common critical categories of Spanish American narrative of the last fifty years: magic realism. This concept has been defined and applied in different ways, inevitably crossing paths with the sister idea of the "marvelous reality of the Americas" [*lo real maravilloso americano*] advanced by Alejo Carpentier. Magic and marvelous realism have been widely used and compared--the latter often being nominally subsumed under the former--and both have undergone much scrutiny and discus-

---

[1] Lorenz qtd. by Bolle 15. Translations from Portuguese or Spanish in the course of this paper are mine.

sion. While terminological and critical ambiguities may, in the long run, limit the usefulness of magic realism as a category, the label has enjoyed undeniable currency for more than three decades. Stylistic and conceptual factors involved in magic realism can surely shed light on the production of João Guimarães Rosa. His historical importance can also be placed in a continental perspective, since his recognition corresponds to the international emergence of Latin American fiction.

This essay will consider how criticism of Brazilian and Spanish American literature has employed "magic realism" with reference to João Guimarães Rosa and how the term might be further applied. The level of Brazilian awareness of magic realism's pertinence to this axial modern writer is gauged, as is the inclusiveness of this critical current born in Spanish America. The discussion covers theoretical overviews of magic realism that refer to Brazil's foremost narrator, as well as instances of interpretation of his fiction via magic realism or related terms. Magic realism is treated, in a general way, as a potential prism to appreciate literary innovation in Rosa, and, in a specific manner, as a conduit leading toward further understanding of some of his salient works. Depending on the latitude given in applying the concept, many of Rosa's works can be viewed in terms of magic realism, but the most profitable application will be to two stories from different stages of his career, "São Marcos" (1946) and "Meu Tio, o Iauaretê" (1962). Appraisal of these two stories of the hinterland will reveal Rosa's guiding linguistic concern and will involve appreciation of continental issues relevant to magic realism.

During the 1960s criticism turns to magic or marvelous realism, in search of the Latin American roots of novels of the "boom" in an attempt to justify their experimental nature, as Roberto González Echevarría has written. He delineates three moments in the trajectory of magic realism: its European origins lie in the postulations of German art critic Franz Roh (1925) and in surrealist André Breton's use of "the marvelous" as a category; the second moment involves Arturo Uslar Pietri's account (1948) of Venezuelan short fiction of the 1940s and the celebrated prologue to *The Kingdom of this World* (*El reino de este mundo*) by Alejo Carpentier (1948), where "the marvelous reality of the Americas" is baptized; the third and longest stage begins in 1955 with an oft-cited though theoretically problematic article by Angel Flores and continues with the critical activity of the sixties (González Echevarría 110-111). Interest in and speculation about magic realism peaked in the 1970s. Confusion arising from terminological imprecision, applications of models, and comparisons with the fantastic was sufficient for a noted critic of Latin American literature to propose abandoning magic realism altogether (Rodríguez Monegal). But the critical bibliography continued to grow into the 1980s, in several cases considerably broadening bases of discussion or conceptual scope.[2]

The discussion of João Guimarães Rosa vis-à-vis magic realism below will be facilitated by general indications of what sort of tricks or marvels are in mind with regard to magic or marvelous realism. The term "magic realism" has been employed least rigorously to refer to any stylized fiction not adhering to the rules of classical realist fiction.[3] As González Echevarría implies, difficulties naturally occur when such terms are used in an effort to account for "narrative that could simply be considered fantastic; that is to say, one that does not depend either on natural or physical laws or on the usual conception of the real in Western culture--a narrative, in other words, in which the relations between incidents, characters, and setting could not be based upon or justified by their status within the physical world or their normal acceptance by bourgeois mentality" (109). These points of departure are most useful, as seen below, within certain hemispheric geocultural boundaries.

Magic realism is generally postulated as something peculiar to the fiction of Latin America or the New World. Objections to such a postulation involve chronological assignments of the marvelous and inverosimilitude: medieval chivalric fiction, time-honored fairy tales and historical chronicles with flights of the imagination, all of European extraction, also defy scientific logic in ways which have been attributed to contemporary Latin American fiction as characteristics of magic

---

[2] For a discussion of the history of the ideas involved in magic realism and their philosophical bases, see González Echevarría 107-129. For general accounts of magic realism, its widespread use, and bibliography, see Chanady, Planells, Zeitz, Chiampi and Gricci, all published in the 1980s. For specific examples of the thinking regarding magic realism in the mid-1970s, see Yates, ed. The Flores paper, "Magical Realism in Spanish American Fiction," was read at the 1955 MLA and published in *Hispania* 38.2 (May 1955).

[3] Cf. D.Y. Young and K. Hollaman, eds., *Magical Realist Fiction* (New York: Longman, 1984) which includes such diverse authors as José Luis Borges, Clarice Lispector, Aníbal Monteiro Machado, Henry James and Franz Kafka.

realism. It is thus important to clarify that magic realism is used with reference to prose fiction of the mid-twentieth century. The master Borges crafted non-realist fiction in the early 1940s that has been called magic realism though he himself called the stories "fantastic." In *Journeys Through the Labyrinth*, Gerald Martin goes even farther back and cites a non-Hispanic starting point. The critic finds the birth of the tendency of "Magical Realism" (144) in the key work of Brazilian Modernism, Mário de Andrade's 1928 rhapsodic fiction *Macunaíma*. Martin further christens the whole of mid-century Latin American production under this rubric. Fully aware of the less than satifactory results of such a stance, Martin offers the following caveat:

> Now that, like "baroque", it [magic realism] has become an almost universal description of the "Latin American style"--exotic and tropical, overblown and unrestrained, phantasmagorical and hallucinatory--it is so ideologically dangerous that it should be rejected. (141)

A factor affecting Martin's acceptance of the term, in spite of the express reservation, is the extent to which it has come to be intimately associated with Latin American fiction, especially from the broad-minded Anglo-American perspective that Martin shares (which may partially explain the natural inclusion of Brazil in the "magically real"). While using conveniently broad divisional strokes, Martin does usefully qualify his magical realism: it is a "consciously mythological conception" (114) involving the "juxtaposition and fusion, on equal terms, of literate and pre-literate worlds" (127) as well as the interpenetration of conscious European dimensions and the native collective unconscious (149), for which reason Martin would prefer "mythical realism" as a general category. In any case, his selection of *Macunaíma* runs contrary to the normal flow of magic realist periodization (focused first on the late 1940s) and characterization, because in Andrade's fiction there is no pretense whatsoever to balance non-magical dimensions and the dominant fictional unreal. The citation of this Brazilian work is noteworthy in itself and anticipates some later considerations of João Guimarães Rosa.

While bypassing Brazilian literature altogether, Amaryll Chanady is more representative in his delimiting of the fictional tendency. He offers a useful summary of majority opinion of magic realism as a mode of presentation operating with autonomous coherent perspectives, one based on an enlightened or rational view of reality and the other on the acceptance of the supernatural as part of everyday reality. Magic realism abolishes the antimony between natural and supernatural planes on the level of textual representation, the reader suspends judgment, and the irrational is not problematic. Unlike the fantastic, the magical-realist mode of literature naturalizes the supernatural or strange.

If this naturalization is to be something peculiar to Latin American reality, one must discriminate features that distinguish the literature of the region from others. Such justification, as with certain strains of romanticism, is to be found in native elements. In this regard, Walter Mignolo has made sensible suggestions regarding magic or marvelous realism, which are used to refer to a certain type of literature in the mid-twentieth century whose ideology corresponds to a search for American-ness [*americanidad*]. Mignolo sees in both terms an expression of a common aesthetic, of efforts to capture certain American realities that are rooted in folk or traditional culture and escape a rational European concept of reality. Here, one must assume, is where fiction goes beyond the linear mimesis of regionalism. In magic realism, two realities are at play: one outlined in the bourgeois "myth of reason" and the other in non-scientific "mythical reason" itself. In the latter, one encounters "a halo of mystery" and "inherent marvel," bases of the ontology of difference in the Americas first postulated by Carpentier. The implication for writing, Mignolo thinks, is that "narrative artifice attempting to resolve the confrontation of these two realities should abandon narration by external observers who, from within the myth of reason, inform us about mythical reason. To the contrary, an effect of co-existence should be created in the text" (40-41). Magic realism, in sum, rejects reporting of occasional non-rational phenomena in favor of integration of transferred Iberian folk, indigenous, mestizo, Afro-American or syncretic belief systems. This is not to say that narrative attention is equally divided between different realms; believable occurrence, in fact, would dominate a survey of narrative attention. But when an oneiric sequence, metamorphosis or possession takes place it is presented as a natural event within the logic of the fictional world.

Such a relation of modes of perception is called "non-disjunction" [*não-disjunção*] by Irlemar Chiampi, Brazilian critic of Spanish American literature, who synthesizes the concept of "marvelous realism" [*o realismo maravilhoso*] from magic realism, marvelous American reality, and related problems. Among the recurring procedures she identifies in Spanish American marvelous realism that may apply to João Guimarães Rosa, two stand out: baroque rhetoric [*retórica barroquista*] and a meta-empirical internal causality. The latter is frequently of a mythological order (158) and structures the characteristic non-antimony of the narration. The former involves technical vocabulary, extended comparison, citation, erudition, etc. that distort signifieds in search of the ineffable in stories of the "denaturalization" of the real.

This baroque angle naturally leads to Lezama Lima, whose speculations about cultural syncretism in the Americas directly relate to the search for continental character that has been associated with magic realism. Chiampi underscores a relevant progression in Lezama Lima's poetic thought: what is called "the voracity of the Americas" is an "incorporative protoplasm" that, having absorbed native and Iberian heritages, was able to create a "gnostic space" open to the production of knowledge and to the proliferation of imagery. This space embodies a singular capacity for "vegetative fecundation," a fertility of consciousness allowing for constant reception and generation of new cultural modalities. It was precisely in the baroque period, Lezama Lima proposes, that a truly distinctive American culture of synthesis was born. A prime example of revealingly unchecked proliferation was the work of Aleijadinho, the colonial Brazilian sculptor of Minas Gerais.[4] Lezama Lima's exemplification has distinct historical resonances in the post-regionalist verbal constructions of the great writer of Minas Gerais, the rural medical doctor turned diplomat, João Guimarães Rosa.

Continuing to relate historico-cultural paradigms to literature, one of several fundamental interpretive currents of Iberoamerican identity postulated by Alfredo Roggiano is the "indigenist." Besides broadly implying mythicality, this approach presupposes, in expressive artistic behavior, a native (or extra-Iberian) baroque that lasted through the nineteenth century and gave rise to a neo-baroque, a revitalization of bases, in Asturias, Carpentier, and Arguedas, prime authors associated with magic realism. The modality envisioned here would be the result of forms and structures of European baroque with referents, signifieds and other contents (magical, religious, aesthetic) of an indigenous baroque. What is perceived is a doctrine of crossing and racial mixture, *mestizaje*, with an emphasis on things American, *lo americano* (Roggiano 16). Abundance and the play of form are wed to items of faith, belief and ritual born outside of the Iberian realm.

---

[4] The preceding account is from Chiampi 125-126. For a discussion of Lezama's ideas of American-ness see Bejel, 123-147.

Such historical angles are also integrated into an expansive scope of concern in the more recent account of Latin America's contemporary narrative by Graciela Ricci. She combines logical, mathematical, psychological, and anthropological problematics in semiotic explanations of homologies of literature and its contexts of what she calls, in consciously combinatory fashion, magic-marvelous realism [*realismo mágico maravilloso*]. In her accommodating interrelation of different narrative visions, she cites João Guimarães Rosa, alongside salient Spanish-language narrators, in the post-war tendency towards questioning of self and of realist mimesis (81), as well as in the effort to produce images of an organic and totalizing reality in which natural and supernatural elements meet in symptomatic "zones of coincidence" (175). For Ricci, a language-centered neo-baroque, and encompassing magic-marvellous realism, are both avenues of access to an overarching cultural consciousness, *ontoconciencia* (153), involving local archetypical awareness and knowledge of syncretic cultural constitutions.[5] Ricci's multitheoretically informed work illustrates the outer limits of a concept with origins, as far as Latin American literature is concerned, in loose, impressionistic historical description. In his account of Venezuelan short fiction (1948), Uslar Pietri used the term "magic realism," for an admitted lack of better words, to describe a characteristic "consideration of mankind as a mystery in the midst of realist data, a poetic admiration of or negation of reality" (161-162). "Magic" here suggests the ethereal, something other than the physical, material plane of scientific explanation, and not necessarily religious, para-religious or superstitious practices or sorcery designed to affect persons, places or events. Both senses, nevertheless, must be kept in mind in a review of critical references to João Guimarães Rosa, for "magic/al" is used repeatedly in the broad, metaphorical sense with respect to a non-empirical plane and territory of wonder.[6] In

---

[5] For Ricci "magic-marvelous realism... is understood as a transforming synthesis; as a conjunction--on the same plane and with the same intensity--of the natural and the supernatural..." (125), which may be delimited as a "zone of coincidence of the rational and the oneiric" (131).

[6] A few examples of the critical metaphors of Rosa's work: in 1963, "a singular atmosphere that takes us away from the reality of the senses... there is always mystery surrounding the landscape, people, acts and words of the narrator. It is a transrealist aura... (Ataíde 143); in 1967,

like fashion, the author's baroque stylizations and utilization of mythical structures are--in general and specific ways--in line with concepts of magic realism outlined above. The essence of a structurally-defined magic realism will continue to be the textual operation of resolved (as opposed to unresolved) antimony of cognitive systems involving events that emerge from a native worldview and defy received reason. To discern and locate the figures of João Guimarães Rosa through the prism of magic realism, then, will entail looking for challenges to mainstream constitutions of the real, a fictional defiance, likely mythologized and baroque, founded in autochthonous outlooks.

* * *

That João Guimarães Rosa should have been predisposed to a magical-realist approach to literature is evident in his acceptance speech to the Brazilian Academy of Letters (1967). Speaking of his hometown in rural Minas Gerais, Rosa says at the outset: "Cordisburgo... where the rain and sun, the clear air and the surroundings quickly reveal a world open, above all, to superior dimensions; they influence a magic notion of the universe." In the conclusion to his address, Rosa summarizes a guiding perception in a simple statement: "the world is magical." Previously, in his most in-depth critical interview (1965), Rosa had related the poetry of his prose to magic and elicited from his interlocutor an allusion to the magic realism of Asturias and, more so, Carpentier. The Brazilian author, perfectly conscious of the comparison, preferred to call his concept "magical algebra" instead of magic realism because "it is more indeterminate and therefore more exact" (Lorenz 89-90). The paradox both confirms the validity of characterizations of Rosa's narratives as lyrical and affirms essential parallels between the master of modern Brazilian prose and Hispanic counterparts, thus opening avenues of inquiry of Rosa's stories and their internal logic.

As for Brazilian criticism, the earliest critical uses of the term magic realism are isolated and predate Rosa's cited comments by some ten years. Independent of conscious employments of the compound

---

"creator of magic worlds" (Oliveira 183); in 1968, "In this way, any interpretation one attempts will turn out to be arbitrary for lack of logic verification in the dynamics of a cosmos all elaborated in magic, legend and myth (Montenegro 274).

term, many critics use "magic" as an adjective to suggest the new and unusual qualities of Rosa's more-than-regionalism in terms of characters, worldview, and language use. More significant from a diachronic point of view is the fact that stories with "magical" associations form part of the author's first collection, *Sagarana*, originally completed in 1937, during the heyday of Northeastern regionalism, but published only in 1946, in a period when such landmark works as Asturias' *El señor presidente* and Carpentier's *El reino de este mundo* appeared.

While such early Rosa stories as "Corpo fechado," which involves sorcery-induced bodily protection, have elements suggestive of the magically real, it is in "São Marcos" that one finds a clear example of a supernaturally-governed turning point. The story, in addition to a literally magic syntagm of transformation, contains a theory of poetry that affirms the centrality and power of language in the story itself and, by extension, in Rosa's fictional system.[7] A brief recapitulation of the story reveals its most pertinent features. The narrator-protagonist of "São Marcos" is openly skeptical of the sorcery practiced in the village where he lives. One day, as he heads for the forest where he scientifically observes flora and fauna, he irritates a local sorcerer. Continuing on his way, he hears the story of a man who managed to flee from prison by means of a magical prayer. Next, the narrator interpolates an account of a poetic exchange: he and an anonymous interlocutor have alternately inscribed verses on huge bamboo stalks; the narrator's key contribution is a roll of names of Assyrian-Babylonian kings; his defense of the naming of the names' "song and plumage" [*canto e plumagem*] as poetry constitutes a modernist *ars poetica*. This episode, together with the effects attributed to ritual verbalizations, underscores the power of language in the story and in the encompassing collection. Later in the forest, the narrator visually perceives natural exuberance in lush and vivid representations that echo the discussion of words' poeticity. At this point blindness strikes the narrator, whose intense focus shifts to auditory perception. Only through chanting the magical prayer is the cause of his crisis revealed, allowing him to make his way to the sorcerer's house, where a sight-restoring struggle ensues. The account of this narrator, the skeptical naturalist poetically aware of local luxuriance, of his experience of transformation implies his admission of the causality of magical spell.

---

[7] See Garbuglio 192ff. and Coutinho 227ff. for synopsis and analysis of the story's theorization of language.

Thus the narration embodies confrontation and textual resolution of the "myth of reason" and the "reason of myth," organizational poles of magically-real structure. Brazilian criticism, of course, has underlined the significance of "São Marcos" as a statement of poetic principles. But the literal sense of magic in the story has not previously been related to magic realism as an emerging Latin American literary mode. Other stories in *Sagarana* may have elements of fable or fantastic grandeur, but none so clearly defines and resolves itself in the terms of magic-marvellous realism.

Rosa's second collection of stories and novellas, *Corpo de baile* (1956), has no supernatural elements per se, but there again critics sensed "magical" airs or atmospheres in the fiction, which may have "marvelous" events in the sense of astounding if not logic-defying. Paulo Rónai finds "Campo Geral" to be "the most magical" of the tales. In the backland setting, "customs are determined not by laws but by odd superstitions, tribal inhibitions, and a strange ethical code." Readers are introduced into "this strange world under the guidance of a child who, being a native of the milieu, accepts its oddities most naturally" (7). This mindset and physical setting are propitious for the magical, but when the young character Miguilim is presented with a pair of eyeglasses, readers understand that what may have been perceived as miraculous now comes into perspective and no question of meta-empirical experience remains. Still, the everyday events in this and other narratives of *Corpo de baile* may be seen to be transformed into symbols via a pertinent approach, as Euryalo Cannabrava would have it: "Magic realism, the key note of this work of multiform aspects, leads the writer to transfigure the themes of everyday life into symbols that form part of fantasies and myths" (265). The approach may even shed light on Rosa's particular literary grace: "The secret of this writer's power perhaps resides . . . in the subtle combination of magic realism and sensory physiology as basic elements of his literary work" (267). In general, Cannabrava is taken by Rosa's literary figures who have some mythical aura, suggest tones of legendary symbols or are creatures of folklore. These somehow contrast significantly, one must assume, with realia on a physical plane. In this critical instance, magic realism is not delimited through integration of worldviews (or anything else), though something along these lines is implied in the term's appearance in opposition to a sensory, tangible level. In fact, one may even wonder where Cannabrava gets the term. For while this commentary may lack pertinent terminological rigor it is notable for the date of the original observation, 1956, making it perhaps the first critical application of the term magic realism, albeit somewhat dubiously, to Rosa. It comes, moreover, before the publication of Rosa's master-piece.

With *Grande sertão: veredas* (1956), critical comparisons with the great Spanish American new novels begin to appear and direct or indi-rect appeals to magic realism are made. Brazilian utilizations and defini-tions of the concept--be they vague, unspoken, implied or otherwise inconsistent--naturally involve references to Rosa vis-à-vis his great novel and other Latin American authors. Bella Josef, for example, finds fertile ground of comparison between Rosa and Asturias, both of whom "grasp reality via the unreal and vice-versa... are committed to their circum-stances and have social foundations imbued with magic realism" (195). This use of the term suggests perhaps no more than something atmo-spheric or tonal. Yet the same critic assigns the broader scope of myth to magic realism (or assumes this meaning to be in the repertory of her readers) when she identifies traits João Guimarães Rosa shares with the novelists of the boom: "...these authors seek collective myth in the sense of a crazed struggle with mythical forces, with heroes led by instinctual forces, undertaking epic struggles. Archetypical characters are created in the abstraction of the concrete in a process of transfiguration of external reality, imbued in the magic realism of a metaphysical world" (190). And what better exemplification of this high-level literary process-ing than the hinterland of Riobaldo in *Grande sertão: veredas*?

It is precisely that literary world to which critic Flávio Chaves refers when he argues that Julio Cortázar's monumental novel *Rayuela* should not be regarded as magic (or marvelous) realism. In contrast to Cortázar, the crucial set of elements postulated by Carpentier--"virgin landscape, fertile mixtures of people, streams of unexplored mytholo-gy"--are seen as central to Vargas Llosa, Rulfo and Rosa (163). The latter's grand protagonist Riobaldo, in turn, would figure among those literary creations to be included in the "epic context of the Americas" (165) so common in the composition of magic realism. This tendency, Chaves asserts, always offers more than "closed realism" and *Grande sertão: veredas* is an "open work: always having something more." In a symptomatic quote, Chaves ascribes a special nature to the discourse of the narrator-protagonist of Rosa's great hinterland: "After all, the word of Urutu-Branco is a magic invitation that resounds and always returns" (131).

Consideration of the local development of the heroic or epic element has led other Brazilian observers to the paradigm of magic or marvelous realism. Dirce Cortes Riedel, for example, studying the chivalric idealization of Medeiro Vaz, concludes that apparently "marvelous" happenings in *Grande sertão: veredas* flow from a tributary of medieval tradition and do *not* represent that undesirable literary effect "against which Carpentier warns us, as it is achieved with tricks and sleight-of-hand."[8] Rosa's literary backland social history might appear "fantastic," if one were not familiar with actual events and the native perspective. Rosa's fictive universe would, by Riedel's reasoning, be an "authentic" case of "marvelous reality of the Americas." From a related angle, João Lopes relies, in a study of an obscure author, on allusions to *Grande sertão: veredas* and to the character Diadorim as "enchanted warrior" to discuss "emblematic figuration" that can be understood as "a procedure of marvelous realism." Here, the specific function of this approach is "not so much the creation of fantastic beings or worlds as the discovery of the invisible and occult relationship between man and his circumstance" (69). Rosa's character Diadorim, in this analysis, is the symbol par excellence of the "enchanted backlands," an angle of perception that links folk consciousness to the critical language of magic realism.

As for as an overall appreciation of *Grande sertão: veredas* via magic realism, the case of José Hildebrando Dacanal, at first glance, would seem to be most promising. His book's title is *Realismo mágico* and his preface seeks to explain how the new Latin American novel exemplified in Rosa and García Márquez needs a new *classification* that transcends the rationality of nineteenth-century narrative. Dacanal further underlines how the historical separation of Rosa's backlands from the "civilized world" structurally parallels the native cultural element (Amerindian or African) necessary for magic realism, of which *Grande sertão: veredas* is called an "essential work" (10-11). Here again, lack of definition soon proves to be problematic, for Dacanal's essay mostly concerns the ontological constitution of the hero in an exo-European, third world context; magic realism figures only in the most roundabout way, in connection to sacred and mythical practices. There is no development whatsover of the questions of perspective of perception or cultural overlays. While Dacanal delivers something other than a justified

---

[8] Riedel 73, referring to the Brazilan edition of Alejo Carpentier *Literatura e consciência política na América Latina*.

interpretation of magic realism, his critical concerns are indeed continental.

From a stylistic point of view, Rosa's master novel does offer rich possibilities. In the above discussion of the story "São Marcos," passages were noted where accounts of perception and lush flora and fauna featured a sensorial and involved literary language that could be called baroque. Such language figures no less prominently in the pages of *Grande sertão: veredas*. Several articulations of magic/marvelous realism, as seen above, bring into play the baroqueness of a seemingly regional rhetoric, and Rosa's qualifications in this respect are many. Severo Sarduy, in fact, detects--in the "baroque exuberance" of the novel in general and in the manipulation of variants of the word "devil" in particular--the fusion of two fundamental oratory supports, substitution and proliferation, which characterize the neo-baroque in Latin American literature (172). For Jorge Adoum, such evidence is so abundant that João Guimarães Rosa is no less than "the most baroque of all writers in any romance language" (205), an author who understood his very task as "seeking and creating an idiom, restructuring or rediscovering his own language" (216). Understanding the choreography of this stance before the instruments of expression could determine how Rosa's greatest novel would fare in an assessment of magic realism as a guiding mode.

A like appraisal of the *Primeiras histórias* (1962) would focus, in addition, on the confrontation of rationality and other states. Critics of the collection have emphasized such common elements as oddity, weirdness or abnormality in a series of strange or unstable characters. Critical interpretations of them have avoided the suggestion of clinical cases (pathology) in favor of a hermeneutics of "the unreal, the irrational, the magical," in the words of a noted critic.[9] In some of the stories involving love, furthermore, there is a magical helper or auxiliary, making the titles conform, above all, to a notion of "modern fairy tales" (Bolle 93). But because individualized eccentricities seem to dominate here rather than any sense of ethnicity, mythologization or relational derationaliza-

---

[9] Paulo Rónai (qtd. by Bolle 10). For his part, Luiz Costa Lima presents the stories as "seeing in creatures the range of mystery, strangeness and perplexity that Rosa sees in the world" (505); the critic sees a rejection of "logical realism" in favor of a "cosmic form of realism." A study of action clarifies dimensions of Rosa's "magico-symbolic preoccupation" (506).

tion, the dominant sense of magical realism developed above does not comfortably fit here. The multiple micro-narratives of *Tutaméia* (1967), in turn, undertake narrative proposals whose innovative character derives from original sources other than magic or marvelous realism, even understood in accommodating terms.[10]

The centerpiece story of the posthumous collection *Estas histórias* (1969), however, exhibits essential characteristics to be considered not only as a clear manifestation of magical realism in the repertory of João Guimarães Rosa but also as an exemplary expression thereof in contemporary Latin American literature. The story is "Meu Tio, o Iauaretê" [My Uncle the True Jaguar (originally published in 1962)]. As in "São Marcos," there is a language-centered theory of narrative imbedded in the telling of this story, as well as a syntagm of transformation crucial to its resolution. Here, in addition, there is a much more pronounced autochthonous element and related mythical underpinnings. The story is cast as the monologue (or implicit dialogue where the interlocutor is silent) of a backlands hunter of jaguars. The narrator is a solitary soul, son of an Indian woman; with developing emotivity, he relates to his listener, a traveler from the city, a series of episodes about hiring out to hunt jaguars, actually hunting them, and victimization of people by animals. Significantly, the language employed is a rural Portuguese contaminated by indigenous Tupy. A process of linguistic transformation becomes progressively more intense, a metamorphosis occurs, and the narrator is transformed into a jaguar before the eyes of the interlocutor, whom the reader then "hears" killing the speaker.[11] By the

---

[10] See Vincent chapters 3 and 4 on *Primeiras histórias* and *Tutaméia* and for a general introduction to Rosa. See Bolle for structural capsulizations of the stories and Merrim for a concise appreciation of Rosa's micro-narratives and their prefaces. In *Tutaméia* there are cases where the *imagination* of a protagonist is greater than a difficulty or becomes reality, achieving the "fantastic or miraculous" (Bolle 128) but these cases are all counterbalanced and do not really involve meta-empirical constructs.

[11] This story could well be analyzed in the terms established by Nancy Gray Diaz in her study of animal form in Latin American literature. Chapter 4 deals with *Macunaíma* and declares the work to be a "forerunner" of Magic Realism (71), more sensible, in our estimation,

end, language has been totally disarticulated; only grunts, noises, vocables and exclamations remain to communicate the final scene.

Sensing the larger literary projection of this act of textual metamorphosis, Haroldo de Campos argues that the story "Meu Tio, o Iauaretê" represents "the most advanced stage of Rosa's experiments," for "the prose incorporates 'the moment of magic or metamorphosis' " (575). José Lino Grünewald, echoing this critical stance, affirms that Rosa's jaguar story best puts into evidence his "preoccupation with acting upon language, a preoccupation even on the level of magic, alchemy." "Magic" is rightly invoked because essential changes are effected in man and his instrument of expression in the story. It is "magically real," it may be added, because of its fusion of outlooks, the meeting of a foundational "civilized" premise of the story and an eventual "savage" event of closure.

Beyond the animal and idiomatic metamorphoses in "Meu Tio, o Iauaretê," Walnice Galvão has studied the story profitably in terms of its operative mythical and cultural paradigms. The structural oppositions that vertebrate the story--white vs. Indian, backland vs. city, America vs. Europe--are directly relevant to its magic realism. Galvão approaches Rosa's dense story via the historically fundamental binomial of the cooked and the raw, noting how "the rejection of the civilized world, domain of the cooked, is accompanied by a return to the natural world, domain of the raw" (13). Fire--which has a predominant function in the story--is the foundation of culture and marks the passage from the raw to the cooked. Rosa's story is based on the myth of the origin of fire, which belonged to the jaguar in Tupy lore and was stolen by humans. Rosa's narrator-protagonist's killing of people has a significant relation to the world of animals, for he is of mixed Indian and white blood, and, as Galvão underscores, he is lost between cultures (26). Furthermore, he combines and juxtaposes lexicons in a linguistic mirror that reflects an Indian-white man-jaguar (33). The mythical elements again demonstrate the underlying breadth of the story and link it to a factor of continental American consciousness, to a search or questioning thereof. Galvão relates the story to a notable presence of the mythical jaguar throughout the lore of the Americas: "the cult of the so-called 'solar jaguar'... points to the extra-Brazilian dimension of the story, American, but above all, Latin American" (13). Aware of these dimensions, Galvão

---

than declaring it to be a starting point of the tendency, for the reasons cited above.

argues that "Meu Tio" must not be considered a mere werewolf tale or fable of licanthropy, but rather "a profound reflection on nature and culture, the theme, after all, of all Lévi-Strauss's work." Rosa's is "an unparalled literary text, a sharp perception of the tragedy that is the extinction of cultures that has taken and is taking place extensively on this American continent, from the Artic to Antartica" (19). Galvão's insight into Rosa's cultural finality connects his fiction to an archetypical narrative situation--the final stage, the beginning of the cycle of death and resurrection--which, in Ricci's mythically-mapped magic-marvellous realism (43, 56), occupies a fundamental place in the governing consciousness of a literary practice.

* * *

If magic realism is held to be a generational attitude towards reality founded on acceptance of the insufficiency of classical realist tenets and of the efficacy of alternative cultural overlays, then the label should clearly be applied to the author who, more than anyone else, led Brazilian letters out of the woods of regionalism, João Guimarães Rosa. The author of *Grande sertão: veredas* is--as a composite Brazilian critic might say--a chronicler who reveals the "magic" world of the hinterland and transcends the documentary mind, discovering real and imaginary places for contemporary readers as Rennaissance explorers discovered and liberally described the virgin coastlands. As some critical citations have indicated, it makes sense to include Rosa in broad definitions of magic realism involving juxtaposition of bourgeois rationality, myth and *mestizaje*, though the number of Brazilian critics who use the term, with whatever precision, is relatively small. In Brazil, Spanish America, the US and Europe, magic-marvellous realism has been primarily associated with Spanish American prose fiction, even though the lines of definition are continental in shape and color and the master story of *El reino de este mundo* has, in Haiti, a non-Hispanic setting. Focusing on João Guimarães Rosa via magic-marvellous realism reveals affinities of aesthetic rupture and affirmation with key Spanish-language writers, shows renovation from a continental vantage point, and facilitates a comparatist approach to the modern literatures of the Americas.

Where magic realism is more strictly defined in terms of incorporation of non-European myth and its textual perspective, João Guimarães Rosa wrote two most pertinent titles: "São Marcos" and "Meu Tio, o Iauaretê." The latter brings together a whole range of possibilities discussed above in relation to the understanding and scope of magic realism as a contemporary literary practice and, with its bodily metamorphosis, can be considered an exemplary manifestation. The former, in turn, merits special chronological consideration. "São Marcos" was published in 1946, the same year as the landmark of Asturias's *El señor presidente*, predating the Guatemalan's *Hombres de maíz* and Carpentier's *El reino de este mundo* (both 1949). Like Asturias's surrealistically-influenced novel of dictatorship, which was begun in a previous decade, Rosa's *Sagarana*, with the poetics of "São Marcos," was written some ten years earlier. In its year of publication, Rosa's story should be regarded as a starting block, a point of departure, a first moment of a creative posture that, by many accounts, is central to an understanding of the modern narrative of Latin America. Magic realism, in the restricted sense employed above, did not proliferate in Rosa's repertory nor in the narrative of his nation, as it did in Spanish America. Yet Rosa's story "São Marcos"--besides embodying, as Garbuglio shows, the genesis of a monumental literary project--could be considered not only as an illustration of a significant commonality on a Latin American level but as one of the earliest contributions to a characteristic and revealing option of midcentury narrative.

It is indicative that both the action and theory of "São Marcos" and "Meu Tio," convoking a magical prayer and exercising a metamorphosed tongue, lead to the centrality of language. Magic realism--understood as the occurrence of trans-empirical events in a fundamentally logical and linear narrative--will not, in the long run, really account for Rosa's literary revolution, for what proves to be foremost in his storied prose are the vertical slices into the paradigms of language. However far one wants to take the issue of magic realism in his prose fiction, its consideration will inevitably reemphasize the author's modernity as a philosopher of literary language itself, as a maker of a new artistic idiolect. Benedito Nunes rightly speaks of Rosa's fiction as "a poetic realism in which the scheme of things and beings is constantly reborn from an originary plot of language," holding that Rosa "uses language not as an exterior instrument to translate a pre-defined world but rather as a kind of tongue in a nascent state that regains the *poiesis* of the Portuguese language" (qtd. by Coutinho 225). João Guimarães Rosa, like Carpentier or García Márquez, is a distinctive poet of narrative prose who merits individualization more than classification. In the spectrum of the prism, magic realism will serve as one angle on the task of explaining the mystery in the universe of a singular writer.

REFERENCES

Adoum, Jorge. "El realismo de la otra realidad." Fernández Moreno. 204-216.

Ataíde, Tristão de. "O transrealismo de G.R." Coutinho. 142-143.

Bejel, Emilio. *José Lezama Lima, Poet of the Image.* Gainesville: U of Florida P, 1990.

Bolle, Willi. *Fórmula e fábula.* São Paulo: Perspectiva, 1973.

Campos, Haroldo de. "A linguagem do Iauraretê." Coutinho. 574-579.

Cannabrava, Euryalo. "Guimarães Rosa e a linguagem literária." Coutinho. 264-270.

Chanady, Amaryll. *Magical Realism and the Fantastic: Resolved vs. Unresolved Antimony.* New York: Garland, 1985.

Chaves, Flávio Loureiro. *Ficção latino-americana.* Porto Alegre: Editora URGS, 1973.

Chiampi, Irlemar. *O realismo maravilhoso.* São Paulo: Perspectiva, 1980.

Coutinho, Eduardo de Faria, ed. *Guimarães Rosa.* Rio de Janeiro: Civilização Brasileira/INL, 1983.

_____. "Guimarães Rosa e o processo de revitalização da lingua gem." Coutinho. 202-236.

Dacanal, José Hildebrando. *Realismo mágico.* Porto Alegre: Movimento, 1970.

Díaz, Nancy Gray. *The Radical Self: Metamorphosis to Animal Form in Latin American Narrative.* Columbia: University of Missouri P, 1988.

Fernández Moreno, César, ed. *América Latina en su literatura*. 3a ed. México, D.F.: Siglo XXI, 1976.

Galvão, Walnice Nogueira. *Mitológica rosiana*. São Paulo: Perpsectiva, 1978.

Garbuglio, José Carlos. "Guimarães Rosa: a gênese de uma obra." *Revista iberoamericana* 98-99 (1977) 183-197.

Gersen, Bernardo. "Veredas no Grande Sertão." Coutinho. 350-359.

González-Echevarría, Roberto. *Alejo Carpentier: The Pilgrim at Home*. Ithaca: Cornell UP, 1977.

Grunewald, José Lino. "Rosa da Prosa." *Correio da manhã* 21 Nov. 1967, 2º cad.- p.1

Josef, Bella. "O romance brasileiro e o ibero-americano na atualidade." Coutinho. 187-197.

Lima, Luiz Costa. "O mundo em perspectiva: Guimarães Rosa." Coutinho. 500-513.

Lopes, João de Oliveira. "O sertão no canto épico e armorial de Janice Japiassu." *Cadernos de literatura* 18 (1984): 61-70.

Lorenz, Gunter. "Diálogo com Guimarães Rosa." Coutinho. 62-100.

Martin, Gerald. *Journeys through the Labyrinth: Latin American Literature in the twentieth century*. London: Verso, 1989.

Merrim, Stephanie. "The Art of Preface in Guimarães Rosa's *Tutaméia*." *Review* 29 (1979): 10-12.

Mignolo, Walter. *Literatura fantástica y realismo maravilloso*. Madrid: Muralla, 1983.

Montenegro, Braga. "Guimarães Rosa, novelista." Coutinho. 271-282.

Nunes, Benedito. "A Rosa o que é de Rosa." *Estado de São Paulo*, 22 March 1969.

Oliveira, Franklin de. "Revolução Roseana." Coutinho. 179-186.

Planells, Antonio. "La polémica sobre realismo mágico en Hispanoamérica." *Revista Interamericana de bibliografía*. 4.37 (1987): 517-529.

Ricci, Graciela N. *Realismo mágico y conciencia mítica en América Latina*. Buenos Aires: Fernando García Cambeiro, 1985.

Riedel, Direce Cortes. "*Grande sertão: veredas*: choques e interação de culturas." *Travessia* 7.15 (1987): 70-84.

Rodríguez Monegal, Emir. "Diálogo de sordos." Yates: 25-37.

Roggiano, Alfredo A. "Acerca de la identidad cultural de Iberoamérica. Algunas posibles interpretaciones." in *Identidad cultural de Iberoamérica en su literatura*. Madrid: Alhambra, 1986. 11-20.

Rónai, Paulo. "An approach to João Guimarães Rosa." Unpublished MS. of address delivered at University of Florida, 1967.

Rosa, João Guimarães. "Discurso de Posse na Academia Brasileira de Letras" in *Correio da Manhã*, 25 nov. 1967, 2º cad. 2-3.

Sarduy, Severo. "El barroco y el neobarroco." Fernández. 176-184.

Uslar Pietri, Arturo. *Letras y hombres de Venezuela*. México, D.F.: Fondo de Cultura Económica, 1948.

Vincent, Jon. *João Guimarães Rosa*. Boston: Twayne, 1978.

Yates, Donald, ed. *Otros mundos otros fuegos: fantasía y realismo mágico en Iberoamérica*, XVI Congreso del Instituto Internacional de Literatura Iberoamericana. East Lansing: Michigan State University, Latin American Studies Center, 1975.

Zeitz, Eileen M. and Richard A. Seybolt. "Hacia una bibliografía sobre el realismo mágico." *Hispanic Journal* 3.1 (1981): 159-167.

HETERONYMY IN GUIMARÃES ROSA[1]

Walnice Nogueira Galvão
Universidade de São Paulo

> E precisaria cada um, para simultaneidades no sentir e pensar, de vários cérebros e corações. Quem sabe, temos? (João Guimarães Rosa, *Tutaméia--terceiras histórias*)

João Guimarães Rosa: noted Brazilian prose writer, credited with the innovation of Brazilian Portuguese in fiction. This name corresponds to a distinct literary personality, as well as to a citizen recognized in social life and a diplomatic career. Could there have been others? Other personalities, albeit in embryonic stages, other repressed voices wanting to make themselves heard but finding no outlet? How could this subject of narrative discourse, so apparently cohesive and unified, have escaped the curse of modernity that makes of the writer a fragmented self?

Guimarães Rosa began publishing his narratives in newspapers and magazines in 1929. He also wrote a book of poems, entitled *Magma*, which has yet to be published. The book was submitted to the poetry competition of the Brazilian Academy of Letters in 1936 and earned first

---

[1] A Portuguese version of this paper was read at the IV International Symposium on Fernando Pessoa, Tulane University, 17-19 November 1988.

place.[2] Despite the award and the critical backing of the jury, the author never sought to have the book published. *Magma* was submitted without camouflage, i.e. it was signed by João Guimarães Rosa. He took a different approach in his first submission of prose fiction to a contest, using the pseudonym Viator (= the wayfarer) for a volume called *Contos* that was presented, without positive results, to the Humberto de Campos prize offered by the José Olympio publishing house in 1938.

The use of a pseudonym was not surprising, some competitions even require one, but the author's subsequent sequestering (in the sense given by Mário de Andrade) was. When the *Contos*, recast as *Sagarana*, were published eight years later (1946), Graciliano Ramos, a member of the jury, revealed that there had been unsuccesful attempts to identify Viator, who had nearly been a victor.[3] The promotor of the competition, José Olympio, had even intended to publish it. And jury member Marques Rebelo, who voted for Viator, wrote years later in his fictional diary, *O espelho partido*--appropriately *à clef* with the treachery that made him notorious--of an encounter he had had with "Magalhães Braga" in which he was treated with the condescension that a modest colleague deserves upon recognizing a genius.

The difference between such a title as *Contos* and *Sagarana* is great, especially if we keep in mind the eight years of re-elaboration, the careful re-writing and selection that eliminated many things from the book. The title *Contos* was indiscriminate; it had already been assigned to countless books and has been to countless others since then. But *Sagarana* reveals a confident writer in command of his talents inventing an original word within a "Guimarães Rosa style" (from *saga*, Portuguese word of Germanic origin, plus *rana*, Tupi suffix meaning "in the manner of" or "what seems to be").

In the meantime, what became of the poet, author of *Magma*, still unpublished? The one whose first complete book was of poetry? Public reception and a critical reputation were born with the publication of *Sagarana*: the Felipe de Oliveira prize was won and two printings sold

---

[2] Opinion of the judges, written by Guilherme de Almeida, in *Em memória de João Guimarães Rosa*.

[3] See Graciliano Ramos, "Conversa de bastidores," in *Em memória de João Guimarães Rosa*.

out in one year. The gaze of the Other constitutes the recognition and establishment of a literary personality, as a *prose writer*.

Ten years elapse between the publication of *Sagarana* and that of *Corpo de baile* and *Grande sertão: veredas* in the same year (1956). The feat is noteworthy: several hundred pages of rich narrative prose with a high level of linguistic invention. There are a few clues as to how much that accomplishment took out of the author in some of the notes from his notebook of the time, "Diário de Paris," which has recently been the object of critical study. Of that preparatory phase, when everything converges in the need to write, Guimarães Rosa says: "my basic anguish is an anxious desire for omniscience" and that by recording things in the diary "I try to avoid the reefs of the incessant storm of my inner life" and "an all-consuming torment, ambitious, insatiable." A letter of the same period tells of his turbulent mental condition while creating: "...I am febrile, full up, with three books ready in my head, a swarm of characters asking to rest on paper. I'm sharpening the pencil to begin the task. It's tough and I've already scared myself before I've taken one step down this painful path that I'm familiar with." The imperative to write, despite the pangs of suffering it brings, is still less harmful than stopping writing when in this state: if the book is not written "it coagulates in me, like a thrombus in a vein, worse than a complex." Driven by those two pains, that of writing and that of not writing, Guimarães Rosa will still publish two books in his lifetime: *Primeiras histórias* (1962) and *Tutaméia -- terceiras histórias* (1967), both of stories. He continues to be, therefore, a prose writer.

Soon after the death of Guimarães Rosa in 1967, a volume in his honor was prepared and published by the José Olympio publishing house, *Em memória de João Guimarães Rosa* (1968), which brings together critical studies, unpublished material, speeches, facsimiles of translations, opinions, manuscripts and a bibliography by Plínio Doyle, who includes interesting information about poems (or better, poets) of the prose writer. The bibliographer states that he followed a clue given by Manuel Bandeira in his *Antologia de poetas brasileiros bissextos contemporâneos* (2nd ed.), in which six poems of Guimarães Rosa's are presented under the anagrammatic pen name Soares Guiamar. From there, Plínio Doyle went back to the sources where the poems had originally been published--1961 issues of *O Globo*--and uncovered twelve more poems and two other pseudonyms, anagrammatic as well. Attention: in all, three new poets emerge in the hide-and-seek typical of anagrams while the prose author continues to brandish his name, by this time A NAME.

The three appear in four pieces Guimarães Rosa wrote for *O Globo* in 1961: "Coisas de poesia" (25 February), "Outras coisas de poesia" (1 April), "Novas coisas de poesia" (20 May), and "Sempre coisas de poesia" (22 July), according to Plínio Doyle. The great majority of the material, but not the pieces on poetry, from this column, which ran weekly from 7 January 1961 to 26 August 1961, goes into the book *Primeiras histórias* and some additional material into *Tutaméia* or even *Ave, palavra*. The pseudonyms are, in addition to Soares Guiamar, Meuriss Aragão (also an anagram of Guimarães Rosa) e Sá Araújo Ségrim (anagram of J. Guimarães Rosa), all of which are coherent in the addition of known last names to invented given names. Plínio Doyle mentions four more poems ("Sextilhas," "Em um álbum," "O burro e o boi no presépio," e "Poemas de Natal") and indicates sources other than *O Globo*.

Before his death, Guimarães Rosa had been preparing two books for publication, both of which appeared posthumously: *Estas estórias* (1969) and *Ave, palavra* (1970). The first book is a volume of stories, like *Primeiras estórias* and *Tutaméia*, which, even discounting the four prefaces of the latter, comprise collections *of stories*. But the second has various, miscellaneous types of text that, strictly speaking, are anything but stories, as varied material published in the press from 1947-1967 is brought together. This is the only book of Guimarães Rosa's of this kind, and it is here that, for the only time, the author himself entrusts some of his poems to the printed page.

In *Ave, palavra* those poets whose elusive profile we had been seeking appear with relative frequency. There is a brief, duly obscure, explanation of each one, in a minimal introit to respective blocks of text. These poets have nowhere near the personalities and detailed complexity that Fernando Pessoa gave to his heteronyms, who even had horoscopes. But the shadow of that poet can be seen in the distance, for he is a *cause célèbre* of whom all informed Brazilian or Portuguese readers are aware. Still, the divergent literary tradition of the two countries should be kept in mind: Brazilians have been much less inclined to use pseudonyms than the Portuguese (Bruneti).

In this last book, there are not three but four anagrammatic poets with the addition of Romaguari Sães, an anagram of Guimarães Rosa, like the first two, rather than of J. Guimarães Rosa, like the third. There are nine poems by Soares Guiamar ("Ou ... ou", "Pescaria," "Teorema," "Parlenda," "Alongo-me," "O aloprado,"[4] "Os três burricos," "Motivos," "Adamubies?") under the general title "As coisas de poesia." The two dates given (25 February 1961 and 1 April 1961) after the name of the newspaper, show that two pieces, both with poems by Soares Guiamar, have been combined into one here; the original titles from *O Globo* are, respectively, "Coisas de poesia" and "Outras coisas de poesia." This may be the origin of some possible confusion since Paulo Rónai, in the introduction to *Ave, palavra*, when he clarifies that he has added some unpublished materials to the body of text left by the author, erroneously includes among them "Coisas de poesia." In addition, a likely typographical error, Plínio Doyle's numbering assigns number 13, "A ausente perfeita," to both Soares Guiamar and Meuriss Aragão (the "real" author). By the latter there are five poems ("Mulher mar morte," "Saudade, sempre," "Saudade, sempre (versão aflita)", "A ausente perfeita," "A espantada estória") under the general title "Novas coisas de poesia," with an indication of the source and date (20 April 1961). They are the same as those listed by Plínio Doyle except that "A espantosa estória" on his list became "A espantada estória" in the book. By Araújo Ségrim, a total of eight poems, divided into two blocks of four each ("Distância," "Recapítulo," "Contratema," "Rota," in the first, and "Aria," "Querência," "Escólio," "Tornamento," in the second). The first block has the general title "Novas coisas de poesia," with an indication of source and date (20 April 1961). The second is called "Quando coisas de poesia" and is labeled *inédito* [previously unpublished]. By Romaguari Sães there are four poems ("Marjolininha," "Cândida," "Presença e perfil da moça de chapeuzinho cônico," and "Marjolininha [9ª]") also labled as *inédito* in a footnote by the author. The general title is "Ainda coisas de poesia." The book, then, enriches the poetic work of the anagrammatic poets not only with another pseudonym (who was previously unpublished) but also with eight new poems. Questions remain: could Guimarães Rosa have written the two groups of poems he labels *inéditos* ("Quando coisas de poesia" de Sá Araújo Ségrim and "Ainda coisas de poesia" de Romaguari Sães) when he wrote all the others and not published them for some reason? Or did he create them expressly for *Ave, palavra*?

---

[4] In the second preface to *Tutaméia*, "Hipotrélico," Guimarães Rosa calls attention to this word, calling it "splendid," as if he had never employed it.

As far as the poets are concerned, the introits provide succinct biographical notes that set up an elegant juggling of masks among them. Perhaps the oldest is Soares Guiamar, since he appears first chronologically; he has retired, no further verse of his is available, and "now he is staying far away, undoubtedly on the banks of Sirimim Creek;" he is more or less Sá Araújo Ségrim's master and is, or wants to be, author of the book *Anagramas*. He has left some well-chosen words about poets and poetry. He is described as "unnoticed, in print, unpublished, out-of-fashion."

The second in order to appear is Meuriss Aragão. "Another pocket poet," he is "young, akward, in his first stage, possibly extinct." The next one, Sá Araújo Ségrim, "suffers alone and writes verse by himself." He also has a book ready, or almost, entitled *Segredeiro*; he is said to be "perhaps a bit of a disciple of Soares Guiamar in light aspects;" he deserves a second look, with nine poems selected by the biographer, who says of them: "being strongly felt things. Being what he doesn't know not about life." The last poet, Romaguari Sães, "the enraptured one," is a "hider of poems." Held to be "a little different" with respect to the group: "He has another music. He has another love, lighter, originary, advanced." He also has things to declare about poetry, in an "interview" of which a lone phrase figures in the introit.

The five introits that present the four poets are duly signed by João Guimarães Rosa, who employs the impersonal or the first person, singular in some cases, plural in others, when addressing the interlocutor *readers*. He seems to want to assure their good will, engage in dialogue with them, ending the introits (with the exception of the first one) with such words as: "See if this will serve." "Might you be in agreement with us?" "However, read it." "Will you approve of it?"

The intricate relationship between prose writer and poets does not end there. In all the books, with the possible exception of *Primeiras estórias*, there is a high degree of intertextuality with poems, backland ditties, occasional verse, spoken, rhymed, or otherwise. The song of Siruiz and "Olererê baiana," the hymn of Riobaldo's band, appear and re-appear in the text of *Grande sertão: veredas*, and serve as emblems of clusters of signification in the plot. In *Corpo de baile*, three of the seven novellas have poetic epigraphs. "Cara-de-bronze" has a folk singer who adds quatrains at frequent intervals, "O recado do morro" may also be analysed as the chronicle of the composition of a song, and at the festivities of Manuelzão ("Uma estória de amor") there is much singing. All the stories of *Sagarana* have poetic epigraphs, some double, some long, all in a folk manner. In *Tutaméia* the use of epigraph is not so systematic, as some stories do not have any. Sometimes one may occur at the end of a story, after the last period, where the author, in a correct neologism, calls it a "hypograph" (cf. "Vida ensinada"). *Estas estórias*, like the general epigraph of *Corpo de baile*, may blend erudite citations into the mix. Only *Ave, palavra* concedes autonomy to the poetic text. Besides the four anagrammatic poets, there are several independent poems; in one of them, "Grande louvação pastoril," a secondary character and singer of praise is a certain "Dr. João Rosa."

In a general way, the game of intertextuality prefers citations that oscillate between personal creation and the folkloric, purposefully throwing off attempts at classification. Personal creations often mimic folklore; only in a few extreme cases can one tell the difference. We must turn to papers in the author's archives,[5] where page after page is covered with notes of quatrains, verses, poems, sayings, which he records incessantly and limitlessly. Even so the difference between collected items and invented items is not clear. Whenever Guimarães Rosa set off a quatrain, or a word, or a locution, or a phrase, to use in his texts, he preceded it with his personal sign "m%", which is found by the thousands in the archives. But this sign designates only "to be appropriated" without clarifying if the item is an invention of the author, a document heard or read by him, or a modified document. Efforts to throw one off the track are clear in the published books: the "citations" are reported to be from sources and names of authors of which one cannot be sure whether they are juggling acts of the writer or not. The epigraph of "O recado do morro" is symptomatic: after a folk quatrain, the indication, in parenthesis, "Counter-song. Pseudofolkloric piece."

Running the risk of collaboration--which critics have already identified as responsible for the multiplication of the heteronyms of Fernando Pessoa, among whom one arose (Bernardo Soares) without the author having included him--I carefully advance the suggestion of another heteronym for João Guimarães Rosa. It is worthwhile to recall, in the case of Bernardo Soares, that his very name is compatible with the others, if we take into account the phonetic analysis done by Jakobson without knowing that another name would surface later.

---

[5] Housed at the Instituto de Estudos Brasileiros, Universidade de São Paulo.

João Barandão is the most ubiquitous of the poets of the prose writer. He does a triple debut in "Cara-de-bronze," in *Corpo de baile*, always with citations "of the *songs of Serão*, of João Barandão." In the first occasion, he appears with a sextine in the third epigraph. The second time, a footnote has a quatrain, and commentary about variants, attributed to none other than Soares Guiamar, the oldest of the anagrammatic poets. The third time, another footnote transcribes a quatrain and a half, this time glossed by the most erudite Oslino Mar. These songs and their author will be mentioned twice in *Tutaméia*. Once in three lines of "Barra da vaca," and a second time in the body of the text of "Melim Meloso," where a quatrain about this extraordinary character is attributed to them; the author adds: "so apocryphal." In *Estas estórias*--which includes a reprint of "Com o vaqueiro Mariano"-- the same verse-maker and the same source in the epigraph to the third part of the text.

In sum, among the pseudonyms examined here--and it is not unthinkable that others may come to light--Viator disappeared as soon as he was supplanted by the equally prose writer João Guimarães Rosa. But Soares Guiamar, Meuriss Aragão, Sá Araújo Ségrim, Romaguari Sães, João Barandão are personas of embarrassed poets, embryonic selves clamoring to be recognized, in the lure of masks and disguises in which they appear, hiding and revealing themselves. Deep within the successful citizen, the acclaimed narrator, there is an (are some) unrealized poet(s) among whom is included the unpublished author of a book of poems, *Magma* by title, that never appeared. "Quem sabe, temos?"
Translated by Charles A. Perrone

REFERENCES

Bruneti, Almir de Campos. "Um Agostinho da Silva, uns Fernando Pessoa." Unpublished paper delivered at the Congresso Internacional Fernando Pessoa, Universidade de São Paulo, 1988.

Em memória de João Guimarães Rosa. Rio de Janeiro: José Olympio, 1968.

Lara, Cecília de. "João Guimarães Rosa na França: anotações do *Diário de Paris*." Unpublished manuscript, 1968.

Perrone-Moisés, Leyla. *Fernando Pessoa--aquém do eu, além do outro*. São Paulo: Martins Fontes Ed., 1982.

IN THE INTER(T)SEX(T) OF CLARICE LISPECTOR AND NELSON RODRIGUES: FROM DRAMA TO LANGUAGE[1]

Ana Luiza Andrade
Universidade Federal de Alagoas

> But in this case the masculine returns to haunt the place of the feminine like a shadow; while, when the affective state is male, the interior body consists of a sort of inverse geometry, an image of the state reversed. (Antonin Artaud, *The Theater and its Double*)

A fundamental concern with human identity led both Clarice Lispector and playwright Nelson Rodrigues to a self-conscious use of the mask as a dramatic device throughout their works. Clarice Lispector once called Nelson Rodrigues "a writer of a thousand faces" ("Diálogos possíveis"). In his theatrical world, the playwright could be considered an actor, for his world was a stage where the human being is, "o único que se falsifica" (Rodrigues, *O óbvio ululante* 67). The choice of the mask, for Lispector, "é o primeiro gesto voluntário humano," her choice of words already implying that language chooses its own disguises (*A descoberta do mundo* 100). At the outset, their inter(t)sex(t)uality is based upon a male/female interplay of masks which in Clarice Lispector's works is dramatized in language and in Nelson Rodrigues' plays is expressed through the sexually charged speech of his characters, as they reflect a sociocultural gender system.

---

[1] The author would like to acknowledge comments and suggestions of Joaquim Francisco Coelho and Fred Clark in the preparation of this article.

But sex is itself a sociocultural representation, as Teresa de Lauretis states in *Technologies of Gender*:

> The cultural conceptions of male and female as two mutually exclusive categories into which all human beings are placed constitute within each culture a gender system, a symbolic system or system of meanings, that correlates sex to cultural contents according to social values and hierarchies. (1-30)

Lauretis's concept that the "construction of gender is both the product and the process of its representation" (5) provides a clearer understanding of what Nelson Rodrigues meant when he said that his theater revolved around "sex, sex, sex."[2] A close examination of his dramas clearly shows sex as a theatrical fiction which, within the playwright's concern for human identity, is as much a sociocultural production as it is a process which reflects a gender system.

Through an inter(t)sex(t)ual study of this nature,[3] one begins to realize that, despite the two authors' apparently disparate public images and texts, there exists, under scrutiny, a common language of the senses which has gone unnoticed, a sign-language as described by Antonin Artaud as that "in which the customary limits of feelings and words are transcended" (41). This inter(t)sex(t)ual approach also helps to clarify certain mystifications surrounding them: Lispector is neither as unreachably philosophical, nor is Rodrigues so despicably vulgar, as their

---

[2] In "Teatro desagradável" Nelson Rodrigues says: "Críticos fizeram uma observação restritiva: minha obra toda gravita em torno de 'sexo, sexo, sexo.' Sendo isso verdade, qual o inconveniente? Já disse que não vejo como qualquer assunto possa esgotar-se e muito menos o sexual" (20).

[3] In Kristeva's words: "The term intertextuality denotes this transposition of one (or several) sign-system(s) into another; but since this term has often been understood in the banal sense of 'study of sources,' we prefer transposition because it specifies that the passage from one signifying system into another demands a new articulation of the thetic--of enunciative and denotative positionality" (*The Kristeva Reader* 111).

critics may sometimes lead us to believe.[4] Rodrigues's theater overtly narrates a reproduction of a gender system, while underneath it questions feminine identity. Lispector's language could be considered an off-stage dramatization of the search for sexual identity, which, in a similar concern for a feminine subject, reveals an underlying split subject in language.

Semiotically, both his theater and her narratives, in their respective scenic/textual languages, intersect in language, as it is culturally defined by the interaction of subject and society (Voloshinov 107). In both their works, sexual identity depends on the subject's entrance into the cultural domain of language, as Lauretis puts it, "subjectivity is produced through language" (Silverman 131). Therefore, an erotics of textual reading which examines the communication between Clarice Lispector and Nelson Rodrigues will consider significant passages from drama to language, which effectively go from a patriarchal eros to a matriarchal logos, from political authority to poetic authorship.

In their work there is a longing for an identical "other" which on the one hand survives as a Greek caricature of ancient sexual roles, as a patriarchal mask which is divided according to a male dominant gender system, and, on the other hand, transforms a feminine "persona," from object to subject, inverting Oedipus's famous question to a question asked by the Sphinx. The answer to this question takes us through the human being's different stages in life, and both Clarice Lispector and Nelson Rodrigues choose adolescence[5] as the decisive human stage for

---

[4] I am referring to the general critical tendencies which usually depart from Benedito Nunes's philosophical criticism on Clarice Lispector. In *O teatro brasileiro moderno: 1930-1980*, Décio de Almeida Prado calls attention to Nelson Rodrigues's vulgarity in a reproachful tone.

[5] In "The Adolescent Novel," Julia Kristeva shows the role of the adolescent as an "open structure" where "The frontiers between differences of sex or identity, reality and fantasy, act and discourse, etc., are easily traversed without one being able to speak of perversion or borderline--and perhaps this would only be because these 'open structures' find themselves immediately echoing the fluidity, i.e. the inconsistency, of a mass media society. The adolescent is found to represent naturally this structure that can be called a 'crisis' structure only through the eyes of a stable, ideal law" (9).

the acquisition of a sexual mask: in Nelson Rodrigues's plays there is a definite search for the feminine identity which ultimately questions sex as power. Similarly, Lispector's sexually aware language surfaces in the act of conceiving words as an initiation into a masculine world of writing.[6]

Coincidentally, their biographies show common life experiences: they both moved from the Brazilian Northeast to the South, and both started out as journalists. A cultural tradition of clearly delineated male/female roles becomes apparent in their newspaper essays. Nelson Rodrigues came from a family of journalists, and easily fell into the bombastic ironic style for which his essays became famous: "Começo aqui a minha grave função homérica. Minha memória é um chão todo juncado de clássicos e peladas fenecidos. Antes, porém, de exumar os velhos jogos, preciso explicar toda a minha função com o fluminense" (*Fla Flu* 11).

Clarice Lispector was introduced to public life through journalism; however, early in her career, her language revealed a conscious effort to break away from the conventional style of the Brazilian "crônica," particularly in establishing a characteristic intimate relationship with her reader: "Vamos falar a verdade. Isto aqui não é crônica coisa nenhuma. Isto é apenas. Não entra em gênero. Gêneros não me interessam. Interessa-me o mistério" (*A descoberta do mundo* 92). The strikingly different styles of Lispector's essays collected in *A descoberta do mundo* and Rodrigues's in *A vida como ela é* significantly represent their authors' conscious adoption of patriarchal gender masks which boldly encourages masculine projection as much as it discourages the feminine. Woman is forced to turn inside herself, to an introversive style, as Clarice Lispector's piece entitled "Anonymity" meaningfully suggests:

> Tantos querem a projeção. Sem saber como esta limita a vida. Minha pequena projeção fere o meu pudor. Inclusive o que eu queria dizer já não posso mais. O anonimato é suave como um sonho. Aliás eu não queria mais escrever. Escrevo agora porque estou precisando de dinheiro. Eu queria ficar calada. (*A descoberta do mundo* 92)

---

[6] For a comparative study of Clarice Lispector's writing as initiation, see Ana Luiza Andrade, "A escritura feita iniciação feminina: Clarice Lispector e Virginia Woolf."

Their difference in male/female roles seems, as the playwright would say, "óbvio ululante." But with Lispector's character Ulisses, one could answer that "o óbvio é a coisa mais difícil de enxergar." And still, Nelson Rodrigues could reply, in reference to himself, that "gênio, santo ou profeta é aquele que enxerga o óbvio."[7] Their own interpretations of the "obvious" not only reinforce the culturally dominant gender-system, but also confirm their not so obviously divergent male/female journalistic styles of projection and introspection.

There is no doubt that the playwright would anticipate, in his theater, "a literature with an eye on journalism" (an expression borrowed from Flora Süssekind) while the writer had a "journalism with an eye on literature." Nonetheless, both writers' works reveal an attempt to remove the sexual mask which was culturally imposed on them: both work on the question of subject formation in the bourgeois family as illustrated by Nelson Rodrigues's play *Álbum de família* (1945) and Clarice Lispector's short stories *Laços de família* (1960).

Álbum de família is a dramatization of incest which belies the three harmonious family pictures opening the first three acts of the play: the characters are striving to maintain their roles as family members. Caught between the double bind of culture versus primitivism, the human drama is reduced to a caricature of patriarchal roles: paternal authority is corrupted by money, while the maternal side is attracted to chaos. The social "persona" parodically mimics a false Unconscious, blindly following the patriarchal model until it is fatally disconnected from the sexual "persona." The play exposes a break between the subject and society while it simulates a social reproduction of the Unconscious, and finally condemns humans to a sexual edge, an everlasting unsettled area in-between sexes. The actors are characterized, but they never fully develop into "subjects" per se. Nelson Rodrigues seems to anticipate Bataille's Christian "eroticism" in that physical continuity can only be

---

[7] In "Vai falar o óbvio ululante," one of Nelson Rodrigues's essays in *Fla Flu e as multidões despertaram!*, he explains what he means by the expression "óbvio ululante" in relation to soccer and says that "only a saint, a prophet or a genius can see the obvious" (109), i.e., can predict, as he does, the victory of Fluminense, a famous soccer team. Clarice Lispector's character Ulisses says that "the obvious is the most difficult thing to see" in *Uma aprendizagem ou o livro dos prazeres* (97).

achieved in death, as sexual intercourse is the ultimate profane expression of discontinuity between humanity and divinity.[8]

In *Vestido de noiva* (1943), a drama representing a search for feminine identity, Nelson Rodrigues falsifies feminine desire as a reflection of his own: the bride's patriarchal mirror becomes a pretext for his interplay of identity and otherness, his own play of sexual masks. Alaide is the bride who looks at herself in a patriarchal mirror, while she is also an anonymous body agonizing in the hospital, after being hit by a car. The playwright manages to cut across both the character's body and mind by confusing stage illumination with the lights in the surgery room, ambiguously penetrating the bride as an erotic object while she pretends to question herself in the mirror, as a subject. In fact, the feminine character is repressed as a subject in the fashion of Bataille's sacrificial victim, she is not only projected as an object of study/desire/consumption, but her body is also parodied, as the dressing/undressing of the bride self-consciously reproduces a theatrical masquerade: it is a play within a play.

In Nelson Rodrigues's theater of sexual masks, it is the desire for a counterpart manifesting itself through a social parody which misleadingly wears a false "persona": *Álbum de família* ridicules the "Oedipus Complex" by denouncing it as a farse in the formative stage of the subject.[9] *Vestido de noiva* epitomizes a theater of deception in the simulated search for a feminine subject as voyeuristically seen through a patriarchally disguised stage setting.

Nelson Rodrigues's characters are destitute of a cultural language, for they speak only of desire. They reflect unfulfilled social de-

---

[8] About the discontinuity of human beings, Bataille says: "Faced with a precarious discontinuity of the personality, the human spirit reacts in two ways which in Christianity coalesce. The first responds to the desire to find that lost discontinuity which we are stubbornly convinced is the essence of being. With the second, mankind tries to avoid the terms set to individual discontinuity, death, and invents a discontinuity unassailable by death--that is, the immortality of discontinuous beings" (*Eroticism, Death and Sensuality* 119).

[9] On the Freudian "Oedipus Complex" as a parodical scenery for a bourgeois theater, see Gilles Deleuze and Felix Guattari. Coincidentally, Nelson Rodrigues deals with the Oedipus complex in a similar way.

sires which are ultimately transferred to the desire for union with the public from whom they are alienated, like incomplete or fragmented beings in desperate search for a "persona." Nelson Rodrigues' bourgeoisie is caricaturesque because it can only imitate cultured subjects: theirs is a fetishistic world in its blind devotion for the profane idolatry of its parts.[10] Not unlike Jean Genet, Nelson Rodrigues propagates "an image of marginal culture which reflects the fears and desires of dominant culture and ideology--'a true image of a false spectacle' as [Genet] would say in *Le Balcon*" (Oswald 140).

Despite the social differences between the characters, both Alaide in *Vestido de noiva* and Clarice Lispector's Macabea in the novel *A hora da estrela* are heedlessly victimized by a male world, in both body and soul, as they are "accidentally" run down in the streets. As a consequence, they are both "erotically" born, to the discovery of their womanhood: Alaide recovers her memory while searching for herself in a patriarchal mirror-stage. Macabea regresses to the instinctive female of the species, as the male narrator witnesses her birth: "...só agora entendia que mulher nasce mulher desde o primeiro vagido. O destino de uma mulher é ser mulher" (*A hora da estrela* 95).[11] In *A hora da estrela*, the male narrator is also representative of a male dominant gender system which deliberately "writes" his victim, as part of a narrative frame.

More obviously, but not less coincidentally, is the fact that the feminine identity comes out, in both authors, in adolescence, as a critical stage in life for the cultural acquisition of the sexual mask. Nelson Rodrigues's monologue *Valsa no. 6* and Clarice Lispector's short story

---

[10] See Michael Taussig for a definition of a fetishism of commodities as a "subordination of persons to things" from pre-capitalist to capitalist societies. Nelson Rodrigues transfers the girl's feeling to the furniture very much in Taussig's sense that "things may well be regarded or spoken of as though they were alive with their autonomous powers" (36).

[11] See also Marta Peixoto's "Writing the Victim in the Fiction of Clarice Lispector." In her short story "A bela e a fera ou a ferida grande demais," in *A paixão segundo GH*, the narrator is a bourgeois woman who recognizes herself as having been an accomplice of the patriarchal mirror, in the social sense: "Ela pensou: o marido o que faria com o mendigo? Sabia que: nada. Eles não fazem nada. E ela - ela era 'eles' também" (152).

"Preciosidade" are not only introductions to a sexually divided world, but they are also instances of victimization. In *Valsa no. 6* the girl's posthumous drama, after being killed by the family doctor, is to remember who she is, similarly to *Vestido de noiva*. She even asks the public to help her remember. Rodrigues exaggerates her chasteness in a typically fetishistic reflection of her body: "Tinha vergonha dos móveis. Digo dos móveis descobertos, sem nenhum pano, nenhuma toalha. Portanto, móveis nus" (*Valsa no. 6* 204).

Unlike Nelson Rodrigues's play, the girl in "Preciosidade" goes through a public initiation in which she is attacked but she keeps quiet about it, at home. There is a difference in the loss/acquisition by these adolescents of a mask which is defined by man: in *Valsa no. 6*, on the one hand, Sonia never reaches womanhood; her memory revolves around her death according to Bataille's sense of discontinuity in the erotic body. On the other hand, Clarice Lispector's language stages the girl's violent confrontation with a male world as indicative of both her entrance into a cultured world and her acquisition of language as a feminine mask, as a self-conscious birth into both womanhood and writing. Intuitively, she knows what is going to happen to her:

> Ela os ouvia e surpreendia-se com a própria coragem em conti-
> nuar. Era o dom. E a grande vocação para um destino. Ela
> avançava, sofrendo em obedecer. Se conseguisse pensar em
> outra coisa não ouviria os sapatos. Nem o que eles poderiam
> dizer. Nem o silêncio com que se cruzariam. ("Preciosidade"
> 102)[12]

Lispector's language transmits both the girls' inner and outer impressions by defining her entrance into a masculine world in terms of listening and being heard, a sexual choice occurring between the public and the private "persona." Unlike the girl in *Valsa no. 6* who dies in the process of

---

[12] In a psychoanalytical sense, Clarice Lispector's initiatory language represents the coming into existence of a speaking subject through the girl's steps which are being heard for the first time. The unconscious emerges as the result of the repression of desire (the girl's "preciousness"), as Jacques Lacan puts it, in the re-writing of the sentence "I am" as "I am that which I am not," meaning "the repression of the desire for the lost mother" (Moi 99-100).

becoming a woman, she knows that her survival depends on the feminine awareness of her condition. Yet, the title "Preciosidade" ironically suggests a useless instinctive mechanism through which a girl has to defend the chasteness she is supposed to lose. By the same token, Nelson Rodrigues transfers Sonia's feelings to a patriarchal stage setting where the furniture comically reflects the "shame" of its nudity to the spectator.

By staging the acquisition of a gendered mask, both Nelson Rodrigues's theater and Clarice Lispector's narratives give us clear indications of their self-conscious intersections as different media--theater and literature--to dramatize culture and gender, critically doubling themselves in a modern process of acculturation. Lispector's language theatrically performs from a conscious to an unconscious level of writing, being able to observe itself in the process, as a spectator, which is concisely stated in *Água viva*: "Fico me assistindo pensar" (69). Rodrigues's dramas also show a mask between the character and the actor, which implicitly lies between an illicit but socially well-known subject and a never accomplished desire for otherness. For him, speech can never achieve the cultural status of language, while Clarice Lispector has just been introduced to it: as a recent adept, she sees herself from the world, in her own writing.

As a result of this critical actor/character division, in the intersections of theater and language, there is a politically representative male/female interplay at the level of textual authorship. Both authors virtually insert and extract themselves from their own dramas by using signatures as parodical marks of their (t)sex(t)ual masks: both attribute authorship to their sexual counterparts, thus relating gender to both sexual authority and authorship. In *A hora da estrela* Clarice Lispector is an accomplice of the writer-narrator Rodrigo de S.M. But she impersonates the "male" as a heteronym,[13] strategically distancing herself as a woman, while she also shares the novel's authorship with him, signing her name in parenthesis: "(na verdade Clarice Lispector)."

---

[13] Here I use the term "heteronym" as a person other than the author (usually referred to the different poets created by the famous Portuguese poet Fernando Pessoa), as opposed to the term "pseudonym" which usually refers to another name for the same author. For a discussion on the narrative structure in *A hora da estrela*, see Marta Peixoto, "Writing the Victim in the Fiction of Clarice Lispector."

Conversely, Nelson Rodrigues uses the name Susana Flagg not only as an attractive female pseudonym, but also as a commercial mask, a fetish-name to be consumed by the reading public. While Lispector's outward distinction between feminine authorship and heteronymity advances her altering disguises in language, Rodrigues's pseudonym is an open mockery. In fact, his novels exaggerate the bourgeois world of his dramas even more, they are *roman rose* per se, since their tranvestite bookcovers simulate an offer for sexual hire suggested in the feminine trademark. It is a kitsch insignia, visibly bordering on the pornographic, in the fine imaginary line left between the outer signature and the real Author, the book and its own body.

Clarice Lispector's sexual parody shows a feminine caricature extracted from traditionally masculine texts, such as the character Lori in *Uma aprendizagem ou o livro dos prazeres*. She puts on a "sexual object" mask by painting another face over her own: "põe sobre si alguém outro: esse alguém era desinibido, era vaidoso, tinha orgulho de si mesmo. Esse alguém era exatamente o que ela não era" (89-90).[14] Trying to inspire confidence by adopting the image reflected by a patriarchal mirror, as the masculine gender of this "alguém" implies, the character finally becomes disappointed with the mask's comic effect. In this novel, the writer parodies masculine as well as feminine styles of writing. As a matter of fact, she parodies a gender system which "writes" established sexual roles in the production of male/female stylized figures. A game of seduction is used as pretext to subvert the epic Ulysses into a woman's apprenticeship: Lori becomes Loreley, the mermaid. Almost as if directly poking fun at the essay where Nelson Rodrigues states his "grave função homérica," the novel's caricatures of both styles finally shows the feminine appropriation of the masculine. Even the apparent inappropriateness of feminine writing, already diagnosed by critics as "anxiety of authorship" is unveiled (Gubar and Gilbert 6), in Clarice Lispector's novel, as one more of her disguises, in a language chosen to seduce through fiction.

Curiously, in one of her short stories "Antes da Ponte Rio-Niterói" (*A via crucis do corpo*) a variation of "Um caso para Nelson Rodrigues" (*A descoberta do mundo* 1973) there is a parody of Nelson Rodrigues's incestuous dramas: the story is a long chain of inbreeding affairs between

---

[14] For a discussion of this novel's theatrical masquerade in its double writing styles, see my "*O livro dos prazeres*: a escritura e o travesti."

lovers and relatives around a particular young bride who becomes handicapped and finally dies. Lispector's language clearly attaches Nelson Rodrigues's mask of incestuous inscriptions when characters are ambiguously defined according to their kinship with one another. Consciously appropriating his style, she reinforces both the mercilessly grotesque and kitsch, against the untouched background of the bride. But above all, she is constantly showing her own anxieties by purposely interrupting the narrative process and excusing herself for not being able to tell a story which is not "de sua safra."[15]

The fact is that, as an apprentice in writing, Clarice Lispector becomes a master of disguises herself, as, among others, the short stories "A imitação da rosa" and "Os desastres de Sofia" could show. In "A imitação da rosa" the feminine mask, as socially defined by a male dominated gender system, gets disconnected from the self: Laura "acts like" a housewife, but her desire to "be like" her roses is stronger. She ends up by playing "the role which is ascribed to her" to perfection, that is, she mirrors the roses according to the chivalric Christian model of "feminine" perfection within the patriarchal stage where she was raised. Clarice Lispector takes the patriarchal parody of "femininity" to its ultimate consequences, for in this "new role" Laura loses her social "persona" in order to be the mystical object of the Other's desire. She impersonates the sacred fetish ("the roses") which stands as a symbol for her own sex, while her social body, alienated from her self, only reflects a mad spectator of the patriarchal mirror ("The Imitation of the Rose" 53).[16]

In "Os desastres de Sofia," more as in *Uma aprendizagem ou o livro dos prazeres*, the gender mask is related to the practice of writing. As the adult woman narrates the story retrospectively, she embodies her own experience as a child in the development of a multifaceted language. The story she tells is a reversal in apprenticeship roles which transforms

---

[15] Clarice Lispector, "Um caso para Nelson Rodrigues," in *A descoberta do mundo*, 715-717, and "Antes da ponte Rio-Niteroi," in *A via crucis do corpo* 65.

[16] For a discussion on the mystic contemplation of the roses, see Marta de Senna, "'A imitação da Rosa' by Clarice Lispector: an Interpretation." See also Ellen H. Douglass, "Myth and Gender in Clarice Lispector." I am also indebted to the ideas presented by Lúcia Helena in "Gender and Narrative Strategies in the 'Imitation of the Rose'."

her old schoolteacher in his own pupil's (herself) apprentice. Unwitting-
ly, one of the most rebellious of his pupils gives him the hope he had
already lost.

After the schoolteacher's death, the child's recollections, as told by
the woman, are changed: the familiar lines of the hungry wolf in the
children's tale "Little Red Riding Hood" reflect her new learnings in
writing as an initiation process in a dominantly male culture. Both the
roles in the tale and in her story intermingle in maturity as they surface
from experience in the two-ply components--the wolf's and the woman's-
-of her dramatic language: "Para que te servem essas unhas longas? Para
te arranhar de morte e para arrancar os teus espinhos mortais, responde
o lobo do homem" (119).[17]

While the question-answer formula is the recognizable aspect of the
dialogue between girl and wolf, disguised in grandmother's clothes
(it is a tale about disguises), the narrator's words have not only transformed the roles which had once reinforced an apprenticeship in the
gender system, but have also acquired new masks which mingle opposite
feelings such as aggressiveness/sweetness, the capacity to destroy/to heal,
to kill/to give birth, to write as though being written.

A masquerade is openly displayed in the novel *Um sopro de
vida*: in the dialogue between an Author and his feminine character
Angela Pralini, Clarice Lispector defines the dramatic sexual bases of her
poetics at the novel's structural level. The interplay of masculine/femi-
nine, subject/object, self/other, takes Angela to subvert Oedipus's bot-
tom question: "Mas eu sou um enigma para a esfinge e no entanto não
a devorei. Decifra-me, disse eu à esfinge. E esta ficou muda" (100-
101).[18] Here the inter(t)sex(t) of Clarice Lispector and Nelson Rodrigues clearly indicates the passage from Oedipus's outer mask, to the

---

[17] Clarice Lispector's language wears a wolf disguise in the search for
identification with the animal instinct in man. For the woman narrator's
zoomorphic identity search, see Anna Klobucka, "A intercomunicação
homem/animal como meio de transformação do Eu em 'Axolotl' de
Julio Cortázar e 'O búfalo' de Clarice Lispector" and Fábio Lucas, "O
impasse da narrativa contemporânea."

[18] Significantly, in *Soulstorm*'s "Explanation" (*A via crucis do corpo*)
there is an obverse side to this viewpoint: "The other person is an enigma. And with eyes that are those of a statue: blind" (4).

Sphinx, as representing the dialogue between interior and exterior. The Sphinx is the feminine enigma. Both their trivializations of Oedipus and Sphinx not only overthrow false idealizations of men and women which imprison the human being, but also show them as part of an erotic and imaginative game consciously staged/verbalized by Nelson Rodrigues and Clarice Lispector in their dramatic exchange of sexual masks.

In fact, a sequence of inter(t)sex(t)ual dislocations from newspaper to theater, from theater to language, and from language to life, uniquely presents these authors as actors in their own representative dramas between self and otherness. Would it be fair to ask, in the fashion of Borges in his well known story about the rewriting of the Quijote: Nelson Rodrigues, the Author of Clarice Lispector, or Clarice Lispector, the Author of Nelson Rodrigues? Once their (t)sex(t)ual masquerade shows them as equals in the erotic search to enter a world which is defined by language, Nelson Rodrigues' characters are marginalized: they pretend to be bourgeois, but they are, in fact, like ghosts of cultural subjects, in their refusal to participate in a gender system. Lispector's language seems to dramatize the birth of a marginalized form into being, as her words attempt to characterize the interstices which permeate a gender system.

In a live interview with Nelson Rodrigues, she considers him a "success" while he feels "defeated," their sexual/textual difference being stressed in between their lines: Nelson Rodrigues ironically confirms his hidden public ambitions by stating that "o único sujeito realizado é o Napoleão de hospício que não tem nem Waterloo nem Santa Helena" ("Diálogos possíveis"). Was Clarice purposely playing the public role of the woman-in-awe of all masculine achievements, while Nelson Rodrigues played the "victim" so he would better identify with her feminine "persona"?[19]

Precisely because he projected himself as a public actor, it becomes difficult to distinguish biography from autobiography in Nelson Rodrigues. He goes as far as dramatizing his own life in so many biographical variations such as the Memórias, A cabra vadia, O óbvio ululan-

---

[19] In Soulstorm (A via crucis do corpo) Clarice Lispector recognizes human failure in all of us, as the woman narrator of "The Man Who Appeared" says: "'we are all failures, we will all die one day! Who, but who can say with sincerity that he has realized himself in his life? Success is a lie'" (33).

te, As confissões de Nelson Rodrigues. In each, Nelson Rodrigues the character is the same, but the interpretations of the facts of his life are different. Conversely, Clarice Lispector never wrote her "memórias," but from an intimate relationship with her language one can notice a reaction against the conventionally biographical literary genre. Her intention, as she states in *Água viva*, was to become "bio," as she participates in the life of words, being able to say "Sou-me" (28-29). Her poetics takes both a conscious and an inverse path from the playwright's "persona", in the direction of the impersonal, the in-between "bio" and "grafia", where the "fact" is defined by the "feeling."

Significantly, the "real" life of these authors/characters ends during a political period in which the Brazilian military dictatorship was still dominant. Again, both the playwright and the writer adopted different masks: his headline projection made him polemically known as a reactionary (Magaldi 69) while her political position emerges poetically from her texts: "Tenho medo de mim. Não sou de confiança e desconfio de meu falso poder. Este é palavra de quem não pode" (*Água viva* 34).

Rooted in the "poetic truth," her language is disguised in apparent fragility so that it can powerfully resist the patriarchal "false identity" attributed to it: "Não minto. Minha verdade faísca como um lustre de cristal" (46). Clarice Lispector's seductive feminine language is poetically born/created from a false truth (a facsimile) which is critically dramatized in the flicker of a resistant crystal.

The playwright's agonistic poetics is rooted, contrarily, in a discontinuous being who creates a false social identity, the stage itself becoming a frame or a symbolic border for the sexual cut which viscerally separates him from the public. Nonetheless, it is a skeletal structure shaping Lispector's poetic question: "Minha liberdade pequena e enquadrada me une à liberdade do mundo -- mas o que é uma janela senão o ar emoldurado por esquadrias?" (25).

The poetic space which is opened by the patriarchal frame of parodying caricatures in Greek masks, results in an inter(t)sex(t)ual mirroring which, ultimately, questions both the figurative image and the mirror as its patriarchal perpetrator, as Clarice Lispector puts it:

O que é um espelho? É o único material inventado que é natural. Quem olha num espelho, quem consegue vê-lo sem se ver, quem entende que a sua profundidade consiste em ele ser vazio, quem caminha para dentro de seu espaço transparente sem deixar nele o vestígio da própria imagem - esse alguém então percebeu o seu mistério de coisa. (78-79)

Upon reflecting a parodic feminine body, the patriarchal mirror is not only unmasked/disfigured as an empty frame but it is also shown in its true material dimension. As a poetic/parodic moment of a loss in sexual identity, both words and things reflect themselves in a "figurativo inominável" of an "espelho vivo" which is transformed as it is being described: "Não, eu não descrevi o espelho - eu fui ele" (80). Step by step, *Água viva* deconstructs this mirror, as it subverts conventional biography which projects the facts of a life, as seen in Nelson Rodrigues's simulations. Instead, the "I" is dramatized either by hiding or by revealing itself behind words, a self-writing, which is the only witness to its own birth and death, a unique testimony of Clarice Lispector's writing vocation.

In the poetic interstices of gender, the dramatization of possible biographies in Nelson Rodrigues's multiple impersonations waylays the virtually impossible biopoetics of autography in Clarice Lispector's language of multiple disguises.[20] Evidently, the difference in gender discloses a generic controversy which, beyond the traditional biographical genre, places both the classical tragedy and comedy in direct confrontation with their original male/female representations. Indeed, these author's/character's adoption of each other's gender masks betrays the traditional Greek use of it, where only male actors were allowed to wear women's masks: Nelson Rodrigues reveals the feminine mask as a masculine falsification, and Clarice Lispector shows the empty façade of a patriarchal mirror.

But their search for identity especially interpenetrates in their own gender's parodies, almost to the point of being the body-doubles of each other's texts: they passionately flesh out intellect from primitive blood ties, showing the politics of human sexuality not in biological difference but in cultural construction. Together, they uncover old mystical images from our unconscious performance of established roles and consciously stage them in a modern setting: from a patriarchal eros, Nelson Rodrigues's alarming play of desire meets Clarice Lispector's sensual

---

[20] I borrowed the term "biopoetics" from Joaquim-Francisco Coelho's *Biopoética de Manuel Bandeira* in the sense that Clarice Lispector's biopoetics mingles life and poetry. It is also "autography" in the sense that it combines "auto" (self) and "grafia" (the written word).

language precisely where there is a conscious feminine struggle between object and subject in the pregnant silence of a matriarchal logos.[21] Mirroring each other in a mutual desire for their sexual counterparts, their texts finally seduce the reader/spectator into participating in their erotic masquerade.

But above all, the staging of their erotic masquerade finally shows that from drama to language, the gender mask plays a pivotal cultural duplicity in human interactions, for as long as it can potentially uncover/cover traditional partitions between being/existing, subject/society, male/female, tragedy/comedy, erudition/vulgarity, it is ultimately unveiling sociocultural desires and the monstrosity of human isolation in a modern world-stage of multifaceted identitites.

---

[21] From Lacan's psychoanalytical point of view, "masquerade is the very definition of 'femininity' because it is constructed with reference to a male sign" (*Feminine Sexuality* 43). Nonetheless, the term "matriarchal logos" refers more specifically to this shifting from object to subject in writing. Clarice Lispector's new identification between womanhood and writing corresponds to what Julia Kristeva has called, in relation to a theory of language, as a feminine *sujet en procés* or a subject-in-the-making (*New French Feminisms* 166). But "matriarchal logos" also implies a more general tendency in contemporary literature, as Fábio Lucas notes in "O impasse na narrativa contemporânea" (61). Lispector's narrative represents this tendency because it not only announces a fall of a dominant practice, but it also prefigures a genesis in the silence of her writing.

REFERENCES

Abjection, Melancholia and Love: The Work of Julia Kristeva. Ed. John Fletcher and Andrew Benjamin. London and New York: Routledge, 1990.

Andrade, Ana Luiza. "A escritura feita iniciação feminina: Clarice Lispector e Virginia Woolf." *Língua e literatura* 15 (1986): 9-21.

_____. "*O livro dos prazeres*: a escritura e o travesti." *Colóquio/letras* 101 (January-February 1988): 47-54.

Artaud, Antonin. *The Theater and its Double*. Tr. Mary Caroline Richards. New York: Grove Press, 1958.

Bataille, Georges. *Erotism, Death and Sensuality*. Tr. Mary Dalwood. San Francisco: City of Lights, 1986.

Coelho, Joaquim-Francisco. *Biopoética de Manuel Bandeira*. Recife: Massangana, 1981.

de Lauretis, Teresa. *Technologies of Gender: Essays on Theory, Film, and Fiction*. Bloomington: Indiana UP, 1987.

Deleuze, Gilles, and Felix Guattari. *Capitalisme et schizophrenie: L'Anti-Oedipe*. Paris: Les Editions de Minuit, 1972.

Douglass, Ellen H. "Myth and Gender in Clarice Lispector: Quest as a Feminine Statement in 'A imitação da rosa'." *Luso-Brazilian Review* 25.2 (Winter 1988): 15-31.

Feminine Sexuality/Jacques Lacan and the École Freudienne. Ed. Juliet Mitchell and Jacqueline Rose. Tr. Jacqueline Rose. New York: Pantheon Books, 1982.

Fla Flu... e as multidões despertaram!: Nelson Rodrigues e Mário Filho. Ed. Oscar Maron Filho e Renato Ferreira. Rio de Janeiro: Edições Europa, 1987.

Gubar, Susan and Sandra Gilbert. *A Madwoman in the Attic: The Woman Writer and the Nineteenth Century Imagination*. New Haven: Yale UP, 1979.

Helena, Lúcia. "Gender and Narrative Strategies in the 'Imitation of the Rose'." Unpublished paper presented at the Colloquium "New Perspectives on Clarice Lispector: Gender, Narrative, Post-Structuralism," Yale University, 2 March, 1990.

Klobucka, Anna. "A intercomunicação homem/animal como meio de transformação do Eu em 'Axolotl' de Júlio Cortázar e 'O Búfalo' de Clarice Lispector." *Travessia* 14 (1987): 161-176.

Kristeva, Julia. "The Adolescent Novel." *Abjection, Melancholia and Love: The Work of Julia Kristeva*. Ed. John Fletcher and Andrew Benjamin. London and New York: Routledge, 1990.

The Kristeva Reader. Ed. Toril Moi. New York: Columbia University Press, 1986.

Lispector, Clarice. *Água viva*. 5a ed. Rio de Janeiro: Nova Fronteira, 1979. English version *The Stream of Life*. Tr. Earl Fitz and Elizabeth Lowe. Minneapolis: U of Minnesota P, 1989.

_____. *Uma aprendizagem ou o livro dos prazeres*. Rio de Janeiro: Editora Sabiá, 1969. English version, *An Apprenticeship or the Book of Delights*. Tr. R. Mazzara and L. Parris. Austin: U of Texas P, 1986.

_____. "Os desastres de Sofia." *Felicidade clandestina*. 4a ed. Rio de Janeiro: Nova Fronteira, 1981.

_____. *A descoberta do mundo*. Rio de Janeiro: Nova Fronteira, 1984.

_____. "Diálogos possíveis com Clarice Lispector: Nelson Rodrigues: 'eu me considero um fracassado'." *Manchete* 838 (11 May 1968).

_____. *Felicidade clandestina*. 4a ed. Rio de Janeiro: Nova Fronteira, 1981.

_____. *A hora da estrela*. Rio de Janeiro: Nova Fronteira, 1984.

_____. "The Imitation of the Rose." *Family Ties*. Tr. Giovanni Pontiero. Austin: U of Texas P, 1972.

_____. *Laços de família*. Rio de Janeiro: José Olympio Editora, 1974. English version, "Preciousness." In *Family Ties*. Tr. Giovanni Pontiero. Austin: U of Texas P, 1972.

_____. *A paixão segundo GH*. Ed. crítica Benedito Nunes. Florianópolis: Coleção Arquivos, 1988.

_____. "Preciosidade." In *Laços de família*. Rio de Janeiro: José Olympio Editora, 1974.

_____. *Um sopro de vida (pulsações)*. 3a ed. Rio de Janeiro: Nova Fronteira, 1978.

_____. *A via crucis do corpo*. 3a ed. Rio de Janeiro: Nova Fronteira, 1984. English version, *Soulstorm*. Tr. Alexis Levitin. New York: A New Directions Book, 1989.

Lucas, Fábio. "O impasse da narrativa contemporânea." *Travessia* 14 (1987).

Magaldi, Sábato. *Nelson Rodrigues: dramaturgia e encenações*. São Paulo: Perspectiva; Universidade de Sao Paulo, 1987.

Moi, Toril. *Sexual/Textual Politics: Feminist Literary Theory*. London: Methuen, 1985.

New French Feminisms/ An Anthology. Ed. Elaine Marks and Isabelle de Courtivron. New York: Schocken Books, 1981.

Nunes, Benedito. *O drama da linguagem: uma leitura de Clarice Lispector*. São Paulo: Ática, 1989.

Oswald, Laura. *Jean Genet and the Semiotics of Performance*. Bloomington: Indiana UP, 1989.

Peixoto, Marta. "Writing the Victim in the Fiction of Clarice Lispector." In *Transformations of Literary Language from Machado de Assis to the Vanguards*. Ed. K. David Jackson. University of Texas: Department of Spanish and Portuguese/Abaporu Press, 1987. 84-97.

Prado, Décio de Almeida. *O teatro brasileiro moderno: 1930-1980*. São Paulo: Perspectiva, 1988.

Rodrigues, Nelson. *O óbvio ululante*. Rio de Janeiro: Livraria Eldorado Editora, 1968.

_____. *Teatro completo*. Org. Sábato Magaldi. Rio de Janeiro: Nova Fronteira, 1981.

_____. "Teatro desagradável." *Dionysos* 1:1 (October 1949) 16-21.

_____. *Valsa no. 6*. In *Teatro completo* Vol. I, *Peças psicológicas*. Org. Sábato Magaldi. Rio de Janeiro: Nova Fronteira, 1981.

Senna, Marta de. "'A imitação da Rosa' by Clarice Lispector: an Inter pretation." *Portuguese Studies* 4 (1988): 159-165.

Silverman, Kaja. *The Subject of Semiotics*. New York: Oxford UP, 1983.

Taussig, Michael. *The Devil and Commodity Fetishism in South America*. Chapel Hill: The U of North Carolina P, 1980.

Voloshinov, V. N. *Marxism and the Philosophy of Language*. Tr. Ladislav Matejka and I. R. Titunik. Cambridge: Harvard UP, 1986.

OSMAN LINS'S *AVALOVARA*: A NOVEL OF LOVE?

Massaud Moisés
Universidade de São Paulo

Perhaps due initially to the qualities of the author's previous work, especially *O fiel e a pedra* (1961), and a maturation of his fictional artisanship and world view, Osman Lins's *Avalovara* (1973), quickly attracted the attention of critics and the public, both within and beyond the borders of the Portuguese language, and became the author's most studied novel.[1] The high point of Lins's trajectory as a writer of fiction, *Avalovara* has attained an international audience that few works of modern Brazilian literature can equal. This in itself--a factor pertaining to a sociology of taste or of reading--is sufficient to evidence the calibre of this strange novelistic construction.

Avalovara's structure derives from the well-known palindrome: SATOR AREPO TENET OPERA ROTAS. The author imagined the five words of the phrase, each with an identical number of letters, arranged in vertical order forming a square, divided in turn into twenty-five others, each occupied by a letter of the palindrome. He then conceived "a spiral that comes from impossible distances, converging on a determined place (or a determined moment). Upon it, delimiting it in part, place a square" (8).

Avalovara can thus be read in several directions, penetrated through any of the points where the spiral crosses the square. Like a kaleidoscope, its verbal and human material reverberates in a thousand facets, giving the impression of a constant, infinite diversity. But precisely because its structure is articulated like a palindrome--which is itself

---

[1] Osman Lins, *Avalovara* (São Paulo: Melhoramentos, 1973). An excellent English-language translation of *Avalovara* by Gregory was published in 1979 by Alfred A. Knopf. All citations in the text refer to this edition [translator's note].

ambiguous, pointing toward an enigma which the novel merely reveals without deciphering (to the contrary)--*Avalovara* preserves a center, toward which it converges and from which it irradiates, like an original nucleus: all entrances, constituted by the small squares containing the letters of the palindrome, lead to the same core, represented by the letter N; everything, the diligent and lucid Narrator explains, dedicated to clarifying (?) the mystery hidden by the palindrome. An intense and perennial dynamism, which the narrative mirrors, guides the combination of letters within the squares with their fulcrum, which is at once centripetal and centrifugal.

What image can or does this kind of *moto-continuo* offer? Like a mandala--the novel can be read in terms of an archetypal interpretation privileging the magical circumference as a primordial expression of Time and Space--the palindromic fable is structured like a reflection of the Cosmos: without beginning or end--"ideally it begins at Always and Never is its end" (6)--the spiral crosses the square of reversible and movable faces, which are set in motion by an internal movement that the impact of the spiral accelerates, without disturbing, however, their fundamental harmony. The reconciliation of the spiral and the square, occurring in a space that the imagination constructs with the help of geometry, represents both the structure of the narrative unrolling before our eyes, astonished in the face of the enigma, and the Cosmos itself.

Thus the novel can be seen as an attempt to narrate/describe the Universe in its palindromic complexity. Admitting that the spiral constitutes a movement outside of the square, which would be merely the visible surface of a dynamism that we can only discern and represent in the (limited?) space of the square: the saga of this effort at representation would consist in *Avalovara* (in the image and similitude of every creator of a novel, if not the Demiurge), just as the visible portion of the Cosmos would show the form of the square to whomever contemplated it, seeking the infinite spiral that animates it. The square, says the Narrator, "will be the enclosure, the precinct of the novel, of which the spiral is the motive force" (9).

We may thus suppose that the spiral's movement in the square corresponds to a geometric representation of the palindrome, such that the (imaginary) center of the spiral and the (virtual) center of the square would coincide with that of the palindrome, the letter N. Here, in the middle of the word TENET (which is palindromic in and of itself), the double center, or, in truth, the only center, is located, since the encounter of the spiral and the square should be prefigured in three-dimensional space (or better, quadridimensional, if we consider the unavoidable presence of Time) and not merely on the surface of the white page. The great enigma would reside, therefore, in this symbolic N, the primeval matrix, the generating nucleus of the spiral and the magic palindrome, as well as the heart of the infinite vortex which is created not only with the spiral's dislocation but also in its collision with the square, without mentioning the abyss that the N becomes when we look at the palindromic square from the periphery to the center, in any direction.

One can thus say that the novel's "problem," both for the Narrator and the reader, is situated precisely in the central N. To reach it, going through the various stages of the palindrome, is the aspiration of both, since this trajectory will lead inexorably to the Nucleus of the enigma and, consequently, of *Avalovara*. Considering the possible readings of this journey--all plausible given the palindromic character of the narrative--we will attempt to see to what extent it is a novel of love (as the author himself has suggested), understanding it not as a sweetened story for dreaming adolescents of the days of our grandparents, but rather as an imperative of the novel's intimate nature, or, in other words, to highlight the complex of feelings and social commitments that are hidden in the amorous relationships between man and woman.

To construct its narrative game (for it truly is a game), the Narrator geometrically divides his task according to the position of the letters in the square, so that the novel reflects the dynamism of the spiral and the square: when it arrives at the N, the Narrator would presumably unveil the enigma of the palindrome, for both himself and the reader. Of course the Narrator plays with marked cards, since he chose the palindromic phrase as the structure of the narrative concerned with unveiling it, and one might guess that he foresaw the semantic content of the nucleus on which his attention and his gaze focused. But it is also true that, by selecting that palindrome, he could not have total certainty of the result of his pilgrimage in the recesses of the phrase (or rather, of the unfolding of the letters in fictive material): a degree of risk accompanied the search, no matter how great an artisanal consciousness we may attribute to him. Or, in the words of the

Narrator himself: "Little is known about the invention or the inventor until he is revealed with his work" (5). And it is precisely in this possible risk (without referring to the possibility of risk present in everything else) that one observes the imposition of a theme that may not be in his plans. At least it would not be in his plans in the way it is presented.

On the other hand, with the purpose of setting the groundwork for our study, we must set aside, not without first registering its presence, the combat (silent and secret, most of the time, yet explicit at some moments) between the "slowly put together" (4), calculated experiment and its concretization as a mimetic fable (somewhat akin to what André Jolles calls the transformation of simple objects in complex narratives). An idea of this conflict can be obtained with the suspicion that, if there is a complete integration of the palindrome and the novel designed to bring it to life, every novel is ultimately structured around a palindrome, albeit often unrecognized as such. Or, inverting the perspective, one might obtain the "same" result (that is, the novel we read under the title *Avalovara*), without appealing to the figure of the palindrome, the spiral or the square.

A clear example of this tension is found in the chapters titled "The Spiral and the Square," in which the Narrator, or more precisely the Author, explains the novel that he is weaving before us based on the palindromic phrase. By doing so, he gives the reader the impression that he is complicating things more than he is elucidating them, in part because he does not have full control of the structure he selects for the occasion (he would probably have it at the end of the narrative, but that would be another story), and also because the explanation suggests something more than he shows and is capable of capturing. One might say that the Author merely intuits, and he intuits more (or less) than he desires, since he supposes to detect something that escapes his comprehension, or he discerns something he is unable to define. And if we take these chapters as "objective" and "rational," it becomes more apparent that the Author was running the risk of being caught up in the web of the palindrome. It takes him ten chapters to explain the spiral and the square, as if the story needed that many or without perceiving that, if his explanation is accepted, the novel becomes obvious, clarified by the Author from within the text, as if it were the univocal and unequivocal illustration of an aphorism.

Even accepting, for now, the intervention of metalanguage as a repercussion of a common tendency of the modern novel, the impression of a dissonance between the palindromic structure and the novel that brings it to life does not disappear. Impelled by the copious number of combinations resulting from the letters inside the square, the Author speaks of the "succession of the constant themes of the novel," and adds, as if to detail the idea in order to prevent possible doubts: "For the square will be divided into a certain number of other squares, ideally equal among themselves. And the passage of the spiral, successively, over each one, will determine the cyclical return of the themes spread out among them, in the same way that the entrance of the Earth into the signs of the Zodiac can generate, according to some, changes in the influence of the stars upon creatures" (8).

At the end of the volume there appears, like a table of contents, an "index of themes," according to the letters R, S, O, A, T, P, E, N. Are they really themes? How can one admit that S, referring to "The Square and the Spiral," is a theme? Is the "The Story of θ, Twice-Born," narrated by the letter O, a theme or a (narrative) complement of R ("θ and Abel: Meetings, Routes, and Revelations"), and E ("θ and Abel: Before Paradise"), of N ("θ and Abel: Paradise"), of A ("Roos and the Cities"), and of T ("Cecília Among the Lions")? And does P ("Julius Heckethorn's Clock") constitute a theme or a parallel story, indispensable for the justification of the clock (a special clock, charged with memories) that witnesses the Lovers' encounters?

Are they various themes, or only one? The secondary situations and/or stories, like that of Nativity, of the Fat Woman or of Julius Heckethorn, seem to function as counterpoints or accessories of the central theme, carried by Abel's relationships with the three women of this life. While they enclose dramatic tensions that inundate with their waters the estuary in which they navigate (or capsize?), Abel and his companions are no more than subthemes. Thus, the clock and the palindrome gain meaning by being understood as metaphors of Time or of Time/Space, at the service of the expression of the novel's argument. In reality, however, there are not eight themes, but rather a single theme and its variations: the recurrences, mentioned in two chapters with the title "The Spiral and the Square," indicate the spatio-temporal variations of a single theme. The women of Abel's life change, as do the cities and corresponding times, but the central axis is represented by θ′, passing through Anneliese Roos and Cecília: the point of departure and return, with its tragic denouement, is in truth indicated by a single binominal. A single theme and its variations: θ′ is designated by a graphic sign, although she is the most constantly present woman and the one who leads the hero to the blind alley, since she summarizes the other women; or, if one prefers, all of the amorous relations reduce, in the final analysis, to a single relationship, between Abel and the Woman, symbolized by θ′.

If our reasoning is correct, one can say that the palindrome has been interpreted erotically in *Avalovara*: without changing a word, the Latin phrase, as well as the two translations adduced by the author ("The farmer carefully maintains his plow in the furrows" and "The Plowman carefully sustains the world in its orbit"), would admit a third interpretation in which an erotic meaning prevails. Understanding the word "*lavrador*" ("farmer" or "plowman") as "lover," everything else gains a highly erotic meaning, which seemed not to be among the author's calculations, considering the translation and the commentary that immediately follows it: "It is difficult to find a more precise and clear allegory of Creator and Creation." He then adds: "Identical is the image of the writer, given over to the obligation of zealously provoking in the furrows of the lines the birth of a book, lasting or with a brief life, exposed, in any case--like meadow and kingdoms--to the same galloping horses" (53). But one thing should have been the plan drawn with a view toward the two versions and the meaning that the author attributes to it, another, quite different, is its perhaps involuntary (but no less important) usage, which he provides throughout *Avalovara*: the erotic meaning prevails, as the frequency of the detailed scenes of sexual relationships indicates. An erotic palindrome, this is the final content of the Latin phrase, erotic by its meaning, deriving from the understanding of "sator" as "lover," and by the fact that the square is able to be read forwards or backwards, up or down, simulating the sexual act or, in other words, the movement of the plow over the N.

In favor of this hypothesis is the author's reference to an imaginary "mystical poem," in which every letter of the square would receive "a mystical meaning":

"A" is the City of Gold; "T," Paradise and Unity--there man comes to know death and is expelled; "R," the divine word, giver of names to things and order to chaos; "E," the human pilgrimage in search of wisdom; "O," the double nature (angelic and carnal) of man; "P," the inner equilibrium or the equilibrium of planets, a total eclipse being the perfect expression to represent the exact, albeit temporary, alignment of errant stars; "N," the communion of men and things. (73)

Why would the author of *Avalovara* dwell on this "erudite" reference if not to "illuminate" the palindrome and, consequently, the novel's structure? One might of course speculate that he did it to throw the reader off the track of the true meaning, which appears later, but to do so would place the very foundations of the narrative in check ("our novel is ruled by a mechanism that means to be as rigid as the one that moves the stars" 53), unless this itself is considered another sign of a false lead. In this case, however, the entire structure of the novel would collapse: to the contrary, the seriousness with which the author undertakes the task of narration, that is, finding a (magical) similarity between the palindrome and the World, would not permit him to construct snares to deceive the reader, especially since his intention (if we are on the right track) was precisely to lead him to assimilate the presence of the palindrome and its implications.

It seems more consistent to believe that the palindrome's erotic meaning arose despite the author. Inclined to tell the story of the Creation, he would be unable to escape the equation man-woman, male-female, from a cosmogonic perspective, as if he were reshaping the world's birth; and by developing this idea, without knowing he drifted toward the novel of love. Without negating the coherence of the initial intent, it adds a more determinate, perhaps unique, meaning: the story of the Creation is the story of the encounter between man and woman, symbolized by Abel and Ø.

Obviously the panorama does not change if we admit that the author *knew* beforehand that everything would converge toward the lovers and their memorable afternoons; it would merely confirm that we are dealing with a novel of love, with the qualification that, in this case, the entire structure of the palindrome would lose the weight that supports it. If the author started from the opposite equation, generating an amorous situation in order to discover in it the enigma of the Creation, with the palindrome and all, we can only believe that this aspect would eventually prevail. Still, by opting for the square based on the Latin phrase, repeatedly crossed by the spiral, keeping in mind that it is a novel of cosmogonic breadth that he coherently attempted to elaborate, he might not perceive that this implied sliding toward a story of love, necessary to the very fulfillment of his cosmogonic intent. But, proceeding in this way, insensibly, but inevitably (there would be no other alternative, since we are dealing with a novel), he allows the erotic aspect to grow in importance.

What is it that the narrator/protagonist searches for in his existential adventure through Europe and Brazil? He says repeatedly that he is searching for the City (with a capital letter): "Go, man, seek the City" (212). What City is he talking about?, the reader may ask, rather perplexed with the indeterminacy. Naturally, the narrator achieves his intention by travelling to Paris, London and other cities; still, if his voyage ended in his contacts with the cities he had dreamed of, we would have no more than a work of novelized travel literature. Abel's City, however, transcends cities. Is it merely their abstraction, a sort of mythical paradigm? Or one of the utopian cities to which the Renaissance gave rise in its search for a perpetually tranquil and content Arcadia? Are we dealing with one of those 16th-century visionaries, dreaming with his City of God? The cosmogonic nature of the novel, clear in its palindromic foundation, could suggest possibilities in this direction, but the analysis of the narrative negates the hypothesis of a Campanellian City-Utopia. First, because the City envisioned by Abel is concrete and accessible to the senses:

> The City that rises up impelling me to find it and that I have engraved in my spirit must be inserted, encrusted in new streets and new blocks, tangled up in another one. I can cross through it and not recognize it. (171)

Finally, the City, "whose image appears to [him] one afternoon, like a miniature, seen through seas and seasons, like the specter of a bird or an ancestor!" (69), little by little merges with the beings who inhabit Paris, London, Olinda, Recife, and São Paulo, or, rather, with the women the narrator knew and loved in his encounters through the world's streets. To such an extent that the woman appears to be made of cities: "Will I be able, however, to describe the cities that float in her body as if reflected in a thousand small transparent eyes?" (20). Immediately converted, for this reason, into Woman, she becomes identified with the City. The women-cities become Woman-City. A long process of discovery presides over this metamorphosis, like that of the chrysalis to the butterfly, but as the spiral continually crosses the square, in its uninterrupted movement, in search of its center, the anxiously sought City is gradually transfigured into the Woman, and vice-versa, in the geography of the Woman's forms Abel slowly outlines the map of the City.

"Roos, she of this city, impresses me by her opposition to shadows. [... A] splendor flows from her skin, as if many candles were lighting her up inside--perhaps the visible expression of what I dream of finding in the City, in a concrete way, thus uniting the expression and its object" (70-71), Abel discovers, still on the surface of the enigmatic being that his Parisian stroll reserved for him one day. And when, after a time immemorial had gone by and the Narrator had already penetrated deep into the palindromic labyrinth, ready to invade its pulsating nucleus, or when his encounters with the Woman had conquered the most salient points of the discovered map, he says: "the City comes to meet the man" (312) as if to say: "the Woman comes to meet the man." From there on, until its archetypal denouement, when the messenger (θ' 's husband) carries out his mission, freeing Abel and θ' from their incessant search, the City reveals itself more and more, to the same extent that the Woman disrobes before Abel's senses, as if the skin hid another being, the City, in a total ecstasy in which erotic plenitude equals the absolute possession of some long-awaited form of knowledge. The traveller finally gets to know the City, or rather, the Woman: "and we know what few or no one, live what they may... oh beauty of your face, sharp and whetted, reigning on a sloping bank, the magic of the City seems to me perilous perfidious infested with stings" (351). But this knowledge cannot go unpunished: the light of the Sun, in excess, blinds. One must pay with death for this wisdom that is finally incorporated, and death comes through the hands of the Messenger, composing an archetypal situation similar to that which expelled Adam and Eve from Paradise. The Narrator confesses, at a certain moment, that we are before a "fable threaded by Death." The carpet of foliage and animals on which the lovers weave their destiny represents Eden: history repeats itself and the fruit of knowledge is the same: Woman or Love.

Through Abel's search, a bird crosses the horizon in a movement that recalls that of the spiral crossing the square. At times it is a "solitary bird" (24) that descends on ϑ' 's womb (31) or on the loving couple (225); other times it is a metaphor for the female sex (65); sometimes there are several, "in pairs" (178), other times an errant bird, "a fugitive from the Ark and the Flood, seeming to return to the wall from which it comes, deviates, flies in the direction of the panels that show the Creation of the World and the Death of Adam, whirls toward them, crosses the sunlit courtyard diagonally, and brushes, on the opposite wall, the tiles of the Tower of Babel" (189). In the midst of the bird's recurrent flights, still far from the final resting place in the last chapter dedicated to "The Spiral and the Square," therefore serving as a summary of the author's metalanguage, Publius Ubonius, who had extorted the palindrome from Loreius, the slave to whom he had promised freedom in exchange for the magical phrase, "dreams of the Unicorn" (71); and it is further declared that the "long mystical poem" had been dedicated to the Unicorn. Finally, the narrator ends his digression by hastening that "the Unicorn circulates among these pages" (73).

While Abel is condemned, like Sisyphus, to rebegin his search until the consummation of his days, the search for the City is likewise converted into a "search for the Name." On becoming aware that he was searching for the Name, the narrator adds, as if to plagiarize the mystical poet: "the author dedicates the work to the Unicorn" (174). Although he dedicates the work to it, he searches not for it, but rather for the Name, as if he were searching for the mystical bird about which he dreams. He seeks the Name, his Unicorn, aware that the Name unleashes the arrival of the sought-for bird. And at a certain moment, his desire is consummated: his Unicorn is Avalovara:

> But the bird, this one, the restless bird you make rise up in me and whose name, I know, is Avalovara, doesn't fall silent or leave or die with your death. (...) I know that the Avalovara is watching over me and transmitting something of your condition to me: by his gaudy feathers, his secret song. (189)

From that point on, the Avalovara will intensify its presence beside Abel and his partners. Slowly, but intensely, the bird allows itself to probe deeper at the same time that the narrator's knowledge of his obsession broadens:

> The Avalovara, frightened, comes down from the clock, flies over Abel's back for a second, and alights on the carpet. Two or three feathers fall off, take flight, return to its body. I make a discovery: it's a composite being, made up of birds as tiny as bees. A bird and a cloud of birds. (225)

Commensal and spectator of the amorous banquets, as if the emissary from an omnipresent Plato, the Avalovara becomes a "real" protagonist. Finally, in the center of the palindrome--the N, identified with the female genital organ (321)--Abel learns the fruit of his anguish: the City, the Woman. Still present is "the bird of birds the plates of rusty metal a bird takes on plumage in our body and a great black bird a bird not visible over the low clouds flies firmly giving out his battered song of raw leather cut with a handsaw" (330). Two birds: one, Avalovara; the other, the annunciation of Death? When Abel and θ', fulfilling their destiny, cross the Styx by the hands of the messenger, they continue seeing "the bird of birds." At this moment, the man (Man) recalls that

> my whole life is concentrated in the act of searching knowing or not what heavy as lead is lost in the clouds the gleaming bird of ignoble song the Bearer in the right hand death the end the conclusion.... (331)

At the same time, "the bird inside of us flaps its wings of silk and sings with a kind human voice" (331): at last Avalovara was inside them. Abel searched for the City, the Woman, the Name, the Avalovara, and he discovers, faced with the imminence of Death, that the bird, his Unicorn, lived within. Rather than being expelled from Paradise, they are punished with Death, but Death is less a punishment than a form of safe-conduct to reach the imagined City. To deserve Eden, woven into the carpet ("The rug is Paradise" 286), it is necessary to die: the discovery of Avalovara encompasses, in the final analysis, the prelude to Death. Thus, the messenger of Death is (also) that of blessedness:

> and we cross a border and we join the rug we are woven into the rug (...) we and the benevolent bird (...) a new and luminous silence comes peace comes and nothing touches us, nothing, we walk, happy, entwined, among the animals and plants of the Garden. (332)

"*Avalovara* a novel of love? Yes, if the Avalovara is understood as a symbol/incarnation of Eros, the bird of Love, bird-Eros, cosmogonically dispersed in women-cities, flying over everything, soaring over the man-woman, male-female encounter, an allegory of the Cosmos, the beginning of Things, the plenitude of Avalovara, through which Eros fulfills its mission and the Universe is organized. A novel of love, because in the beginning and the end is the Word, embodied in Avalovara, the Word reincarnate in which the oracle is realized. The novel of Avalovara or of Eros: that is the narrative's message, the mirror of Man's pilgrimage in the face of Destiny. The novel of Avalovara, the saga of the first man and the first woman, reproduced *ad infinitum* in all men and women, in all Abels and Annelieses and Cecílias, for Time and Humanity are fulfilled. A novel of love, yes, because every novel pretends to be about Love and hopes to surprise the flight of the Avalovara, even though it may reject the mythical bird or repudiate its reason for being. A novel of love, an emblem of all novels, because everything is summarized, in the final analysis, in the union of Man and Woman.

MEMOIRS TOLD TO THE MIRROR: AUTRAN DOURADO AND DARCY RIBEIRO

Fábio Lucas
Universidade de Brasília

This essay is a reflection on the relationship between the narrative text and the memoir, the confession, the historical testimony and the creative imagination, based on a reading of Darcy Ribeiro's *Migo* (1988) and Autran Dourado's *Um artista aprendiz* (1989).

Novel and History

In *Vanguarda, historia e ideologia da literatura* (1985) I discuss the correlations between History and Literature in some detail. Without repeating the arguments outlined there, I will briefly reexamine the issue of the scale of observation that creates the phenomenon, for every time we change our scale of observation we perceive new phenomena.

In chapter 9 of his *Poetics*, Aristotle showed that dramatic works need an air of plausibility. How can one confer plausibility to a chain of events except by showing that they in fact occurred? Narrated events are at times organized like a simple account, in which the narrator functions as the cold mirror of the past, and at other times like a report, in which the narrator is no more than a participatory mediator of the visions he or she intends to communicate.

In the first case, the introduction of artistic content into the account "dramatizes" History. It creates either a novelized History or subgenres such as biography or autobiography. In the second case, the success of the narrative derives from its historicity. It produces the historical novel, where novelistic action is interwoven with past, empirically documentable facts, or the confessional novel, where the focus falls exclusively on the action of the narrator, who is purposely confused with the author. To confess consists in delivering to someone else the "self"

165

which is not yet revealed, but rather reconstituted by the self-evaluative discourse.

In an essay on generational novels set in the geographical and historical scenario of Belo Horizonte, in the state of Minas Gerais, and concentrating on the period that goes from Eduardo Frieiro to Luiz Vilela, I attempted to show how each literary generation delegated to one of its writers the task of defining its most illustrious names, its values, aspirations and shortcomings, in a rite of passage with a strong tendency for repetition (cf. "Aspectos da ficção mineira pós-45").

In the present study I am interested in exploring the hypothesis of epochal evocation in a gesture of retaking time and exorcising traumatic situations, considering the city of Belo Horizonte, its habits and its projections in two different sensibilities in terms of literary formation. One may verify the recurrence of themes, situations, and places, in which knowledge and emotions are experienced for the first time in a game of initiation characteristic of the city. To this end I will examine the formational novel of Autran Dourado and Darcy Ribeiro's confessional novel. Both refer to the same period of the city and use similar personalities, places, events and circumstances.

Dramatic realism, which renders the novels artistic, reinforces the conviction that the works are "literature," "fiction" in the imaginative sense of the term. But the limit between emotion and reason permits us to invoke the historiographical residual the novels reflect, while keeping in mind that the works do not exist because of statistical virtues or by way of an encyclopedic collection of data.

The study, therefore, does not attempt to be a map, report or an x-ray. By dealing with literary works, the psychological and ideological mechanisms that involve or shape them are presented with extreme polysemic breadth, since they enclose the prismatic variety of the life they attempt to represent.

Plato and Aristotle distinguished between *diegesis* (simple relating) and *mimesis* (poetic imitation). In the Mineiro novelists what would be pure information, or the sum of data about the student and petit-bourgeois atmosphere of the state capital, is no more than the motivating impulse of novelistic realization. The revisited past is enriched by psychological perspective and literary order.

Fictional works with an evident retrospective purpose are generally based on a discourse which, returning to past situations, tends to cover the same paths, much like Gadamer's fusion of horizons. It thus provides the benefit of catharsis, for the spirit needs to find refuge from disasters whose symbolic representation has a liberating effect.

In Autran Dourado, the fusion of horizons occurs from the perspective of the past or, more precisely, horizons are fused so that the past resuscitates. With Darcy Ribeiro the fusion of horizons implies the primacy of the present, for it actualizes the past, which is contemplated in the light of present interests. In Dourado, the narrative leans toward the past's mythic force, while in Ribeiro the contemporary values of writing, which are judges and selectors of the revival of the past, prevail. Autran Dourado's text is guided by an invisible unity. That of Darcy Ribeiro by a polyhedral conception, although the narrative flow is linear in causal and temporal terms.

Fiction and Memory

As long as the novel has been understood as the epic form of the bourgeoisie (Hegel), the representation of life through narrative has been linked to the description of the quotidian. The story of the short-lived myths adopted by natural societies, linked to the cycles of the sun and the moon, or of days and nights, is retold. But the invention of the hero individualized each narrative, although the daily forms of life codified by bourgeois society did not abandon the inevitable cycle of days and nights. It tends to relate the individual, exclusive, and irreversible trajectory of the protagonist.

Memory is at the base of the oral narrative tradition. The famous invocation of the prototypical peasant who, in his tales, revives the community's immemorial past and of the sailor who, in his adventures, makes distant places near, shows that the use of memory is a factor used to captivate the attention of the listening public. Ancient and distant episodes are "recalled" for the listeners' delight, often during the long nights of winter.

Memorialism is part of literature itself. When one says "memoirs" one refers to a literary genre defined as "historical, written, or testimonial narrations" or "writings in which the author narrates facts more or less associated with his person." The word "memoir," in many cases, maintains synonymity with "telling" and "narration."

In mythology it is said that Cronos, having devoured his sons, had to vomit them up on Zeus's order. The symbol helps us to search for the return path often taken to past situations in order to revive or reintroduce them in the present. One seeks especially "to vomit" an unforgettable young man who has passed from childhood to adulthood, a "son" devoured by Cronos.

Referring to man's surviving biological memory, Sándor Ferénczi mentions ancestral traumas like the drying of oceans or birth in which the human beings simultaneously suffer the anguish of passage from the maternal womb to extra-uterine life and have the sensation of freedom that birth provides. He then outlines the hypothesis of the voluptuous tendency for repetition. People devote themselves to recreating the same inaugural scene in the hedonistic search that compensates for prior traumas and in the pleasure of again feeling the felicitous freedom from a great danger.

We see, in novels such as *Um artista aprendiz* and *Migo*, the desire to recompose a prototype of ideation: the youthful years. There is a certain egotistical function in this, the impulse of giving one more opportunity to the already formed Ego. Thus the practice of a certain psychological archaism, for rites of devouring ancestors were not uncommon.

According to Sándor Ferénczi, based on the alternation between differentiation and integration proposed by Spencer, "necessity obligates organisms to change, suppressed desire impels them to return incessantly to the abandoned situation and, in a certain sense, to its reintegration."

Autran Dourado's narrator specifies the material of his artistic elaboration:

> A ação se passava principalmente no passado. Aliás o passado sempre lhe interessou mais do que o futuro, dele é que se nutria. Com que se faz um romance, ele se perguntava e ele mesmo respondia - com a memória e a imaginação. (*Um artista aprendiz* 176)

Both Mineiro novelists, with their memorialism, register the physical and cultural landscape of Belo Horizonte in a moment of great political agitation. Here we are interested in the works' poetic substratum as well as the biographical, sociological, and literary consequences of the narration.

Autran Dourado's Formational Novel

In *Um artista aprendiz* the narrator performs an alchemical procedure which transforms lived situations into recalled emotions and then into elements of a novelistic texture. Dourado does not hide the weight of his reminiscences in the novel's elaboration: "Só na memória inconsciente e na imaginação é que as coisas regressam, ele aprenderia depois. Mas voltam contaminadas, deformadas pelas lentes das lágrimas ou do tempo" (5-6).

Articulating his story of apprenticeship, after the publication of twenty works, including novels and essays about the literary profession, the novelist dialogues with his earlier production, fuses memory to imagination and combines events that really occurred with others that are invented. The objective of *Um artista aprendiz* is to describe the artist's development and, primarily, to invoke a commitment he had attempted to pursue throughout his life: to become the most important novelist of his generation.

As a novel of formation, apprenticeship or evolution (as Wolfgang Kayser would have it), Autran Dourado's text narrates the protagonist's sentimental, spiritual, political and human awakening. Art consists of transmitting to the reader the rhythm of temporality that "forms" the narrator. The *Bildungsroman* would be a narrative subject to an "open end," although Autran Dourado circumscribes his narrative with the conclusion of the "artist's" commitment with the obstinate finality of possessing a "technical knowledge" that he would transport to his work, "pouco importando o preço que tivesse que pagar" (254). Thus, he describes the dreams of the young writer, foreseeing himself as "o maior da sua geração," even though he recognizes the difficulties beginning with his initiation, his "aprendizado da dor" (10). "Quem sabe," the narrator questions, invoking Scheherazade, "os romancistas só escrevem, só contam as suas histórias pra continuar vivendo?" (24).

Besides the title, other signs are left to the reader's perception for information about the experimental years of João da Fonseca Nogueira, who functions as a sort of alter-ego of the novelist. Distinguishing between truth and fantasy is a difficult task. The artist's creative imagination, in effect, starts from the real and elaborates it, just as it ferments the imaginary and renders it real and concrete.

The narrator of *Um artista aprendiz* understands the moving frontier and returns to it, for he ends up citing himself in other novelistic adventures. In the character's retrospective consciousness, the theme is presented from the outset:

> Pra mim o imaginado vira o acontecido, é duro separar um do outro, do sonho então nem se fala, as coisas, as pessoas principalmente se fundem numa só massa, névoa aquosa dentro de mim, se dilatando, se espalhando, tudo de cambulhada, a gente sofre pra burro, o que realmente vivi? o que foi que eu inventi? (4)

Thus instead of a temporality of memory, jumping from a remote era to the present, it occurs to him that "era impossível distinguir as coisas que realmente aconteceram daquelas que ele fantasiava na livre associação de idéias, se lembrava melhor das coisas que nunca aconteceram" (4).

For Autran Dourado's readers this passage sounds rather familiar. It comes from an epigraph from Mark Twain, placed before *O risco do bordado*: "When I was younger, I could remember anything, whether it happened or not; but now my faculties are declining and soon I will only be capable of remembering things that never happened." In *O risco do bordado* there is also the first phase of the character's sentimental education, distributed among the display windows of the prostitute Teresinha Virado and the girl from the circus, Valente Valentina, as well as in the ardent apparition of Tia Margarida.

Finally, the first imprecision of *Um artista aprendiz* resides precisely in the limit between the character's speech and the author's secret confession. Are the exorcised ghosts real or imagined? Thus we arrive at a second level of ambiguity.

In *Um artista aprendiz* Autran Dourado travels the roads of passage from innocence to worldly knowledge. Some vestiges are clear. After the title come dedications to Artur Versiani Veloso, who initiated him in the study of philosophy, and Godofredo Rangel, who provided his literary education. Both become characters in the novel, redressed as Sinval de Sousa and Sílvio Sousa. And on pages 99 and 100 there is a clear questioning of the novel that deals with the man's beginnings and describes his formative age.

The character notes the reading of Flaubert's *L'Éducation sentimental* and Goethe's *Wilhelm Meister*, the latter often cited as the true creator of the *Bildungsroman*, despite some who recognize precursors in Eschenbach's *Parzival* and Grimmelshausen's *Simplizissimus*. Nevertheless, the genre lends itself to narrating the consequences of external

effects on the character's emotional, psychological, and personality transformations. The child becomes a man by learning, and he discovers
himself through experiences of love, friendship, politics, and life's hard
reality, all of which is more pertinent to thematics than to the work's
formal structure.

In Dourado, the novel takes a hybrid form. Part of the narrative
may be considered a *roman à clef*, since real people appear under fictitious names. The whole generation with which the novelist lived and the
books he read in his early years in Belo Horizonte are also reflected in
the work.

What was his apprenticeship? The primary vectors converge in
his amorous experiences, his philosophical-literary culture, and politics.
By adopting a content that is more memorialistic and less directed at
effects, less constructed to please the reader, Autran Dourado creates a
novel in which verism becomes more evident than verisimilitude.

Unlike Fernando Sabino, who uses the same social framework
in *O encontro marcado*, designating a generation troubled by religious
and existential doubts, Dourado contracts his creative impulse, curbs his
imagination and develops a tremulous narrative with jumps in the causal-
temporal structure. As an example one might take the death of Teresa,
at the end of chapter 8.

The only fully developed instance of an amorous relationship is
the maturing of the main character's love for Aurelia Sousa e Silva. The
others are fortuitous and shallow. (A parenthesis: what strange event
leads the author to always put the Sousa's on the side of good? Sinval de
Sousa, Silvio Sousa, Aurelia Sousa e Silva...).

The narrator's literary formation becomes clear through the
abundance of literary judgements. There appear portraits of Oswald de
Andrade, Lúcio Cardoso, and Graciliano Ramos. Artur Versiani Veloso
(Sinval de Sousa), who had inspired another novelist, Ciro dos Anjos,
appears to Dourado, perhaps because of generational factors, as a friend
and partner in liquid and literary libations rather than as a guide or
mentor.

In their novels of generational testimony, Fernando Sabino and
Ciro dos Anjos retain the group spirit, something that does not happen
to Autran Dourado. The associative spirit is more difficult for him. For
this very reason, the best moments of his fiction are concentrated in the
narration of the variable movements of consciousness. His partners in
youthful adventure do not receive a clear outline or a life of their own.
They are far from types such as Rosalina and Juca Passarinho (*Ópera*

dos mortos), Maria (*A barca dos homens*) and so many other children of the novelist's imagination.

The third element of his formation is politics. The main character realistically recalls everything his initiation and militancy in the Communist Party meant to him. What does it mean for a son of a family from a decadent rural aristocracy to enter and leave the Communist Party at the end of the Vargas dictatorship? In this regard, the novel's explanation seems rushed. At that time hundreds of young people passed through the same experience. In some, who subsequently fell into the opposite camp, the marks of the Party are noticeable throughout their life.

While the friends in Fernando Sabino's novel have their encounter marked by the shadow of a religious institution, reestablishing the cycle of the traditional reencounter, Dourado's narrator tells of leaving the Communist Party like someone who sheds his skin or retreats from a youthful fantasy. The character's mission is elsewhere. His mature commitment was to the art of writing, and his goal was to become the best of his group, no matter what the cost.

Why did hundreds of young people who were not politically inclined enter the Communist Party at the end of the dictatorship and during the cold war, only to become disillusioned and leave shortly thereafter? *Um artista aprendiz* does not provide an answer to this question. It is a novel of formation, not of social or political criticism. It's a shame. We would like for someone with the acute vision of Autran Dourado to analyze the seduction the Party had for an entire generation of rebellious petit-bourgeois young people in the 1940s when the Party, like a forbidden fruit, held a degree of fascination that many political parties are unable to attain today.

In a peripheral, dependent, poor society dominated by an oligarchy with a low level of technical and political aspirations, the Communist Party offered an alternative to the reigning obscurantism. It organized resistance, set itself up as a counter-power, and promised a utopia. To the young spirit, such ingredients were sufficient. Many were not prepared for the sacrifices it represented.

Um artista aprendiz is an extremely perceptive testimony about what happened to Brazil in the 1940s. Between the lines one of the masters of Brazilian fiction provides an account of affective castration, intellectual limitations, and political repression.

Darcy Ribeiro's Autobiographical Chronicle

Migo escapes from the typical model of the novel of apprentice-ship even though it dedicates a substantial part of the narration to the recovery of the past with a well-defined date and place. The realist concern is evident: the novel opens with a comment on the diaries that Eduardo Frieiro burned one day, despite his wife's protests. The novel regrets that the writer destroyed years of confidential writing concerning the daily life and provincial intrigues of Belo Horizonte.

The question raised by Darcy Ribeiro consists in defining the genre he is engaged in, refusing to destroy notebooks of confessional writing:

> Só sei mesmo desse meu livro - diário? romance? biografia? - é seu nome provável: Migo. Não sei bem por quê. Será talvez para expressar minha identidade mais íntima: a-migo, co-migo. Lembra também inimigo. Que mais? Sei lá! Migo seja, isso me basta. Suspeito também que Migo seja eu. Sou eu. Como todo romance, este, se sair, será uma autobiografia inventada, de mentira. Impostada. (13)

Alongside the intrepid narrative of many adventures, almost all dealing with erotic triumphs, it includes the destructive marks of time: "O tempo me gasta, tão lentamente, tão silenciosamente, que eu mal sinto. Mas não pára de me carunchar, mansa, devagar, inexoravelmente" (29).

There also appears the idea that writing is the narrator's salvation:

> Acho até bom demais viver enrolado no meu cipoal de palavras e figurações, feito delas, que são a carne do meu espírito. De todos os destinos que poderia ter sido e vivido, gozado e sofrido, prefiro este. (123)

What kind of past or essential truth was discoverable for him to restore in life? This is where writing and the cultural residuals of Minas Gerais join in the same purpose: "O escritor que sou tem seu limite precisamente nesse confinamento mineiro em que sempre vivi atrelado. Como saber do humano, se dele só sei a humanidadezinha nossa, geralista" (133).

What is the goal of Darcy Ribeiro's rather cynical narrator? He states it himself: "Nesta altura eu penso no Rosa e me encolho todo. Preciso é ser ainda maior que ele. O maior dos escritores brasileiros. E por que não do mundo inteiro?" (369). One can see that *Migo*'s narrator has an ambition analogous to that of the narrator of *Um artista aprendiz*, perhaps with an even greater emphasis.

In its hedonistic search for life's pleasures, Darcy Ribeiro's narrative impulse is governed by that voluptuous tendency for repetition noted by Sándor Ferénczi. This is clear in the following passage:

> Tire da vida o gozo que sua vida pode dar a você. Só a você ela pode dar. Singela ou enroscada, sua vida é a única coisa que você tem. O que temos que fazer, você e eu, é nos assumirmos e gozar o gozo possível, ainda que seja apenas um gozinho à toa. (133-134)

Within the novel's labyrinthine perspective, we can go down recurring or iterative paths. The narrator in reality attempts to relate the road to maturity, the way a repressed Mineiro learns to be a man. The young macho discovers himself and his own social role through amorous experiences, relationships and life's arduous trials.

Migo's most notorious particularity consists in the frequent and direct intervention of the non-fictional world in the work of fiction. The narrator is not constrained by the possibility of defining people according to a point of view in which the narrator becomes confused with the author. Satirical opinions are given to the reader as if decontextualized from the fiction.

Besides this, the journalistic quotidian of the period of the novel's composition interferes in the narration, as if plausibility increased by such techniques. Example: the inclusion in the novel of the death of Hélio Pellegrino. The beginning is of an unexpected colloquialism: "Puta merda: Zélia do Jorge me disse hoje - 24 de março de 1988 - aqui em Paris, que Hélio morreu, ontem, no Rio" (176-177). *Migo* is a confessional fantasy in which the novelist combines nostalgia with his testimony about the writers and politicians that comprise the climate of the period that influenced him.

The fictional printworks become amusing to the extent that the reader, on attaining a certain intimacy with the characters, runs into personalities of Brazilian life, especially Mineiros. Thus, the reader finds the death of Tancredo Neves, along with José Sarney, José Aparecido de

Oliveira, Aureliano Chaves, Ulisses Guimarães, Leonel Brizola, members of the Communist Party in Minas (Armando Ziler, Fritz Teixeira de Sales, Bimbirra, etc.), as well as the intellectual group from São Paulo composed of Mário de Andrade, Oswald de Andrade, Sérgio Buarque de Hollanda, Antônio Candido. The novel also evokes Eduardo Frieiro, Artur Versiani Veloso, Emílio Moura and Guimarães Rosa as well as contemporaries of the narrator/author such as Ciro dos Anjos, Hélio Pellegrino, Fernando Sabino, Otto Lara Resende, Autran Dourado, João Etienne Filho, Edgar da Mata Machado, Morse Belém, Amaro Xisto de Queiroz and Dantas Mota. Some of them appear in mischievous or at least curious circumstances. For example, Vivaldi Moreira appears offering the narrator a chair in the Academia Mineira de Letras; Ciro dos Anjos and Otto Lara Resende serve as examples of talented Brazilian mulattos; Paulo Mendes Campos is portrayed as an innocent Bohemian poet, "o melhor de nós;" Amaro Xisto appears in the title of two novels imagined by the narrator: *Amaro* and *Xisto*.

Admiration for Juscelino Kubitschek is unlimited, comprising the character's moments of happiness, as is his sympathy for Leonel Brizola. His vibrant love for Tiradentes, Aleijadinho and baroque churches spills out onto the page. In literature, Drummond stands out in the protagonist's cult. In terms of his philosophical background, Arthur Veloso and Carlos Campos are prominent. About the former he testifies:

> Era o único intelectual daqui que assumia suas leituras e suas tesões. Ambas desvairadas. Foi o horror indignado e o espanto invejoso dos letrados de sua geração e o pastor-fauno, da nossa. Vendo sua coragem de ser e de viver, plena, fazíamos das tripas coração pra nos assumir. (19)

Later he comments that Veloso was the one who kept him from falling into the arms of Bloy, Péguy and Maritain. About Carlos Campos he informs us that he was: "[o] único sábio verdadeiro que conheci e freqüentei. Uma vida toda de ler, de meditar" (88).

One should also note among the novel's literary components, as an intertextual practice, the insertion of evocative verses at the end of each chapter, generally from the work of Carlos Drummond de Andrade, Camões and Manuel Bandeira.

Not everything is successful in the novel. Despite prolonged reflections on the genre, the written word, and literature's regenerative function, the work presents a certain lack of harmony. For example, the insistent and unwise exhortation of the reader in a sort of proselytizing loquaciousness or a search for complicity. A rhetorical trick that works at some moments and doesn't at others is that of arbitrarily shifting the narrative perspective to different characters. Another obsession consists in transcribing scenes and more scenes of sexual acts without the composition of an erotic plot, without love, in the fashion of a "subliterature" for men only in which women appear without life, like inflatable dolls.

Like a story told before a mirror, *Migo* is not lacking direct nominal references to its author, Darcy Ribeiro, as well as marketing appeals to characters created by him in other novels. Ironically, the final chapter, with its conclusion so convenient to the narrator, is titled "Requiem."

Migo avoids the characteristic "open end" of formational novels. Ribeiro closes his plot with a sort of happy ending, since the denouement of the dramatic situation that involves the main character opens the doors to the realization of his erotic fantasy.

Cybernetic Places and Cultural Redoubts

We have already seen how the narcissistic condition nourishes the voluptuous ego of narrators. What does João da Fonseca Nogueira in *Um artista aprendiz* intend? And the protagonist of *Migo*? Each one, in his own way, wants to be the best novelist of his time, which implies a dynamic force, a desire for perfection only realized by the legitimate heirs of Prometheus.

The substratum of meditations on the art of writing, in both, makes clear the intention of self-realization through the narrative discourse. One should note, in truth, that the introduction of non-fictional material in the novels does not reach the point of becoming a mixture of fiction and prescription. In a certain sense, Autran Dourado and Darcy Ribeiro adopt a relativist attitude in relation to life's ethical, political and social precepts.

Both explore, however, the lustral waters of Minas Gerais. Their fantasy, their search for identity, their self-contemplation in the autobiographical mirror pass through the intention of defining their *mineiridade* between phases of apology and repulsion. Autran Dourado's profession of faith is unequivocal: "Quero me encharcar de Minas, entender a nossa terra. É duro pra burro entender Minas, a gente carece de amar primeiro, disse ele. Somos um país singular no Brasil, tudo que dizem da gente é verdade e é mentira" (209). He includes his literary ambition in this: "E ele lhe falou da sua ambição: escrever um grande painel de Minas, algumas coisas de grandioso, uma coisa forte, à Goya." At the end of the novel, the character registers the following: "Não viverei mais com a visão do horizonte barrada pela Serra do Curral, dizia pensando em deixar Minas Gerais. Mas levarei Minas comigo, como o rio que para ser fiel à sua fonte toma a direção do mar" (254).

For Darcy Ribeiro, Minas Gerais is a land of challenge which the main character at times caustically unmasks while at other times exalting it with the fervor of an energumen. *Migo*'s epigraph is illustrative and is certainly part of the novel, giving it its first significative intention and providing a first glimpse of the fluidity and indefinition of *mineiridade*:

> Minha gente eu vou m'embora
> Mineiro tá me chamando
> Mineiro tem esse jeito
> Chama a gente e vai andando

The character's profession of faith is simple:

> Meu país, minha patrinha, pra valer, é Minas. Essa Minas de pedra e de ferro, atarrachada no meio do Brasil. Uma França, de tamanho; meia Espanha de população. Três séculos de história civilizada. Dez mil anos de civilização índia. E ninguém sabe o que é, nem onde é. (148)

Another character, Uriel, on a visit to the narrator, goes directly to a critique of his cultural heritage:

> Aqueles mineiros antigos, falados, eram homens de virtudes, se diz. Alguns queriam ser e parecer honestos, sérios, confiáveis, sem vícios nem joças morais. Eram os tais do fio de barba branca valendo promissória. Esse pendor será, talvez, um eco do escravismo que deu sustentação moral, tanto à romanidade como à mineiridade. Nos dois casos é uma mentira. Nunca houve gente orgiástica como a romana com toda a sua mania de falar em virtude. Minas não é tão orgiástica assim. Por covardia amofinou e está até perdendo a eloquência no elogio da

virtude. Há é muita hipocrisia nesta terra minha, muito mais que boemia. (206)

The state's intellectual mentality is treated with sarcasm, from which not even Veloso escapes: "O que o saber mineiro produz mesmo são mistificações. Nisto somos riquíssimos. O produto mais acabado do esforço de Minas pra gerar intelectuais é gente como o Veloso, inteligência vadia, eruditíssima. Inutilíssima" (199).

From there the narrator goes on to the destruction of the myth of the Mineiros' conciliatory nature. Their talent is, rather, for acquiescence and graft, always attentive to fawning and sinecures. All of this occurs, of course, in a context of controversies. Thus we have a confrontation of two versions of Minas:

Ser mineiro pra Guedes é assumir nosso passado lusitano, com arfante orgulho dele: enforcando, esquartejando. Pra mim é dar uma de Tiradentes para mudar. (...) Quero é ver, redivivos, os Filipe dos Santos, os Joaquim José e os Antônio Francisco: criativos, veementes, vibrantes. (311)

After exploring the function of writing and the weight of Minas's cultural heritage, Autran Dourado and Darcy Ribeiro turn to the topographical excavation of Belo Horizonte. We see clearly how cultural redoubts and cybernetic spaces merge, the latter considered to be those that favor or propitiate encounters between characters and the circulation of knowledge, culture and emotions.

Autran Dourado's character describes his first encounter with the city and mentions the Rua da Bahia, the heights of Av. Afonso Pena, and its growth after it ceased being the "cidade vergel." Darcy Ribeiro goes directly to the "umbigo feio da cidade," Praça Sete. With inspiration he associates the image of the revisited plaza to the character's psychological structure: "Lembrei-me da sapataria antiga que ali havia. Ali, também, vi os primeiros bondes quando cheguei a Belô. Saudades? Qual! Gostei de estar ali, olhando e vendo o presente, lá fora, e o passado, cá dentro" (204).

For those who know the history of Belo Horizonte, there is a difference between remembering the Rua da Bahia or Praça Sete first. Darcy Ribeiro's character also refers to another, newer place, the Savassi, the symbol of contemporary consumerism, which is so important in Roberto Drummond's pop fiction.

The points of convergence the city presents to the writers are always the same: the Parque Municipal, the Praça da Liberdade, Av. João Pinheiro, the old Faculdade de Direito (Praça Afonso Arinos), the Igreja de Lourdes (where, in *Migo*, a wedding has Juscelino Kubitschek as godfather), Rua Pernambuco, Rua Magnólia, Rua Angustura, and the Faculdade de Filosofia (FaFi).

In *Um artista aprendiz*, Rua Guaicurus, the street of prostitutes, appears as the locale of sexual initiation. The narrator recalls the streets perfumed by magnolias, which is a typical reminiscence of Belo Horizonte, as one sees in Ciro dos Anjos's *O amanuense Belmiro*. Autran Dourado's main character frequents the Parque Municipal, the Clube Acaba Mundo, the Minas Tênis Clube, the ice cream shops and bars Nova Celeste, Elite, Trianon, Gruta Metrópole, Tip-Top, Monsa.

He recaptures the intellectual atmosphere by remembering the Agir and Oscar Nicolai bookstores, the municipal library, and the Faculdade de Direito. He even recalls the light at the Casa Bleriot, which illuminated Belo Horizonte's nights.

Literary personages fill the novel's pages: Ciro dos Anjos, Bueno de Rivera, Aires da Mata Machado, Graciliano Ramos, Lúcio Cardoso, Hélio Pellegrino, Fernando Sabino, Otto Lara Resende, Francisco Iglésias, Sílvio Felício, Murilo Rubião and others, who are presented either with their own names or hidden behind fictitious ones.

Thus, in both *Um artista aprendiz* and *Migo* the themes and characters adhere to the landscape and its strategic places to amalgamate the novelists' cultural memory as a *locus* appropriate to the flowering of the inventive project. The faculties, bars, buildings, parks and houses evoke the people of their existential perambulations, helping them find the sanctuaries of their literary and artistic vocation as well as their amorous and political destination.

The circulation of knowledge also has appropriate sites--schools, bookstores, libraries--just as their professional, philosophical and political formation depends on new, more or less institutionalized places. The same can be said about spaces of leisure--cinemas, theaters, clubs, dance halls, and bars--in which romantic selections are concretized. There being a coincidence of time and space, it is natural that the confessional narratives of apprenticeship would indicate the same ideological sources and the same meeting places.

To conclude, we can say that the confidential dimension of the narrative shortens the distance between creation and memory, between the narrator's sphere and the author's field of evocation. The search for the recognition of the self by others is put in parentheses, and the text is sought as the liquid surface in which Narcissus contemplates himself. In this contemplation the process of self-recognition and the evaluation of the appropriate social forces, to which the narrator had to adapt or which he was stimulated to change, can begin.

To exorcise their ghosts, Autran Dourado and Darcy Ribeiro had to weigh the dimensions of the inherited cultural ruins of three cybernetic stadia, considered as the places to which people return to meet others and provide an outlet for the flow of communication. Thus, Minas Gerais and Belo Horizonte appear like geometrical spaces for the passage of the ideologies and utopias of the two young artists in the process of formation. They offer cybernetic places for debates and the exchange of ideas: faculties, bars, cabarets, boarding houses, and student apartments. Companions and friends would converge on these sites and establish the elective affinities that would help them in their initiation into the mysteries of life: love, politics, social and economic relations. A space of learning the novels describe as the center of gravity of their plots as well as their existential nucleus.

Confession Before the Mirror

We thus have two novelists, Autran Dourado and Darcy Ribeiro, who elaborate their memoirs before the distorted mirror of fantasy and disguised as a narrative of formation, in the first case, and self-evaluative fiction, in the second. In both cases, creative prose is mixed with auto-biographical testimony.

In order to read themselves, the novelists also read the people and places that form the structural framework of the self in formation, and they question the genre that they chose as a vehicle in their return to the past. The mirror they contemplate, however, contains the narrative of the rite of passage from the state of innocence to adulthood. The narrator's self is presented as shaped by contemporary interests. The verbal repetition of the past is given a content of purification.

The search for self implies a reevaluation of *mineiridade* as a psychic value and socio-cultural entity. The image of the self, surrounded by Minas Gerais and Belo Horizonte and by the cultural redoubts and the people responsible for their initiation, also provides an image of the present, in which the future is envisioned: the project the novelists have delegated to themselves of writing a perfect novel, the best of their time.

Such a commitment to perfection, touched by dramatic situations, makes the flame that Prometheus took from the gods shine and evokes the "blind faith" that he proudly inscribed in the hearts of men.

REFERENCES

Dourado, Autran. *Um artista aprendiz*. Rio de Janeiro: José Olympio, 1989.

Ferénczi, Sándor. *Thalassa: ensaio sobre a teoria da genitalidade*. São Paulo: Martins Fontes, 1990.

Lucas, Fábio. "Aspectos da ficção mineira pós-45: romance de geração." *O eixo e a roda* 5 (1986): 43-69.

_____. *Vanguarda, história e ideologia na literatura*. São Paulo: Ática, 1985.

Ribeiro, Darcy. *Migo*. Rio de Janeiro: Guanabara, 1988.

LITERATURE, FILM AND POLITICS IN BRAZIL: REFLECTIONS ON THE GENERATION OF 1968

Randal Johnson
University of Florida

> Estavam jogados entre a ditadura e a linguagem cinematográfica. (Márcio Souza, *Operação silêncio*)

With the process of redemocratization in Brazil, which began in the mid-to-late 1970s under the names *distensão*, then *abertura*, many literary, theatrical, and cinematic works appeared concerning the difficult period of authoritarian rule that followed the military's 1964 overthrow of João Goulart. Opposition to the regime is a central theme in such novels as Antônio Callado's *Bar Dom Juan* (1974) and *Reflexos do baile* (1976), and Artur José Poerner's *Nas profundas do inferno* (1979), among many others.[1] It is also obviously central to the many memoirs or "political testimonies" of participants in the armed struggle against military rule such as Fernando Gabeira's *O que é isso, companheiro?* (1979), Alfredo Syrkis's *Os carbonários* (1980), and Alex Polari's fictionalized *Em busca do tesouro* (1982), to mention only the most well known.[2] Opposition to military repression has also been expressed in

---

[1] As Joan Dassin has written, with such works it is clear "that fiction... took to heart the self-assigned task of describing, analyzing, and perhaps exorcizing the effects of repression on Brazilian society" (42, n. 1).

[2] Dassin's essay is perhaps the best study yet undertaken of the politicial testimonies published in the late 1970s and 1980s by participants in the armed struggle. It focuses primarily on three areas typically ad-

such films as Francisco Ramalho Jr.'s *Paula* (1980), Leon Hirszman's
Eles não usam black-tie (1981), Roberto Farias's *Pra frente Brasil!* (1982),
Oswaldo Caldeira's *O bom burguês* (1983), Eduardo Coutinho's *Cabra
marcado para morrer* (1984), and Nelson Pereira dos Santos's cinematic
version of Graciliano Ramos's *Memórias do cárcere* (1984). All of these
works in different genres and media--and I have failed to mention numerous theatrical works on the same subject--attempt to put the events
of the period of dictatorship in critical perspective.

Two of the most intriguing of such works are Renato Tapajós's
Em câmara lenta (1977) and Márcio Souza's *Operação silêncio* (1979).
The two novels have much in common. Taken together they constitute
a rich discussion of the complex relationship between literature, film, and
politics under military rule and an acute dissection of the perplexities and
dilemmas of the generation that matured in the repressive atmosphere
of military-ruled Brazil.

Both novels were written by writers from northern Brazil--Souza
from the state of Amazonas, Tapajós from Pará--who were living in São
Paulo in the period leading up to and following the 1964 coup d'état.
They were both active in student politics, and they were both subsequently arrested for suspicion of belonging to the same clandestine organization. Tapajós and Souza were also active in filmmaking or film-related
activities, and the cinema is a central metaphor in both novels.

Renato Tapajós began his filmmaking career while a student at
the University of São Paulo with short documentaries such as *Vila da
barca*, *Universidade em crise*, and *Um por cento*, all of which were connected with the student movement. After an interval lasting until 1976,
he made the prize-winning *Fim-de-semana* in collaboration with the
university's film school. A number of his films have since been produced
in conjunction with the Metalworkers' Union in São Paulo.[3] Márcio

---

dressed by such memoirs: "1) the personal choice to join the armed
struggle; 2) the fears engendered by that choice; and 3) the nature of the
resistance that developed..." (17).

[3] Renato Tapajós was born in 1943 in Belém. He went to São Paulo
in 1962 to study engineering, but eventually decided to study sociology at
the Faculdade de Filosofia, Ciência e Letras of the Universidade de São
Paulo, where he became active in documentary filmmaking. Among his
films are *Acidentes de trabalho* (1978), *Que ninguém nunca mais ouse*

Souza's first published book, *O mostrador de sombras* (1967) is a collection of essays on film. He participated in numerous film productions, and in 1973 he directed a cinematic version of Ferreira de Castro's *A selva*. Among his short films is a 1969 documentary titled *Bárbaro e nosso: imagens para Oswald de Andrade*.

The centrality of the cinema to these two novels is homologous with its centrality in Brazilian cultural discourse in the period between 1960 and 1985, especially under the leadership of the internationally-acclaimed Cinema Novo movement. One might argue that in this period the cinema supplanted traditional fictional narrative, just as popular music replaced poetry, in what Pierre Bourdieu would call the "hierarchy of cultural genres." João Guimarães Rosa once remarked, in fact, that if he had to begin his career again, he would be a filmmaker and not a writer. As *Operação silêncio*'s protagonist Paulo Conti says, *"Deus e o diabo na terra do sol* [Glauber Rocha, 1964], *Vidas secas* [Nelson Pereira dos Santos, 1963], *O desafio* [Paulo César Saraceni, 1965] foram filmes que criaram as condições de se eleger o cinema brasileiro como ponta de lança da cultura nacional" (10).

Em câmara lenta and *Operaçao silêncio* are critical portraits of what the latter's narrator calls the "generation of 1968," a generation of young artists and intellectuals whose politics developed in the post-1964 period. *Operação silêncio*'s protagonist, filmmaker Paulo Conti, informs us that he was born in 1966 when he enrolled in Social Sciences at Faculdade de Filosofia in São Paulo. The narrator of *Em câmara lenta* also traces the roots of his political militancy to student politics.

It is a generation that lived through the early years of military rule, the increasing polarization of political forces in 1967 and 1968, and the repression and torture of the period governed by the Fifth Institutional Act (1968). It grew up debating the highly politicized films of Cinema Novo, the plays of José Celso Martinez Correia's Teatro Oficina, and the protest music of Chico Buarque and Geraldo Vandré. It is also a generation faced with tragic options: silence and conformism or revolt.

---

duvidar da capacidade de luta do trabalhador (1979), *Linha de montagem* (1982), and *Em nome da segurança nacional* (1984). The script of his *Fim-de-semana* can be found, along with a detailed description, in *O filme curto*, vol. 2, 88-98.

Renato Tapajós began writing *Em câmara lenta* while in prison for alleged "subversive" activities (Machado 73).[4] In the book's short introduction, the author himself describes its purpose:

> O romance é uma reflexão sobre os acontecimentos políticos que marcaram o país entre 1964 e 1973 e, mais particularmente, entre 1968 e 1973. Seu aspecto fundamental é a discussão em torno da guerrilha urbana que eclodiu nesse período, em torno da militância política dentro das condições dadas pela época. É uma reflexão emocionada porque tenta captar a tensão, o clima, as esperanças imensas, o ódio e o desespero que marcaram esse extrema tentativa política que foi a guerrilha. (x)

Janete Gaspar Machado has suggested that like traditional journalistic reporting, *Em câmara lenta* fulfills the function of divulging information, but in this case information that could not be printed in newspapers because of strict press censorship (76). In this sense--and in this sense alone--the novel has affinities with the *romance-reportagem* that began to take on increasing importance during the military dictatorship by assuming what has been called a "para-journalistic" function. Given its autobiographical nature, however, the novel is actually closer to--and in many ways anticipates--the memorialism of Gabeira's *O que é isso, companheiro?* and Polari's fictionalized *Em busca do tesouro*, described by the author as "Uma ficção política vivida."

Like *Em busca do tesouro*, Tapajós's novel relates what must seem to many to be a "political fiction," but one the author and many of

---

[4] Tapajós was arrested by Operação Bandeirantes (OBAN) on 31 August 1969 on suspicion of belonging to a proscribed political organization, the Ala Vermelha of the Partido Comunista do Brasil. While in detention, "foi espancado e submetido a 'pau-de-arara' e a choques elétricos, ocasião em que presenciou outros acusados neste mesmo processo sofrendo as mesmas violências; ...foi levado ao DOPS e, de novo, espancado; ...sua esposa, presa na mesma ocasião, sofreu choques elétricos e, colocada ao lado do interrogado, [foi] tratada de maneira aviltante; ...foi ameaçado de retornar à Operação Bandeirantes ou ser entregue a um 'Esquadrão da Morte', se não concordasse com [o] auto." *Projeto Brasil nunca mais*, Tomo V, Vol. 3 ("A Tortura"), p. 563.

his contemporaries experienced. Similar to Callado's *Reflexos do baile*, Tapajós's novel attempts to reconstruct the recent past through a fragmented narrative structure which alternates--in the fashion of cinematic cross-cutting--multiple perspectives and time frames. An objective third person narrative voice traces the events that lead to the decision to take up arms against the regime, recounts some of the clandestine organization's activities, and relates its growing difficulties as the military offensive becomes increasingly successful. Although not presented in chronological order, these segments situate the action in time and space: the coup d'état of 1964 (63-66), the 1968 street battles between left and right leaning students in São Paulo (32-37), the December 1968 decree of the Fifth Institutional Act (43-50), and so forth. In these segments, a number of the most important figures are given first names--the guerrilla leader Fernando, his companion Marta, Lúcia (who follows her father's advice to go to Europe shortly after the AI-5)--but the main character is referred to only as "he" (*ele*), as in the following episode involving student street battles:

> Ele correu para a banca de jornais que havia na esquina e abrigou-se ali. Um coquetel Molotov explodiu a poucos metros, um ruído de sopro e a chama lambendo a parede. Olhou a rua, avaliando: por toda a extensão em frente à escola, os estudantes corriam, desviando-se dos projéteis que vinham dos telhados do prédio em frente, o prédio do Mackenzie. (32)

Additional segments with an omniscient third person narrator recount a failed attempt, by "seis estudantes e um venezuelano," to establish a guerrilla *foco* in the Amazon region. Although never specified as such, these segments clearly suggest the Partido Comunista do Brasil's effort to initiate a *foco* in the Araguaia region in 1970. Because of strict censorship, the events of the Araguaia region were not widely known by the Brazilian public until 1979. These segments are thus the closest to the *romance-reportagem* genre.

Em câmara lenta incorporates yet a third set of fragments narrated in the third person, this time in an indirect free style reflecting the consciousness of the participant-narrator. Chronologically, these fragments occur at a moment when the clandestine political organization has been decimated by the military and defeat is inevitable. The book's opening segment, punctuated by the phrase "É muito tarde," exemplifies this narration:

É tarde demais, mas é preciso continuar vazio, um sentimento
oco. Agora não dá para fazer nada, nem por ela nem por ninguém e o que fecha a garganta é o cerco, as armas sem nome,
as mãos sem nome, as peles vazias que se movem como se
fossem gente, o isolamento; cada dia mais perto, há quinze dias
nunca admitiria isso, embora já soubesse há muito tempo.
Nada deu certo, o fogo de artifício iluminou o céu, mas pouca
gente entendeu, nem podia entender e agora estamos sozinhos...
(14)

Through these fragments, the narrator provides a sense of the political
and existential crisis the characters--and the historical actors they repre-
sent--go through when faced with their own defeat. They had started out
idealistically thinking they could in fact change the world, but many of
their friends, colleagues, and loved ones were now either dead, in prison,
or in exile. They move forward almost through force of habit and a
sense of inexorability:

Para que continuar se não há mais esperança? Se já se sabe que
os gestos se despiram de tudo e são apenas aquilo que parecem:
gestos. Para que continuar? Um único motivo: não há nada
além disso que possa ser feito. O compromisso com os com-
panheiros já se despiu de todos os seus conteúdos e se tornou
apenas compromisso. Mas, mesmo assim, vazio, é ele que per-
mite a única possibilidade de olhar o mundo e aceitar uma
prorrogação do fim inevitável. (139)

Through these self-critical fragments, the novel gives a sense of the
tragedy of what the author, in his preface, calls the "ingênua generosida-
de daqueles que jogaram tudo, inclusive a vida, na tentativa de mudar o
mundo" (xi).

Other segments have a first person narration, normally introduced by quotation marks, in which the narrator recalls his youth, his
graduation from high school, and the events leading up to his political
radicalization. These segments are highly self-reflexive and critical, as
when the narrator reflects on his decision to "make the gesture" of getting involved in politics:

Eu me sentia disponível diante do mundo, e inquieto por causa
disso. Toda beleza era triste porque não decifrada--a avenida,

a praça e a praia, aparências de um mundo subterrâneo. Um mundo desconhecido, um mundo que eu precisava conhecer, para transformá-lo. Ou destruir-me. Esperávamos o sol, tomando cerveja no quiosque da praça. 'Buscaba el amañecer / Y el amañecer no era." Ainda não. Mas virá. Meus amigos daquele tempo não fizeram o gesto. Eu acabei de fazê-lo. Quem conheceu a morte sabe que o único crime é permanecer na superfície da vida. (31-32)

Although never clearly stated as such, the text suggests that these sections were written in prison as the author/narrator attempted to bring all the fragments together and make sense of the events of the preceding years:

> Hoje eu olho para essa parede em minha frente, a mesma parede de todos os dias, onde desfilam rostos conhecidos e ela me devolve, em suas manchas, os fragmentos do passado. Fragmentos: as peças do jogo de armar. E uma tênue linha de ligação, um fio quase invisível capaz de organizar as peças--a tensão. Cada momento não existiu isolado, nem se ligou linearmente aos outros. Eu, o lógico, o cartesiano: dilacerado. (112)

The past comes before him in fragments, as if they were pieces of a game or a puzzle he is attempting to put together. But wholeness is illusory: "Chave eternamente provisória, porque o jogo de armar é interminável: o próprio fato de organizar as peças representa a criação de uma peça nova--e exige uma nova solução" (113).

Toward the end of the novel, the "objective" third person, the indirect free third person and the first person narrative voices come together and fuse--only to separate again in the final section--in an episode in which the narrator and Marta meet in an apartment and make love. Marta had been the companion of Fernando, who had been killed by the military:

> Ela vestia uma blusa leve, clara e era noite de ano novo. Parecia uma rocha de firmeza, nunca duvidava da revolução, da vitória e reanimava a todos quando as coisas pareciam ir mal. Não permitia que ele vacilasse e ele seguia em frente apoiado na certeza dela. Terei te conhecido realmente, companheira?

Ou tudo isso era o imenso esforço que você fazia para enfrentar o mundo? (165)

By the time the first person narrator recalls the events of his political militancy, Marta had been arrested, tortured, and murdered by the police.

Marta's capture and death are related in yet another set of fragments narrated in the third person, each of which begins with the words, "Como em câmara lenta," which give the book its title. The first of these segments, which are the most dramatic and brutal of the novel, is but a paragraph long, and subsequent fragments gradually expand, providing more and more details of her refusal to cooperate with the police and the increasingly sadistic methods of torture used against her. Marta suffered the same fate as Patrícia in *Operação silêncio*: a "coroa de ferro... tinha estourado a cabeça" of both Patrícia and Marta, who may represent one and the same person (*Operação silêncio* 5, *Em câmara lenta* 172).

As a response to the knowledge of what happened to Marta-- "Agora eu sei. E saber não deixa mais nada além do ódio" (173)--the first person protagonist-narrator goes out into the streets and knowingly walks into the gunfire of a police ambush, committing what the third person narrator calls, in the book's last sentence, "a deserção definitiva." *Em câmara lenta*, in short, is a novel about tragic options forced by a sociohistorical context beyond the characters' control. It is in many ways an extremely pessimistic novel of disenchantment, disillusion and despair, an expression of anguish at the personal destruction and pain that was all too common in Brazil's recent political history. At the same time, however, it is a novel that recognizes that something must be done and that the only thing that cannot be accepted is the "deserção definitiva" of death.

Em câmara lenta's link to the cinema is structural, visible primarily through the cross-cutting of chronologically and spatially dispersed fragments and the constant, slow-motion repetition of the events leading to Marta's death. Márcio Souza's *Operação silêncio* renders the link much more explicit. Although it too deals with the armed struggle against the regime, it broadens the context to include the sometimes virulent, highly politicized artistic debates that also characterized the generation of 1968, "a geração que pensou colocar a revolução popular de uma outra perspectiva; atacando o revisionismo e a mentira da coexistência pacífica" (82).

Operação silêncio's title refers ironically to the code names of the many military operations unleashed against the regime's opposition, the most notorious of which was OBAN, or Operação Bandeirantes. Its protagonist, Paulo Conti, survived the repression, survived the armed struggle in which he did not directly participate, and survived the adversities faced by his generation. In *Em câmara lenta*, Tapajós writes what could be a description of Conti's situation:

> Olhar pra as pessoas que passam ao lado da rua: todos andam normalmente, não existe por aqui uma guerra? Não, não existe. Existem apenas combatentes derrotados, sobreviventes que teimam em ser apenas isto: sobreviventes. (85)

Conti survived, but has not been able to escape the doubts and perplexities of the generation. *Operação silêncio*, which is largely filtered through his consciousness, is his attempt to come to grips with what happened. As the narrator tells us:

> [Conti] Sabia o quanto tempo estivera abandonado, pensando de uma maneira pequena e constrangedora; estivera acuado e sem forças, mas agora podia desenhar para si um perfil mais adaptado ao tempo, um novo sumário de tudo o que tinha compartilhado, de todos aqueles momentos precários em que tinha sido jogado... o fascismo não estava derrotado; sabia o quanto essas remissões feriam... é que talvez através delas ele pudesse encontrar o caminho de volta, retornar à trajetória que iria esvaziar essa intolerável sensação de silêncio... (93)

Conti survived; many of his friends and loved ones did not. He survived in part because his chosen area of struggle--the cinema--did not involve taking up arms.

Operação silêncio is a discussion of art--specifically the cinema-- and revolution. But revolution means different things to different social and political sectors. Paulo Conti, the narrator, writes, "Sonhou com uma Mitchell; a *revolução redentora*, REVOLUÇÃO, agora uma palavra seqüestrada, ainda não tinha terminado; agonizava" (1). To which revolution does this passage refer? To the so-called "revolution" decreed by the military in 1964, or the "revolution that never was," the insurrection proposed by certain sectors of the Brazilian left in the post-1964 period?

The military had not only taken power, it had also confiscated the left's language. As Paulo Conti thinks to himself:

> ...E esta palavra, revolução, o que significava no Brasil, seqüestrada pela ditadura e amordaçada por um tratamento reacionário martelado na cabeça... a luta armada parecia um delírio e os verdadeiros revolucionários isolados como terroristas pelos terroristas. (82)

Although the novel discusses armed struggle and the intense ideological debates that led up to it, it neither romanticizes nor advocates armed struggle. Rather, like *Em câmara lenta*, it sees it as the tragic and frequently suicidal option it was.

Operação silêncio has a minimal plot. It is an admixture of *roman à clef*, essay, screenplay, and Oswaldian farse and is divided into two parts: I. "O sobrevivente Paulo Conti;" and II. "O rio de sangue."[5] In the first part, Paulo Conti walks through the streets of downtown São Paulo to the apartment of his producer Melusine, also known as the Embaixatriz, to discuss the possibility of directing an historical film. As he walks through the city, Conti recalls in chaotic fashion the events of the last ten years. Melusine, in the meantime, talks to her niece and awaits the arrival of her life-long friend, General Braylly, who will invest in the film.

The first part is divided into multiple fragments, many no more than a paragraph in length, each of which is introduced with a subtitle reminiscent of the writings of Mao Zedong. Such subtitles are often used with parodic effect, such as when the title is longer than the section's content:

A GRANDE REVOLUÇÃO CULTURAL PROLETÁRIA DESEJA APERFEIÇOAR E FORTALECER A DITADURA DO PROLETARIADO
Patrícia queria sair da casa dos pais. (46)

In some fragments, cinematic cross-cutting occurs at the level of the phrase, as in the following sequence which cuts between the Embai-

---

[5] Márcio Souza had at one point planned to make a film with the title *O rio de sangue*.

xatriz in her apartment and Conti in the street (spatial dislocations, or "cuts," indicated by "[/]"):

> A Embaixatriz tinha acordado cedo naquele dia, o apartamento estava sombrio, as janelas fechadas, as cortinas protegendo de luz a grande sala de estar. Ela, ainda de *robe de chambre*, está caminhando entre os móveis, sonolenta. Vai até a parede da sala e coloca um quadro na posição certa. Observa com um misto de ternura e sono o quadro: é uma fotografia do seu casamento. [/] Conti via que era uma doença que exatamente se coadunava com a manhã, se isso quisesse dizer alguma coisa! Mas o medo, companheiro dos sobreviventes, é que fazia Conti se sentir assim, enquanto a cidade se excitava, [/] enquanto a Embaixatriz ouvia o silêncio de sua casa entrecortado pelo rumor da rua lá embaixo. Era estranho que num apartamento tão grande ela não mantivesse criadagem, só ela e Maria, afilhada, companheira, empregada doméstica. [/] E assim, Conti e as mulheres estavam, é claro, tomados pela mesma poalha de vômito. (6)

Narrative fragmentation in the novel's first part takes many other forms as well, juxtaposing and alternating diverse forms of discourse, ranging from traditional narrative and description to poetry, diary entries, dialogues, and a multiplicity of references to the major figures and works of contemporary Brazilian and international pop culture.

In the novel's second part, written "de um só fôlego," Conti enters Melusine's apartment and talks in a rather bizarre and sexist fashion with her niece Maria. As General Braylly arrives Conti climbs atop a grandfather clock--reminiscent of the skyscraper in Oswald de Andrade's *Serafim Ponte Grande*--and observes his conversation with the Embaixatriz. Finally, Conti begins to shout obscenities at the producer and the general, who march in goose step around the apartment as the telephone transmits the socialist International hymn.

The second part consists largely of long, Joycean sequences without punctuation interspersed with dialogues and different forms of cinematic inserts. Cross-cutting in time and space creates an unlikely dialogue between the hard-line general, who used to play torture when he was a child, and the armed opposition to the regime, equating, to a degree, the opposing extremes. Flashbacks have Paulo Conti in Lima, Peru, narrating the storyline of *O rio de sangue* to a friend. The proposed film traces the massacre of the Incas by their Spanish conquerers, drawing parallels between the violence imposed on the Incas and that imposed on the Brazilian people by the military.

The central focus of *Operação silêncio* is the cinema, and more specifically the relationship between cinema and politics. Its dedication reads "à Ida, em 24 fotogramas por segundo." Its protagonist, Paulo Conti, is a filmmaker. Like poet Paulo Martins in Glauber Rocha's *Terra em transe* (1967), Conti is an artist torn between art and politics. As he walks through the streets of São Paulo he recalls the endless discussions held with friends and particularly with film critic PPP, a thinly disguised Paulo Emílio Salles Gomes.

They had frequently discussed the transformation--due to external circumstances--of the Cinema Novo movement from a well-intentioned political cinema to a cinema characterized by what Conti calls "irrational individualism." Although in the early 1960s it had been a major force in Brazilian cultural discourse, by the late 1960s Cinema Novo had lost its political perspective. It was concerned with reaching a broader public and no longer attempted to make film an area of political resistance.

> Conti sabia que muitos já tinham descoberto o ridículo na pregação de um púlpito visual. Será que estavam cansados de gritar no deserto e agora fazem filmes desertos? Desertores? Será que o martírio tinha chegado ao extremo? (4)

In his discussions Conti had attempted to rediscover the possible political uses of the cinema.

> Era necessário que numa situação como aquela, alguém tratasse de discutir a prática do cinema (política, engajamento, luta armada); alguém tinha de tentar chegar direto ao assunto. Falar de cinema era falar de política, a eficiência ideológica estava densamente incorporada à idéia de cinema e não se podia pensar o cinema sem essas coisas. (22)

The contradictions of the cinema, and especially political cinema, go far beyond the projected image. How can one create a cinema that challenges capitalism, the novel asks, when that cinema's modes of production are capitalist? Conti criticizes Brazilian cinema, and especially Cinema Novo, for having supported itself through the exploitation of the surplus value of the film crew's work (33). Politics, he suggests, rests not so much in the images of the film as in the movement of capital in its production. An unresolvable contradiction exists in the hope of creating a revolutionary cinema in a reactionary industry. But the contradiction goes even deeper. Due to an historical lack of production capital, Brazilian cinema has turned increasingly to the state for protection, subsidies, and production financing.[6] "E quem era o Estado," Conti asks. "O fascismo, a contra-revolução armada e na ofensiva" (67).

Although Conti criticizes the lack of political efficacy of Brazilian cinema, he in fact embodies its major contradictions. While hoping to create new forms of transformational cinema, he supports himself by writing scripts under a pseudonym for Good Beaver Productions: "comédias ditas de costume, massagistas, empregadinhas violadas por patrões" (5). The historical film he hopes to make is to be co-financed by the Embaixatriz and General Barylly, the encarnation of the authoritarian state. But Conti is aware of--and torn by--these contradictions. He likens the cinema to the myth of Sisyphus: "se estavam certos, estavam equivocados; carregar os sintomas da crise até o cume da violência nacional e deixar rolar de volta para baixo, perplexos" (60).

This perplexity belongs not only to filmmakers, but to many Brazilian artists and intellectuals who try to reconcile their art and the political conjuncture. *Operação silêncio* places the situation of Brazilian cinema into historical context, discussing the role and responsibilities of intellectuals vis-à-vis the reality of underdevelopment. Especially significant, in this sense, are the pages devoted to Euclides da Cunha, Graciliano Ramos, and Oswald de Andrade, three cultural and intellectual models.

According to Souza's rather convoluted indirect stream-of-consciousness prose, Euclides da Cunha was a victim of the tremendous gap between the imported philosophical and political ideas of Europe and the violence of Brazilian reality. He is an example of what Roberto Schwarz has called "as idéias fora do lugar." Da Cunha's Republican zeal crumbles when faced with the reality of the Brazilian backlands:

> Euclides da Cunha engavetava os logaritmos e escrevia
> no *Estado de São Paulo...* que o movimento de Canudos era

---

[6] For a discussion of cinema/state relations in Brazil, see Randal Johnson, *The Film Industry in Brazil*.

uma nova Vandeia e então re-escreveria tudo perdendo o zelo republicano frente à fome que sentia o camponês e frente ao medo e ao ódio dos revoltados... a defasagem só podia levar ao desespero que se apossou de Euclides até marcá-lo como um vingador irritadiço... (117-118)

The silence imposed after 1968 is likened to the silence imposed on Graciliano Ramos in the 1930s. And yet this silence, according to *Operação silêncio*, was unable to still Graciliano Ramos's critical realism. The act of writing, for Graciliano, became a means of existence against the dictatorship of Getúlio Vargas, a way of continuing to be a man and an artist. Graciliano wrote *Memórias do cárcere*, the narrator suggests, "embora e porque a ditadura possuísse cárceres e força para encarcerar a literatura" (132).

But Oswald de Andrade is, for Paulo Conti, the most perfect model for Brazilian intellectuals, since he had managed to bridge the gap between the artist and his time. Oswald's art

> ...representava um vínculo entre ele e o seu tempo escapando da defasagem e por ela se convertendo e se transformando e revolucionando de tal forma que em 1968 começaram a dizer que o Brasil tinha parado em 1930 exatamente por estar no palco do Teatro Oficina *O rei da vela*. (123)

Oswald managed to bridge the gap between his art and his epoch because he knew that art is an agressive weapon that can only assume transformational attitudes when subversion touches the very essence of art itself. But the novel suggests that Oswald has not yet been completely digested by Brazilian intellectuals. His work, says Conti,

> ...tinha sido tão forte que a sua reabilitação atual provocou os transtornos conhecidos e acabou jogando os intelectuais de encontro a sua própria condição revelando que continuavam decidindo sobre eles mesmos e sobre a sua época de uma forma totalmente solitária e aventureira. (116)

Like *Em câmara lenta*, *Operação silêncio* raises more questions than it answers. Through its complex discussion of art and politics, however, it suggests that the writer or filmmaker should follow Oswald de Andrade's example and strive to bridge the gap between art and contemporary society, creating works which are ideas in motion, "realizando e antecedendo a transformação" (32). Both works are testimonies of the failure to "realizar a transformação" through armed struggle against a repressive, authoritarian regime. Both novels are tortured reminders of the human costs of that struggle which, through discursive practices, has shifted to the level of the symbolic.

REFERENCES

Dassin, Joan. "Fear and the Armed Struggle in Brazil." Unpublished paper prepared for the Social Science Research Council Seminar on "The Culture of Fear," Buenos Aires, 30 May-1 June, 1985.

O filme curto. 2 vol. Org. Carlos Roberto Rodrigues de Souza. São Paulo: Secretaria Municipal de Cultura, Departamento de Informação e Documentação Artísticas, Centro de Pesquesa de Arte Brasileira, 1980.

Johnson, Randal. *The Film Industry in Brazil: Culture and the State.* Pittsburgh: U of Pittsburgh P, 1987.

Machado, Janete Gaspar. *Constantes ficcionais em romances brasileiros nos anos 70.* Florianópolis: Editora da Universidade Federal de Santa Catarina, 1981.

Polari, Alex. *Em busca do tesouro.* Rio de Janeiro: Codecri, 1982.

Projeto Brasil Nunca Mais. 12 vol. São Paulo: Arquidiocese de São Paulo, 1985.

Souza, Márcio. *Operação silêncio.* Rio de Janeiro: Civilização Brasileira, 1979.

Tapajós, Renato. *Em câmara lenta.* 2nd rev. ed. São Paulo: Editora Alfa-Omega, 1979.

THE PRISON-HOUSE OF MEMOIRS: SILVIANO SANTIAGO'S *EM LIBERDADE*

K. David Jackson
University of Texas at Austin

> ...que par pudieras ser entre mil pares
> (Orlando Furioso a Don Quijote de la
> Mancha)
>
> Mas julgue-o quem não pode experi-
> mentá-lo (*Os Lusíadas*)
>
> enovelo-me ou libero-me (*Em liber-
> dade* 233)

Simulation and "De-writing"

In his 1981 fictional work, *Em liberdade*, Silviano Santiago (b. 1936) confects counterfeit memoirs of renowned author Graciliano Ramos (1892-1953).[1] Ramos's *Memórias do cárcere* (1953) serve as

---

[1] Memorialism is a strong tradition in modern Brazilian literature. Antecedents include literary texts--from Machado de Assis (*Memórias póstumas de Brás Cubas*) to Modernist works (Oswald de Andrade's *Memórias sentimentais de João Miramar*) and contemporary prose (Sérgio Sant'Anna's *Confissões de Ralfo*)--historical and political memoirs, such as recent works on early anarchist and communist movements in Brazil (corresponding in part with Graciliano's memoirs of the Vargas "Estado Novo" of 1937-45), and personal or cultural memoirs, exemplified by Pedro Nava's sweeping six-volume series.

Why is memorialism a dominant trend in Brazil, even gaining strength in current letters, while it is weakly represented in Spanish

Santiago's model to exemplify in contemporary Brazilian prose one of the most prominent currents of the postmodern aesthetic, the reproduc-

---

American literature? One theory would be the "search for identity" that has especially characterized Brazilian civilization since colonial times, expressed in the phrase of historian Stuart Schwartz, "Who Are We?" The memoir could be related in this context to the tradition of colonial chronicles of discovery or description. For more than two centuries these descriptive essays directed the narrative voice toward a single absent and distant center, which was the Portuguese king and court, thus supporting a strong literary tradition joining the epistle, almost in the form of a travel diary, to the descriptive essay.

In a study of poetry and fiction in autobiography, Antônio Candido finds a form of confessionalism in colonial letters that treats reality with techniques of the imagination and inscribes personal events with universal significance, within a sophisticated form of dialectical movement (52-53). Candido traces the Brazilian memoir as creative literature, raising the local to the universal and the particular to the generic, through the Arcadist Cláudio Manuel da Costa's "mini-autobiografia" (*Apontamentos para se unir ao Catálogo dos Acadêmicos da Academia Brasílica dos Renascidos*), Modernism's Drummond (*Boitempo, Menino antigo*) and Murilo Mendes (*A idade do serrote*), and Pedro Nava's contemporary memoirs (*Baú de ossos*). As shall be seen, Santiago draws Cláudio Manuel da Costa into a fictional structure that Edelweiss has termed an "alterbiography."

Alfredo Bosi (470-78) discusses the memoir in the context of contemporary psychological or intimist literature, whose model is nineteenth-century interior realism (Chekhov, Machado de Assis, Eça de Queirós, etc). The psychological dimension tends to interiorize the chronicle, which treats themes of childhood and education as dramas of social consciousness or private desire and emotion. While writers such as Cyro dos Anjos used the classical rhetorical devices of the memoir, producing elegant prose, reliance by others on the interior monologue indicates a passage from psychological to metaphorical and metaphysical prose, while still maintaining the structure of the memoir, as exemplified in works of Osman Lins, Autran Dourado, and Clarice Lispector.

tion of the real through simulation.[2] The aesthetic of simulation, whose principles Jean Baudrillard describes as the signs of ritual, excess, and equivalence, provides one of the most accessible critical approaches to Santiago's postmodernist strategy, which could be termed the "de-writing" (implying borrowing or cannibalization) of a noted memoir.[3] As a simulacrum, Santiago's fiction is built first of all on the interplay of language, memory, and history as found in Graciliano's prison memoirs: *Em liberdade* questions the relationship of history and fiction, of speech and language, of thought and reality. The restraints and limits set on literary language by Santiago--the challenge to composition that "imprisons" the memoir--are inherent to the act of simulation, where the linguistic sign functions through an oxymoron of confined freedom (the latitude to produce an "exact" copy) that, on a more abstract level, parallels the author's problematization of mimesis: "[the] sign is free only to produce the signs of equivalence" (Baudrillard 86). Simulation ostensibly binds the imagination to the limits of Graciliano's inimitable style and perspective, which paradoxically become the subject of imitation, while equivalence suggests linguistic ambiguity and conceptual repetition.

---

[2] Following Jean Baudrillard's analysis, writing as simulation produces hyperrealism and the joy of an excess of meaning: ". . . a thrill of vertiginous and phony exactitude, of alienation and of magnification, of distortion in scale, of excessive transparency all at the same time" (50). Secondly, simulation is both ritual and illusion. Reality is ritualized as "a striking resemblance of itself" (45), while language constructed on other language produces the illusion of referentiality: "the metalinguistic illusion duplicates and completes the referential illusion" (148). Thirdly, for Baudrillard the art of simulation is capable of representing a "social microcosm" (23), thus attributing to the text the status of a critical consciousness.

[3] Derived from early modernist practices, the procedure at work, described in terms of Gregory Ulmer's essay on the "lessons of the modernist revolution in representation" (87), can be traced to the primacy of geometrical fragmentation in techniques of collage and mime: "The deconstruction is accomplished in fact by borrowing the very terms used by the host work itself... and remotivating them, detaching them... from one conceptual set or semantic field and reattaching them to another..." (93).

Assuming a postmodern stance,[4] Santiago's work exploits illusions of equivalence and verisimilitude among several carefully constructed yet "artificial" conceptual or semantic areas, thereby confusing testimony with invention, matrix with sequel, authenticity with illegitimacy, host with parasite, convention with counterfeit, and narration with simulation. *Em liberdade* affirms the ambiguity and even reversibility of these categories by reproducing Graciliano Ramos' voice in a narrative that purports to be a recuperation of the master's yet unrevealed memoirs of Brazilian life in the late 1930s while maneuvering within a prison-house of restrictive forms and frames that challenge the writer to act through disguise and duplicity in the role of artist and performer, the absent eminence behind the text. Santiago's counterfeit or false memoirs of Graciliano Ramos free the pseudo-narrator from a literal prison-house only to lead him, along with his postmodern readers, into other prison-houses of language and of genre--respectively, Graciliano's characteristic style and the nature of the historical memoir. Working within the limitations of chosen linguistic and generic models, Santiago's diary amounts to a portrait of the postmodern writer as escape artist.

"Ficção e Confecção" [Fiction and Confection]

In his prison memoirs, Graciliano Ramos recalls the mysterious, threatening telephone call at the beginning of 1936 that would interrupt his life, culminating on the 3rd of March with his arrest by an army lieutenant and long peregrination from the headquarters of the 20th Battalion in Alagoas to the prison colony on Ilha Grande, near Rio de Janeiro: "Comecei a perceber que as minhas prerrogativas bêstas de

---

[4] For a view of the postmodern aesthetic in Brazilian literature and culture, sources include the special issue of the *Revista do Brasil: literatura anos 80* (Ano 2, Nº. 5, 1986) edited by Heloísa Buarque de Hollanda, Flora Süssekind's *Literatura e vida literária* (Rio de Janeiro: Zahar, 1985), Rodolfo Franconi's "Erotismo e poder na ficção brasileira dos anos 80" (Diss. Vanderbilt, 1987), *Cultura brasileira: tradição/contradição* (Rio de Janeiro: Zahar/Funarte, 1987), and essays by José Miguel Wisnik and others.

pequeno-burguês iam cessar, ou tinham cessado" (1: 22).[5] The interrelationship between fiction and confession in this and other works by Graciliano Ramos has been well documented in critical interpretations:

> Ficção e confissão constituem, pois, na obra de Graciliano Ramos, pólos que ligou por uma ponte, tornando-os contínuos e solidários... (Candido 81)

As Candido observes (75), literature is both a form of resistance and a source of equilibrium against the disorder Graciliano perceives in social constrictions and personal experience. Skepticism and negation in the portrayal of experience further conceal a primary or primitive current that rejects all social conventions and motivation: "Que sou eu senão um selvagem, ligeiramente polido, com uma tênue camada de verniz por fora?" (Candido 23). Memoirs are in this sense perhaps his greatest works of fiction, rejecting the values and norms of society while unifying the contradictory impulses of his world view:

> Daí a importância das *Memórias do Cárcere*, onde se encontram homem e ficcionista, e o pessimismo de um é completado pela solidariedade participante do outro.... (Candido 81)

The prison memoirs, begun in 1947, lacked only the final chapter at the time of the author's death in 1953, as testified in a postscript by his son Ricardo Ramos. Having noticed over a period of time his father's apparent reluctance to finish the memoirs, he asked what the nature of the last chapter would be. Graciliano replied, "Sensações de liberdade" (2: 306). The missing final chapter forms the nucleus of Silviano Santiago's fictional work, *Em liberdade* (1981), whose introductory materials recapitulate the above information and identify the text as Graciliano's "lost" manuscript, a diary covering his first two months and 13 days of liberty, from the 13th of January to the 26th of March, 1937.

---

[5] The same quote, but without the adjective "bêstas," is repeated in the "editor's" note to *Em liberdade* (11).

Postmodern "Grands récits": Imprisoned Memoirs

This essay explores interpretations of *Em liberdade* as ritual and illusion, departing from theories of postmodern culture put forth by Arthur Kroker and David Cook, according to which Santiago's work can be said to construct, necessarily within a negative dimension, one of the "grands récits" of the age of a new primitivism:

> We're living through a great story--an historical moment of implosion, cancellation and reversal; that . . . traces a great arc of reversal, connecting again to an almost mythic sense of primitivism as the primal of technological society. (15)

In Santiago's text primitivism is centered in an historical retrogression linked by Kroker and Cook to a will to self-liquidation, itself congruent with the pessimism and skepticism of Graciliano's memoirs: "[t]he governing logic of technological society is *the hyper-atrophication of emotional functions and the hyper-exteriorization of the mind*" (Kroker and Cook 15). Another primitivist vein of the postmodern in the work, set forth in an essay by Santiago, is represented by the location and (re)production of a permanent discourse of tradition within modernism's aesthetic of transgression and destruction (Santiago, "Permanência" 115). In this case, the historical memoir or confession serves as a primary model underlying the regressive simplicity of the modern primitive. Yet a third level of primitivist reading, suggested by the same essay, can be found in the utopian and anti-normative orientation of Graciliano's memoirs: an indigenous primitivism, the "saber selvagem" emanating from the "criminally" different, recapitulating the language of Oswald de Andrade's radical "Manifesto Antropófago," is posited as the Carib and cannibal rebellion against concepts of an imported European and alien culture ("Permanência" 127-28). Santiago's memoir is constructed, as a consequence, not on the apparent tradition of confession but rather through postmodern confection using ingredients of primitivism and simulation. The present analysis will carry Santiago's careful use of simulation into the field of metaphor, as developed in Hayden White's "visual icons," while allying Brazilian primitivist thought with Michel Serres's illuminating work on parasites. Santiago's "magical escape" from a self-imposed prison-house of writing, itself a simulation, will be viewed through the conversion of history and language into myth and the formal exploitation of contradictions and self-conscious play in neo-baroque antitheses.[6]

Two Brazilian Prison-Houses

Fredric Jameson's *The Prison-House of Language* argues against the "attachment to the essentially cryptographic nature of reality," as seen in Lévi-Strauss (142), and critically examines the notion of the predominance of language over history in modern formalist thought. The critique could well accuse Santiago's self-conscious and referential memoir on several points: first, in the epistolary novel, as in the memoir, "real" events are replaced by literary ones, as the writer calls attention to the activity of writing itself, which becomes the new subject (199-200). Secondly, the binary structure equates perceptions of identity and difference, since "every linguistic perception holds in its mind at the same time an awareness of its own opposite" (35); and, finally, an alleged defect in the structure itself controls analysis by confining investigation and truth to an infinite, regressive sequence of metalanguages (208). *Em liberdade* constitutes Santiago's fictional "reply" to these charges by casting the mythical with the existential and reviving neo-baroque play with language and experience.

---

[6] According to the *Princeton Encyclopedia of Poetry and Poetics*, baroque style can be viewed as "an eternal phenomenon, recurrent in all ages" (67). Traits of the baroque revived in Santiago's work include its conceits and wit, "rhetorical figures such as metaphor, the element of time, the dramatic situation. . . and the implied world view;" especially apparent is "a tendency to manipulate time and exploit its paradoxes" (67). The illusion of socio-literary identity in Santiago's prose notwithstanding, a central concern is resolution of the problem of opposites (68), linked to an outlook of disequilibrium and disillusionment, represented by freedom and imprisonment, skepticism and commitment, individual and archetypal, etc. The term neo-baroque has been applied to other contemporary Latin American writers.

Linguistic and Generic Models

Throughout the diary, Santiago's narrator constantly reflects on the prison-house of language and genre, which becomes the principal theme, overshadowing simulation of the sociopolitical environment of Rio de Janeiro in the 1930s. The narrator becomes aware of a fictional trap in the architecture of his diary: Is the writer to be a mere scribe of events, a privileged recipient of history following a score already composed; or can his imagination be called original, shaping an intrinsic language that would invariably transform the diary into a novel that, ironically, no longer narrated the truth? Is there a logic in the narrator's selection of events, or is meaning controlled by chance, embedded in a second or subtext to the diary (125)? These are questions of writing itself, the suggestion that the text, indeed all of writing, is a fiction among fictions, whose true or pre-text, if it exists, is beyond the reach of our "frightful nothingness."[7] What might seem initially to be a principle of legitimacy and difference in Santiago's text is revealed by this line of inquiry to be one of identity and convergence. The reader asks "Who is the true author of the diary?" and the narrator answers "The story writes itself." By choosing to write in a double prison-house, that is, recasting Graciliano's memoirs as history and story, memoir and fable, event and simulacrum, Santiago provides the reader with the subtext of his own release, as author, from structures of entrapment and enclosure.

Literary hesitations and doubts about the nature of the historical memoir as a genre can be found in the opening chapter of the actual *Memórias do cárcere*: the inevitable and corrosive passage of time; the disproportion between narration and events; possible effects on the lives of living personages who could be misrepresented, etc. On a purely literary level is what Graciliano himself perceives to be a prison-house of the memoir as a genre, its capacity to deform or distort events, and the oppression of literary language through laws of grammar and syntax.

---

[7] "[C]ar j'entrai tout à coup dans un néant affreux," writes Santiago's narrator, quoting "uma passagem das Cartas Persas, de Montesquieu," while perhaps considering himself to be the "persa alagoano (que) se vestia de canibal caeté na noite carioca" (58-59). Graciliano suggests in his memoirs that through the difficult act of writing an author may emerge "lentamente daquele mundo horrível de treva e morte" (*Memórias* 1: 9).

Of the first of these, he writes, "Repugnava-me fazer do livro uma espécie de romance" (7), a recognition of the inevitable literariness of the memoir that converts history into fiction through the act of writing. Graciliano addresses the problem of language in what could be taken as a statement of the rules of the game for his future textual double: "começamos oprimidos pela sintaxe e acabamos às voltas com a delegacia de ordem política e social, mas, nos estreitos limites a que nos coagem a gramática e a lei, ainda nos podemos mexer" (8). Liberty is to be found in the narrow ground for maneuvering within fixed limits: "Liberdade completa ninguém disfruta" (8). The prison memoirs, in their literal and figurative enclosures, embody the principle of neo-baroque literary play that epitomizes Santiago's textual labyrinth.

Yet another germ of the conceptual play in the contemporary text is expressed by Graciliano in his unexpected baroque approximation of the notions of prison, pleasure, and freedom: "Naquele momento a idéia da prisão dava-me quase prazer: via ali um princípio de liberdade" (1:19). The confining freedom of prison would exempt Graciliano from the unpleasant bourgeois duties of his office and the horrors of provincial political bureaucracy, while granting him the only time and tranquility possible in which to correct the manuscript of an unpublished novel. In a structural inversion typical of carnivalization, freedom and pleasure come into being through imprisonment. The situation is already a double one of fiction within fiction, approaching a continuum, as Graciliano describes his character's desire to write a novel that could reach beyond the humid, black prison bars that confine him (1:19). It is, after all, the act of writing that leads to the atemporal and ahistorical consciousness of freedom. As in a baroque conceit, *Em liberdade* strives for expressive freedom through a structure of limitations and enclosures either inherent to or imposed upon history and writing. The prison-houses of the text, intimate counterparts that make the principle of liberty possible, explore the interplay between historical memoir and fiction in a way that considers both to be paradigms, forms, or patterns that underlie the myth of experience and the art of representation.

History and Myth

In his essay "The Historical Text as Literary Artifact," Hayden White questions the basis of historical consciousness and writing, in particular the relationship of the historical narrative to literature, by comparing historical documents to literary texts. In his structuralist view, White finds that "verbal fictions," comparable to the function of myth in literature, form the external models of historical representation:

> Viewed in a purely formal way, a historical narrative is not only a reproduction of the events reported in it, but also a complex of symbols which gives us directions for finding an icon of the structure of those events in our literary tradition. (88)

More than a reproduction of events, the narrative "complex of symbols" contains the icons of a particular literary tradition that endow the unfamiliar with meaning. The mythic structure, embedded in pure form and language, diverts discursive writing into stories and fictions. To read the prison memoirs of Graciliano Ramos, following White's concept, would be to winnow out the patterns and forms of cultural convention capable of revealing structural icons that are encoded in the memoir as genre. In turn, these icons function as the deep framework for interpreting the structural meaning of socio-political and literary reality.

In "Narrativa histórica e narrativa ficcional," Benedito Nunes further provides a critical basis for assessing the fictional component of historical and scientific narratives, which are themselves interrelated:

> A História, investigação e registro de fatos sociais das civilizações, recorre a leis gerais, que são próprias - ciência, e também utiliza a ficção; a ciência pode limitar-se ao registro de fatos, e a Ficção, por intermédio do romance, do drama, alcança, honrando a observação aristotélica de que a poesia é 'mais filosófica do que a história', um nível de generalidade semelhante ao do pensamento científico... O caráter de ciência, conquistado pelo conhecimento histórico, não suprime a base narrativa, que mantém o seu nexo com o ficcional. (12)

The fictive in the historical, the implications of its narrative bias, is yet another prison-house for the author of memoirs, since writing is considered by White to be alienated from the deeper symbolic truths of language and form.

Verbal Icons: The Drop of Sweat and the Key

The episodes of the drop of sweat and the key in *Em liberdade* function as White's verbal icons, quasi-parables of the condition of the symbolic forms underlying writer and written. In a short entry to the diary titled "Antes do jantar," reminiscent, as is much in Graciliano, of Machado de Assis, the narrator notices that a drop of sweat produced by the intolerable heat of a tropical afternoon has fallen onto the written page:

> Calor insuportável hoje pela tarde. Enquanto relia algumas páginas deste diário, esperando a hora do jantar, o suor foi tomando conta do meu rosto, até que pingou uma gota na página escrita. Fiquei pensando nela e na sua curta e passageira existência. Ao contrário do arabesco no papel feito pela tinta da caneta, a gota de suor vai desaparecer tão logo passe a limpo este manuscrito. (99)

The drop of sweat and the page, the liquid and the solid, constitute a microcosm of the antithesis between categories of individual and generic, transitory and conventional: the drop of sweat will evaporate, while the writing will be carried into type, print, multiple editions with neatly formed words. The human dimension of the writer, however, is limited to the drop of sweat and its short, passing existence:

> Se todos os praticantes da literatura pensassem um minuto nas implicações deste corredor da produção e da indústria do livro, deixariam com que a maioria dos seus escritos tivessem a transitoriedade de uma gota de suor na página escrita, em uma tarde de calor insuportável. (99)

Such is the prison-house of a writer faced with the dilemma of literary production.

The metaphor of the keys in "Quarta-feira de cinzas," another entry in the diary, carries the concept of incarceration to the level of societal myth:

> Não é conseguindo que se abram as portas da prisão que se chega mais depressa à liberdade. É não deixando que as pessoas mais chegadas venham correndo fechá-las de novo. A

saída da cadeia se dá através de um corredor com milhares de
portas semelhantes e abertas. Todos os amigos estão prepa-
rados para serem carcereiros: cada um fecha uma das sucessivas
portas. Este é o lado trágico e infeliz da situação. O problema,
para mim, foi sempre o de enxergar, primeiro, a chave da cela
na mão da pessoa com quem ia conversar. Antes que fizesse
uso da chave, lançava-me contra ela impetuosamente, arrebatan-
do-a. Assim, fui evitando que as portas que transpunha no
cotidiano fossem fechadas. (145)

The most certain path to liberty, states the narrator, does not lie in
getting the prison doors to open or even in the social world, where every
person is prepared to become a jailor by shutting each of the doors of
being or possibility. Incarceration is the narrator's structural icon of
social interchange and history, revealed through the unsuspected use of
the keys, far beyond their original and apparent social purpose. The
icons of the drop of sweat and the key represent the enigmatic, coded
nature of experience, resolved through allegory, and further constitute a
defense of the "prison-house" in face of the challenge posed by Jameson.

Flypaper and the Prison-House of Language

The narrator's parable of the flypaper illustrates the revolutionary potential of form against repression. Entering a tavern in suburban
Maceió, Santiago's narrator, an upstanding citizen, orders cheap *cachaça*,
to the consternation and hostility of the bartender. A bum at the corner
table, however, receives attentive, even obsequious treatment. The
narrator becomes aware of the shameful barriers that separate him from
society's lower depths. Now defending the bum from the hostile opinions
of the bourgeoisie, the narrator notes his uncommon verbal aptitude, his
ability to tell rich stories that fill time with the food of his imagination:
"The doughy speech of the bum":

Aproximando-se do vagabundo, conversando com ele, desco-
bre-se que tem uma qualidade rara na nossa sociedade que se
urbaniza: mercê de uma facilidade verbal incomum, é sempre
capaz de narrar histórias com facilidade e jeito, com ares de
quem mantém contato diuturno com o ofício da ficção. É capaz
de passar horas alimentando com a sua imaginação o tempo,

tornando-o estofado e prazeroso, de tal forma que o correr das horas passa desapercebido do ouvinte. É a maneira que encontra para 'prender' o grupo e minimizar as agruras da solidão noturna. (75)

The narrator is entranced by the directness of the bum's critical vision, the existential perceptiveness of his marginality, and becomes trapped like a fly or mosquito on his inverted literary medium, flypaper:

A fala pastosa do vagabundo (sempre motivo de asco) é pastosa porque tem o ponto da cola e do açúcar. Suas narrativas são como o papel pega-mosca, onde o mosquito desprevenido cai e de onde não consegue mais alçar vôo.
Quantas noites fiquei preso no papel!" (75).

Graciliano's own explanation of his uncompromised freedom of observation and description in the prison memoirs can be related to the bum's irresistible storytelling and social marginality:

Tendo exercido vários ofícios, esqueci todos, e assim posso mover-me sem nenhum constrangimento. Não me agarram métodos, nada me força a exames vagarosos. Por outro lado, não me obrigo a reduzir um panorama, sujeitá-lo a dimensões regulares, atender ao paginador e ao horário do passageiro do bonde. Posso andar para a direita e para a esquerda como um vagabundo, deter-me em longas paradas, saltar passagens desprovidas de interêsse, passear, correr, voltar a lugares conhecidos. Omitirei acontecimentos essenciais ou mencioná-los-ei de relance, como se os enxergasse pelos vidros pequenos de um binóculo; ampliarei insignificâncias, repeti-las-ei até cansar, se isto me parecer conveniente. (9-10)

The telling of pleasurable stories, the flypaper narratives of 1001 nights, is capable of inverting the prison-house of social difference through the introduction of a parasitical metaphor.

"Escritofagia": Host/Guest, Eater/Eaten

In the essay "The Critic as Host," J. Hillis Miller considers the implications of M. H. Abrams's statement that "any history which relies on written texts becomes an impossibility." Miller addresses questions of textual identity and difference in the context of historical referents by using the critical metaphor of host and parasite. Santiago's narrator touches on the same theme by defining the reader as a parasite on the memoir, a voyeur who invades "real" action with his imagination:

> Sem o perceber, o ouvinte já se imiscui parasitariamente na ação real, esquecendo-se de que, para ele, é apenas imaginária. Somos todos *voyeurs* da conquista alheia, invejosos; ou então corpos no palco para os demais *voyeurs*, orgulhosos. Se não vemos o quadro pintado com as palavras alheias, é porque estamos narrando a ação. (narrar é mais importante do que experimentar). (30)

If, as in Brazilian *antropofagia*, the cannibal/narrator can be defined only in relation to his supposed opposite, a victim/reader who will serve as his food, the primary text may already support an uncanny alien meaning as a necessary and dangerous counterpart, its difference.[8] The parasitical relationship is described by Miller as one of double antithesis:

> 'Para' is an 'uncanny' double antithetical prefix signifying at once proximity and distance, similarity and difference, interiority and exteriority, something at once inside a domestic economy and outside it, something simultaneously this side of the boundary line, threshold, or margin, and at the same time beyond it, equivalent in status and at the same time secondary or subsidiary, submissive, as of guest to host, slave to master. (441)

Following his argument, the dynamic of both cannibal and parasite would question boundaries and limits, suggesting their interpenetration. The

---

[8] This is the concept of difference developed by Jacques Derrida in *L'Ecriture et la différence* (Paris: Éditions du Seuil, 1967); *A escritura e a diferença*. Trans. Maria Beatriz Marques Nizza da Silva (São Paulo: Perspectiva, 1971).

apparent polarity of the relationship host/guest, or eater/eaten, with its superimposition of intimate kinship and ritual enmity, is transmuted into the complexity and openness of reciprocal obligation, in which one element fulfills the role of the other. If in the world of literature the text becomes a food needed by each, thus establishing an interplay of asymmetrical relationships, in the Brazilian context writer and reader can equally and interchangeably be identified as "escritófagos," or cannibals of the written word.

The relevance of the cannibal model to Santiago's memoir can be further intensified by returning to the bum and the key in the light of Michel Serres's work, *The Parasite*. The bum's "doughy speech" is both a food and a medium of exchange, placed by social convention outside the reach of hosts or bourgeois diners. Following Serres, the bum pays for his food with words:

> The parasite is invited to the table d'hôte; in return, he must regale the other diners with his stories and his mirth. To be exact, he exchanges good talk for good food; he buys his dinner, paying for it in words. It is the oldest profession in the world. (34)

The parasite thereby invents something new by changing the order of things. The bum/parasite not only exchanges his voice for matter (sound for solid) but also speaks in a logic previously considered irrational and ungovernable. Dependent on the host's table for trapping his food with words, the bum's revenge is the flypaper of his irresistible tales. As Serres observes, "Each society allows a linguistic specie that can be exchanged advantageously for food. Influential and powerful groups are able to diffuse a forced lexicon in that way" (34). As are lexical and economic relationships, language and specie are subject to the laws of the prison-house.

Turning to the case of the key, the narrator exhausts himself by seeking to conquer the social and existential barriers imposed by those who wield it through his copious use of conventional language: "Essa corrida com barreiras tornou-me um ágil atleta da palavra. . . Lança-va-me à conversa com a desenvoltura de um advogado baiano" (146). Words are the specie through which the prisoner/parasite attempts to reenter the world of social exchange, as he puts it, with the tactics of a general but avoiding the word "cadeia" at all costs (146).

> Tornei-me palavroso, bom papo e curioso de todo e qualquer
> assunto que viesse do meu interlocutor. Ganhava terreno, avan-
> çava, conduzia a batalha a bom termo, via-me vitorioso. Um
> general teria inveja das minhas táticas de conquista do adversá-
> rio na chamada vida social. (146)

But because the prisoner lacks the bum's saving indifference, he therefore cannot find the free language he seeks. Santiago's postmodern
narrative in this sense expresses both the alienation of the different and
the convention of imitation.

For a literary author, Miller considers the parasitic system by
which the host becomes the food to argue in favor of the "hyperbolic
exuberance" of a given text or language taken to its limits.

> [Deconstructive strategy] provides a model for the relation of
> critic to critic, for the incoherence within a single critic's lan-
> guage, for the asymmetrical relation of critical text to poem, for
> the incoherence within any single literary text, and for the
> skewed relation of a poem to its predecessors. (444)

The weight of the prison-house of language can thereby be reduced or
disguised, he asserts, by its translation into an expansive universe,
through the mutual reversibility of roles, and by the metamorphosis of
historical description into myth:

> The complexity and equivocal richness, my discussion of 'para-
> site' implies, resides in part in the fact that there is no conceptu-
> al expression without figure, and no intertwining of concept and
> figure without an implied story, narrative, or myth, in this case
> the story of the alien guest in the home. (443)

Neo-Baroque Sleight of Hand

Santiago places Graciliano's latest memoirs within an elaborate
neo-baroque frame whose counterfeit purpose, while transparent to the
reader, is to affirm the text's legitimacy through a carefully prepared
provenance. The "editor" of *Em liberdade* who has come into possession
of the manuscript states the case for its authenticity: revised and typed
by Graciliano in 1946, it was confided to a friend to be kept until 25

years after the author's death; in 1952 the author decided to burn the diary and so instructed his friend, who lied in saying that he had carried out the request. Because of the editor's acquaintance and long conversations with the unnamed friend, upon the latter's death in 1965 his widow, having found the editor's address on top of the manuscript, mailed it to his teaching post at Rutgers University.

The editor affirms the impeccable credentials of his dossier: he has guarded the manuscript in secret another 15 years; he has obeyed the author's 25 year restriction before publication; he has even after a fashion "solicited" the originals from the author, who never denied other manuscripts to an editor; he has not revealed the friend's name; and he has accepted responsibility for the consequences of his act. Yet even within the legalistic presentation of facts, dates, and events, the editor hits upon uncanny literary parallels that suggest deceptive, recurring patterns or rhythms: the friend whose lie saved the diary is compared to the story of Max Brod and the works of Kafka; the editor himself is at work on a presumably unpublished chapter of Gide's *The Counterfeiters*. Perhaps the editor has confused his editing of a true counterfeit with the interlacing of footnotes in the Brazilian manuscript that identify marginal notations, erasures, arrows, parentheses, quotations, additions in red ink, or the use of a different kind of paper. As if to define mimesis as sincere deception, the editor reminds the reader that his Graciliano considered the manuscript at hand, his final chapter, to be the contrary of what a reader habituated to prison memoirs was prepared to accept: "Não vou dar-lhe o livro que exige de mim. Dou-lhe em troca o que você não quer... Estou trabalhando com a sua decepção. É ela a preciosa matéria-prima deste diário" (128).[9]

---

[9] While toying within the prison-house of textual criticism, the complex frame of *Em liberdade* at the same time firmly places the memoir in a central tradition of Western fiction that questions the nature of authorship and writing. In the prologue to the *Ingenioso hidalgo Don Quijote de la Mancha* (1605), the narrator exploits mimesis: "que en [la orden de Naturaleza] cada cosa engendra su semejante." Pronouncing himself devoid of the talent necessary to write the discreet and intelligent book of his dreams, the author is reduced to dissimulation of tradition: "Pero yo, que, aunque parezco padre, soy padrasto de Don Quijote, no quiero irme con la corriente del uso . . . ." The play between author, narrator and text--where the appearance of truth coexists with the dis-

Recurring Rhythms: Memoir and Myth

The historical memoir can be displaced by the establishment of a rhythm underlying the recurrence of events that casts the diary into literature and myth. This rhythm is achieved in Santiago's diary by the introduction of a countertheme from colonial Brazilian history that also expresses the metaphor host/guest and the aesthetic of simulation. In early March, 1937, the narrator of *Em liberdade* has a dream, presumably triggered by too much champagne and whisky, that draws him back to 1789. The dream's main character is also a prisoner writing a diary, none other than the poet and rebel Cláudio Manuel da Costa (1729-89)

---

guising of fiction--is a practice firmly established in Portuguese literature from the *cantigas de amigo*, where the voice of a young maiden flows from a masculine pen. In Renaissance prose, the *Prymera parte da cronica do emperador Clarimundo donde os Reys de Portugal descendem* (1522), a chivalric novel by humanist João de Barros, presents itself as being a translation of a previously existent Hungarian manuscript that relates the life of a fictitious "Emperor Clarimundo," who in turn is the false father of Count Henry of Burgundy, who is the true father of D. Afonso Henriques, the first king of Portugal. This fiction did not pretend to deceive its cultured readers; its purpose was to create a textual mythology capable of transforming history into legend, transfiguring royal characters into heroes of magical adventures of chivalric novels. Disguised in verisimilitude, the author of this "translation" made use of fiction in order to candidate himself to the post of royal historiographer, which he became as author of the *Decades of Asia*, texts which themselves relate the truth of distant lands unknown to the author: *Asia de Joam de Barros dos fectos que os Portugueses fizeram no descobrimento e conquista dos mares e terras do Oriente* (1552). To the extent that the chronicle approximates fictional narrative to contemporary history, the *Decades*, like the memoir in question, "translated" distant historical reality, veiled by time and the seas, incorporating it into the problematics of European narrative traditions. Portuguese historiography took on mythological proportions.

of the *Inconfidência*.[10] For lack of paper the character writes on a wooden table, and his desire to write is further frustrated because the same words keep repeating. The narrator recognizes that the character is in truth himself, Graciliano, writing Cláudio's diary of persecution during the colonial *Inconfidência*.

This realization shocks the narrator out of his stupor, and he decides to confront the dream by marshalling his forces to produce a story of significance and imagination.

> Escrevo estas miudezas que me afligem e devem afligir o leitor.
>
> Por que não escrevo algo mais significativo? Por que não enfrento o sonho, como a um touro, e com ele construo um espetáculo que se chama conto? (202-203)

He gathers up and examines all the data at hand about the rebellion of Vila Rica and begins to deconstruct the existing history of the event, in which he recognizes the mythical glorification of a martyr, and returns to a literary examination of the memoir and the poet:

> Quero repensar, sem preconceitos, toda a trama urdida por isso a que chamamos de tradição histórica... Proporei, com o conto, uma nova interpretação da ação dos homens, tentando elucidar o raciocínio e a motivação que se encontram por detrás dos atos e palavras. O trabalho da imaginação entra nesse momento. (206)

The narrator's obsession with the writing of Cláudio's story is comparable to the "thermal excitement" (190) brought about by Serres's

---

[10] Cláudio Manuel da Costa (1729-89), Brazil's greatest neoclassical poet who studied Law in Coimbra (*Obras* 1768; *Obras poéticas*. Ed. João Ribeiro. Rio de Janeiro: Garnier, 1903), was one of the *árcades mineiros* of Vila Rica. Arrested and interrogated during the Inconfidência, he was found dead in his jail cell. Santiago's text exploits Costa's personal and historical affinities, as author and sacrificed member of a national liberation movement, with Graciliano Ramos' prison memoirs of some 150 years later.

parasite, who produces fluctuations in systems and messages and places human actions and relations in a different light:

> The parasite is an exciter. Far from transforming a system changing its nature, its form, its elements, its relations and its pathways. . . the parasite makes it change states differentially. . . . The parasite intervenes, enters the system as an element of fluctuation. [It] changes its energetic state. (191)

Related to fluctuation and continuum is the narrator's revised description of duple memoirs: "escrever a sua vida como se fosse a minha, escrever a minha vida como se fosse a sua" (209). The narrator's rethinking of historical tradition recapitulates Santiago's own repetition of the prison memoir by examining the relationship of its internal antitheses: history/story, fact/myth, etc. The historical memoir is thereby revisited and validated as dream or story of multiple meanings.

Ghost Writer/Writer Ghost

Em liberdade is (re)constructed as an individual literary memoir of collective language, generic experience, and literary form: "Graciliano redige, mas quem escreve é Cláudio" (234). If Graciliano's prison memoirs, in their unconfoundable "dry and concise" style, were the work not of a ghost writer but a writer ghost, the reader could better recognize the antithetical nature of the deceptive question posed by Santiago's text: "Who is the writer of *Em liberdade*?" Cláudio's text resonates in Graciliano's prison memoirs, and, by projection, in Santiago's contemporary simulation, making of all three moments participants in a Brazilian paradigm of socioliterary crime and punishment. Story, myth, and archetype are restored as shaping forces of the historical memoir.

Through a neobaroque play of forms, Santiago's fiction revives yet another, postmodern dimension of the memoir: the status of art, or art object. Through their rich artistic imaginations, both Cláudio Manual da Costa and Graciliano Ramos would be capable of envisioning a utopia of liberty in the national prison-house of slave labor and social convention. Their superimposed memoirs of imprisonment or persecution as an art of writing, filtered through the recurring metaphor of national experience in the 1960s and 70s, recapitulate an open-ended and paradoxical apprenticeship of individual craft to demanding models. Through an art of imitation, Silviano Santiago encounters a carefully constructed freedom in the mythical forms of writing itself, one of the possible answers to the prison-houses of literature and experience.

REFERENCES

Baudrillard, Jean. *Simulations*. Trans. Paul Foss, Paul Patton and Philip Beitchman. New York: Semiotext(e), 1983.

Bosi, Alfredo. *História concisa da literatura brasileira*. 2a ed. São Paulo: Cultrix, 1977.

Candido, Antonio. *Ficção e confissão*. Rio de Janeiro: José Olympio, 1956.

_____. "Poesia e ficção na autobiografia." *A educação pela noite & outros ensaios*. São Paulo: Ática, 1987. 51-69.

Foster, Hal, ed. *The Anti-Aesthetic: Essays on Postmodern Culture*. Port Townsend, Washington: Bay Press, 1983.

Edelweiss, Ana Maria de Bulhões Carvalho. "Em atenção à palavra do outro - Alterbiografia: a autobiografia 'Em liberdade'." M.A. Thesis, Pontifícia Universidade Católica, Rio de Janeiro, 1990.

Kroker, Arthur and David Cook. *The Postmodern Scene: Excremental Culture and Hyper-Aesthetics*. 2nd. ed. New York: St. Martin's Press, 1988.

Lyotard, Jean-François. *La Condition postmoderne*. Paris: Minuit, 1979.

Miranda, Wander Melo. "Contra a corrente: a questão autobiográfica em Graciliano Ramos e Silviano Santiago." Ph.D. dissertation, Universidade de São Paulo, 1987.

Miller, J. Hillis. "The Critic as Host." *Critical Inquiry* 3 (1977): 439.

Nunes, Benedito. "Narrativa histórica e narrativa ficcional." *Narrativa: ficção e história*. Ed. Dirce Côrtes Riedel. Rio de Janeiro: Imago, 1988. 9-22.

Princeton Encyclopedia of Poetry and Poetics. Ed. Alex Preminger. Princeton: Princeton UP, 1974.

Ramos, Graciliano. *Memórias do cárcere*. 2 vols. 5th ed. São Paulo: Martins, 1965.

Revista do Brasil: literatura anos 80 2.5 (1986).

Santiago, Silviano. "Para além da história social." *Narrativa: ficção e história*. Ed. Dirce Côrtes Riedel. Rio de Janeiro: Imago, 1988. 241-56.

_____. "Permanência do discurso da tradição no modernismo." *Cultura brasileira: tradição contradição*. Rio de Janeiro: Zahar, 1987. 111-45.

Serres, Michel. *The Parasite*. Trans. Lawrence R. Schehr. Baltimore and London: Johns Hopkins UP, 1982.

Ulmer, Gregory L. "The Object of Post-Criticism." *The Anti-Aesthetic: Essays on Postmodern Culture*. Ed. Hal Foster. Port Townsend, Washington: Bay Press, 1983. 83-110.

White, Hayden. *Tropics of Discourse*. Baltimore: Johns Hopkins UP, 1978.

THE HURRIED MIDWIVES OF TIME: BRAZILIAN FICTION IN THE 1980S

Silviano Santiago
Universidade Federal Fluminense

> Com efeito, na medida em que o ato criador incorpora a metalinguagem [...] a literatura se pensa e se critica. Que resta então a fazer? Que sobrará para a "velha crítica", aquela que se exerce fora da obra e que pretende ser seu conhecimento e sua avaliação? (João Luiz Lafetá, *1930: a crítica e o modernismo*)

Human beings are decimal creatures. Faced with years ending in zero they begin to look backwards, and they review the past with the arrival of years ending in one. They discover that Time exists, passes and leaves definitive and enigmatic marks, and they begin to interpret their memory of facts that have gone by and will not come again. Driving the car of life forward, their eyes get lost (while sighing heavily with affliction) in the rear-view mirror, recalling events of a year, a decade, a century earlier.

Brazilians are decimal and hurried creatures, perhaps in a radical effort to disprove the thesis that we are citizens forming a nation without memory. In his novel *Galvez, imperador do Acre* (1976), Márcio Souza ends the 19th century on 31 December 1899. In *Aos trancos e barrancos* (1985), Darcy Ribeiro kicks off the 20th century on 1 January 1900. They are complementary writers. There may even be here a legitimate Tupininquim contribution to historical chronology. If Christ, as they say, was born in Bahia, it was in the year zero. Are we or are we not hurried midwives of Time?

Silviano Santiago

Parodying Drummond, I confess that I stroked a typewriter, drove a Volkswagen Beetle and learned at the tables of a bar that I am a decimal, green and yellow creature. The decade of the 90s begins on the first day of January, 1990. So let's go to a review of the 80s.

Affirmative responses to two questions--Is a book a commodity? Is the writer a professional?--indicate an important about-face in literary production of the 80s. The writer could no longer enter the labor market or the market of consumer products without consequence. This is the cause of a reversal with profound repercussions in the world of letters. In the 1980s writers had to change their behavior not only in relation to publishers, but also in relation to the reader. To satisfy the former, they had to rethink the notion of literary text inherited from the great writers of this century. Thus they could affirm that their originality resided in their disobedience to the scriptural rules of the recent past, in the deviations they initiated.

In their relationships with publishers, writers began to demand a contract as well as its fulfillment. To improve the relationship with possible readers, they opted to direct their work not to the initiated (the "happy few," as Stendahl and T.S. Eliot have said), but to readers of average taste.

* * *

Criticism of the work of contemporary artists is always a provocation. Foolish is the critic who claims to make categorical and definitive judgments. Even more foolish is the artist who believes it. Criticism of contemporaries is similar to the coil in a water heater: it makes the stagnant water in the tank rise from room temperature to boiling. Criticism serves to elevate the ambient discussion to the heat of reflection. If the coil receives its energy from an electric source, criticism receives its energy from a library. Borges is absolutely correct when he says that "to organize a library is a silent manner of exercising the art of criticism." The term "library" need not be understood here in a "private" sense. In hard times, one may recommend the use of the adjective-- imaginary--which André Malraux used to describe museums. Private or imaginary, it matters little of which library we are speaking.

Despite the fact that he is not just any collector, the critic does not fail to use the tricks of an obsessive collector of knowledge. To be accepted as part of a whole, he organizes--and will reorganize infinitely until his death; each new item has to be responsibly examined and evaluated within the spirit that inspired the collection. So-called common readers often lack this responsible care with "tradition" (they of course do not lack perspicacity, sensitivity, intellectual curiosity, and so forth). Criticism calls on the reader to assume a lasting commitment with his/her/our/the public's library and with the book he or she has just finished reading. Does it go on the shelf or not? The critic--and any reader who wants to be a critic can be one--thus works with a stock of information that is qualitatively superior to that of the so-called common reader. On the other hand, it is always worthwhile repeating that the work of art (be it a book, a painting, a popular song) is not made only for critics, but rather for any and everyone.

One of the basic criteria that anchor critical work is that of predictability (in the composition of the text, the creation of characters, the treatment of dialogue, the invention of the plot and its development, etc.). It is not easy to present this concept theoretically, despite the efforts of the Russian formalists at the beginning of this century to configure its opposite: unpredictability. The critic does not have the right to approach a work naively. It is not the first time nor the last that he will read a book. Perhaps for this very reason there is, in the way he approaches a text, a compulsion to find in repetition the pleasure of a difference that will awaken him to knowledge. Often he is not enthralled by the seriousness of that which is apparently profound, and other times he lets himself be facilely seduced by trinkets that a less perverse reader will judge to be mere tinsel.

The critic is a reader who is more sensitive to unpredictabilities and less patient in relation to the predictabilities that a text may present. What the text transmits to him as profound may be a mere cliché, even of the most common kind, and there is no way not to turn up one's nose. What is given as frivolity can be that which sensually involves the most demanding and sophisticated reader.

Predictable/unpredictable: there is no doubt that this double criterion becomes the basis of the judgement that serves to value or devalue the contemporary work of art. But the critic must take care to use the criterion without manichaeism, which can lead him to close himself in the rigid and programmatic principles of avant-garde art, such as they were established at the beginning of the century. Considering the avant-garde spirit indispensable, but not limiting ourselves to it, we must conclude that predictability is not necessarily a defect, just as unpredictability is not necessarily a quality. Each case has to be considered individually, and it is for this reason that the art of criticism is the exercise of discernment in the organization of a library.

* * *

In comparison with the artistic production of the heroic period of Modernism, more recent literary production has worked with a higher degree of predictability. This step backwards, this reversal (if one wants to be more radical), did not occur by accident. It reveals a change in the writer's behavior on both the existential and professional levels that ends up being reflected in the conception that the writer begins to have of the text as a whole. In other words, it is reflected in the role conferred on the book-object (work of literature) in contemporary Brazilian society.

To admit a higher degree of predictability (in the composition of the text, the creation of characters, the treatment of dialogues, etc., etc.) presupposes that in the 1980s the writer has accepted his entrance into the market of cultural goods as a form of struggle. Was this good or bad? We should avoid definitive judgements and attempt to characterize the situation. The writer accepted the idea of becoming a professional of letters, and not a mere dilettante. He agreed to examine, before writing the text itself, the function of a book in a peripheral consumer society, bombarded from all sides by the foreign best-seller. Instead of welcoming freedom (total, irrefutable, maddening, etc.) at the absolute moment of engagement with language, he stood aside during the process of creation, in order to admit as well that he had to include practical considerations about the act of writing.

The forms in which redundancy and predictability can appear in a literary text to more easily seduce the reader are multiple. A few, varied examples will suffice. They can be in the way in which Autran Dourado (in *Lucas Procópio*), J. J. Veiga (in *A casca da serpente*), and Antônio Torres (in *Balada da infância perdida*) rework their own fictional obsessions, creating small new worlds within a larger universe. They may be in the borrowing of some elements from detective fiction, as in the latest novel of Antônio Callado (*Memórias de Aldenham House*), or in Lygia Fagundes Telles (*As horas nuas*), or in Rubem Fonseca (*A grande arte*, *Vastas emoções e pensamentos imperfeitos*). They may be in way in which from book to book a trilogy is constructed, as in the cases of João Gilberto Noll and Sérgio Sant'Anna. They may even be in the return to the laws of the historical novel with a nationalist tinge, as in

João Ubaldo Ribeiro (*Viva o povo brasileiro*) or Nélida Piñon (*A república dos sonhos*).

Instead of being committed exclusively to the text he or she produces, with its originality and aesthetic efficacy, the writer of the 1980s multiplies the number of commitments to assume. He accepts entering a network of interests of which, at the extremes, both the publisher and the reader are part. The gratification does not derive just from the satisfaction of having written a text according to intransigent and personal values, but rather from the multiple and different critiques and forms of recognition received in the production, commercialization and consumption of the book.

From the publisher the writer wants a good contract; from the press, good publicity; from booksellers, good commercialization; from readers, a place on the best-seller list; from critics, a positive evaluation of the book's quality. Publisher, the press, booksellers, readers--all are indispensable elements. Criticism, regrettably, has been dismissed.

* * *

In less interesting authors, the exemption from critical evaluation is the direct consequence of the desire to write a lively (and not current) book that runs without obstacles along the rules of the marketplace, pretending that it is entering into full competition with foreign works. In more interesting authors, the exemption can be the way the creator faces the difficulty that any criticism (national or foreign) finds in keeping up-to-date in moments of crisis, or in times of transition and change. In these moments, instead of occupying the privileged space of reflection that helps the author face the possible deficiencies of his work or the problems it presents, and instead of aiding the public to better evaluate the work's importance, criticism becomes a retrograde activity, insisting on values of the past and not the values it has come to depend on. In the glorious period of the avant-garde, criticism's task of staying up-to-date occurred in an aggressive and programmatic manner by the manifesto(s) produced by emergent groups.

Throwing grouchy criticism into the corner and not wanting to penetrate the authoritarian snarls of the literary manifesto, the writer in the 1980s, in the effort to modernize the field of comprehension of the contemporary work of art, decided to take up again the modernist tendency to thematize the art of criticism in the literary work itself, making it self-reflexive. In the best texts of the last decade can be found the principles for a new criticism which, without glorifying the multiple "spurious" commitments in which the writers have become involved, discusses with intelligence and precision the status of the work where these commitments are inscribed. The play between the novelistic intrigue (with a greater degree of predictability) and its self-criticism, between the "anecdote" and "reflection," as Machado de Assis would say, makes the work less "spurious" than the commitments assumed by the writer.

* * *

The 1980s brought back the confluence of literature and the contemporaneous reader. Information about the vacuum of readership in which the modernist writer worked is well-known. A vacuum that provided him with an enviable and indomitable freedom in his dealing with language. From commitments to language one moves to a commitment to the work's contemporary reader. Yesterday as today it is good that the institutions of knowledge do not easily and proudly match with contemporaneity. But it is not good that they relegate criticism to a third plane, as if the contract signed in a public square between the writer and the reader somehow stained the pleasure of reading that supposedly exists only in the great works of the past. Without doubt it is more gratifying to work with the greater authors. And perhaps more important. But how does one justify the divorce between literary production in the 1980s and contemporary criticism?

The 1980s will be remembered by this divorce. Regrettably. João Luiz Lafetá asks, in the epigraph to this essay, what remained for "old criticism" in the face of the modernist contribution which had strategically incorporated metalanguage in the creative act. He responds that what remained was the same as before: "to reflect on the development of the literary tradition, to judge, delimit positions, enlighten both authors and public, justify, condemn." But to these tasks a new one has been added: it has also fallen on criticism "to say explicitly whether the work manages to go beyond itself."

The incorporation of metalanguage in the poetic text has been taken up again by the new authors, but in another context and aesthetic proposition. The question remains current: the first part of the answer is still and always will be current. But will we be able to explain the new responsibilities of criticism, at the risk of wanting to endlessly repeat the modernist creed, even when the work at hand has distanced itself from it?

Even yesterday frogs croaked in the marsh: today's criticism is remiss, lazy, supercilious. Cranky voices have cried that it is today's literature that is uninteresting, poor, superficial. The adjectives have been exchanged in innumerous pamphletary articles. Why pamphletary language, if today we have a criticism with a university and lay background that can elevate the level of ambient discussion to that of reflection. A task for the 1990s. Without doubt, grateful artists would thank the critics, for what is at stake is the legitimacy of their profession and the quality of the product they manufacture.

CONTRIBUTORS

ANA LUIZA ANDRADE, professor of Brazilian and Comparative Literature at the Universidade Federal de Alagoas, taught at Harvard and Yale after receiving her Ph.D. from the University of Texas at Austin in 1982 with a dissertation written under the direction of Fred P. Ellison. She is the author of *Osman Lins: crítica e criação* (1987).

JOÃO ALEXANDRE BARBOSA is professor of Literary Theory and Comparative Literature at the Universidade de São Paulo and currently serves as the director of the Editora da Universidade de São Paulo. His books of literary criticism include *A tradição do impasse* (1974), *A imitação da forma* (1975), *As ilusões da modernidade* (1986) and *A leitura do intervalo* (1990). He was E. L. Tinker Professor at the University of Texas in 1986.

HAROLDO DE CAMPOS, Professor Emeritus in the Program for Graduate Studies in Communication and Semiotics a the Pontifícia Universidade Católica in São Paulo, is a poet, essayist, and translator of poetry. Among his books of poetry are *Xadrez de estrelas* (1976), *A educação dos cinco sentidos* (1985), and *Galáxias* (1984). His essays include *Metalinguagem* (1967), *A arte no horizonte do provável* (1969), and *Morfologia do Macunaíma* (1972). He has translated Pound, Joyce, Goethe, Maiakovski, and classical poetry from Greco-Latin, Chinese, Japanese (*Hagoromo*) traditions as well as from the Bible ("Ecclesiastes"). He was visiting professor at the University of Texas in 1971 and E. L. Tinker Professor in 1981.

WALNICE NOGUEIRA GALVÃO is professor of Literary Theory and Comparative Literature at the Universidade de São Paulo. Her books include: *As formas do falso* (1972), *No calor da hora* (1974), *Saco de gatos* (1976), *Saptamatr* (1978), *Mitológica rosiana* (1978), *Gatos de outro saco* (1982), and critical editions of Euclides da Cunha's *Os sertões* (1985) and João Guimarães Rosa's *Grande sertão: veredas* (forthcoming). She was a visiting professor at the University of Texas at Austin in 1978.

231

K. DAVID JACKSON is professor of Luso-Brazilian Literature at the University of Texas at Austin. His books are *Prosa de vanguarda em Oswald de Andrade* (1978) and *Sing without Shame: Oral Traditions in Indo-Portuguese Creole Verse* (1990). With Al Bork, he co-translated Oswald de Andrade's *Serafim Ponte Grande* (1979), and he co-edited, with Merlin Forster, *Vanguardism in Latin American Literature: An Annotated Bibliographical Guide* (1990).

RANDAL JOHNSON is professor of Brazilian Literature and Culture at the University of Florida. His books include: *Brazilian Cinema* (co-edited with Robert Stam, 1982, 1988), *Literatura e cinema: Macunaíma do modernismo na literatura ao Cinema Novo* (1982), *Cinema Novo x 5: Masters of Contemporary Brazilian Film* (1984), and *The Film Industry in Brazil: Culture and the State* (1987). He is also the editor of Pierre Bourdieu's *The Field of Cultural Production: Essays on Art and Literature* (1992). He received his Ph.D. from the University of Texas at Austin in 1977, writing a dissertation under the direction of Fred P. Ellison.

NAOMI LINDSTROM is professor of Latin American Literature at the University of Texas at Austin. Her books include *Literary Expression in Argentina* (1977), *Macedonio Fernández* (1981), *Women as Myth and Metaphor in Latin American Literature* (co-edited, 1985), *Jewish Issues in Argentine Literature* (1989), and *Jorge Luis Borges* (1990). She co-translated, with Fred P. Ellison, Helena Parente Cunha's *Woman Between Mirrors* (1989).

FÁBIO LUCAS is professor of Brazilian Literature at the Universidade de Brasília and author of *O caráter social da ficção do Brasil* (1985), *Vanguarda, história e ideologia da literatura* (1985), *Do barroco ao moderno--vozes da literatura brasileira* (1989), *Crepúsculo dos símbolos--reflexões sobre o livro no Brasil* (1989), *Poesias de Emílio Moura* (1991), *Fontes literárias portuguesas* (1991), and *Mineiranças* (1991), among others. He was a visiting professor at the University of Texas in 1972.

PEDRO MALIGO is assistant professor of Brazilian Literature at Michigan State University. He received his Ph.D. from the University of Texas at Austin in 1988, writing a dissertation on Amazonian literature.

MASSAUD MOISÉS is professor of Portuguese Literature at the Universidade de São Paulo. Among his many published works are: *A litera-*

tura portuguesa (1960), *A criação literária* (1967), *Pequeno dicionário de literatura brasileira* (1967; with José Paulo Paes), *Dicionário de termos literários* (1974), *Literatura: mundo e forma* (1982), and *História da literatura brasileira* (5 vols; 1983-1989). He has been visiting professor at numerous American universities, including the University of Texas at Austin (1971).

CHARLES A. PERRONE is associate professor of Brazilian Literature and Culture at the University of Florida. He has published two books on Brazilian popular music, *Letra e letras da MPB* (1988) and *Masters of Contemporary Brazilian Song: MPB 1965-1989*. He received his Ph.D. from the University of Texas at Austin in 1985.

AFFONSO ROMANO DE SANT'ANNA is a poet and professor of Brazilian Literature at the Pontifícia Universidade Católica (Rio de Janeiro) and the Universidade Federal do Rio de Janeiro. He currently serves as the President of the Brazilian Fundação Biblioteca Nacional. His works of poetry include *Canto e palavra* (1965), *Poesia sobre poesia* (1975), *A grande fala do índio guarani* (1978), *Que país é este?* (1980), *Política e paixão* (1984), and *A catedral de Colônia* (1985). He has also published numerous critical studies, including *Análise estrutural de romances brasileiros* (1973), *Por um novo conceito de literatura brasileira* (1977), *Música popular e moderna poesia brasileira* (1978), *Carlos Drummond de Andrade--análise da obra* (1980), and *O canibalismo amoroso* (1984), among others. He was a visiting professor at the University of Texas at Austin in 1977.

SILVIANO SANTIAGO is a novelist, poet and professor of Brazilian and Comparative Literature at the Universidade Federal Fluminense in Niterói. His works of fiction are *O banquete* (1970), *O olhar* (1974), *Em liberdade* (1981), and *Stella Manhattan* (1985). Among his many books of criticism are *Uma literatura nos trópicos* (1978), *Vale quanto pesa* (1982), and *Nas malhas da letra* (1989). He has taught at Rutgers and SUNY Buffalo and was visiting professor at the University of Texas at Austin in 1976.